Praise for
God Distorted

GW00645536

"John Bishop tears away those misconceptions, disto:
have in the way of a dynamic relationship with God. By highlighting how significantly
the relationship with our earthly father distorts our view of our heavenly Father, *God
Distorted* leads readers on a path of healing and better understanding of God the
Father."

—MARK BATTERSON, *New York Times* best-selling author
of *The Circle Maker*

"John Bishop writes from his personal life and his years as a pastor to describe the incredible importance of accepting our Father's love into the deep places of our lives. So many
of our challenges come back to how we view God, and John clears the way for us to see
God in all of his power, love, and fame. This is a powerful book and a great resource."

—JUD WILHITE, author of *Pursued* and senior pastor
of Central Christian Church, Las Vegas

"A. W. Tozer asserted, 'What comes into our minds when we think about God is the
most important thing about us.' *God Distorted* helps us discover and replace the warped
perceptions with God's perfections. Writing with great vulnerability out of his personal
journey, John guides us to letting go the 'daddy damaged' idols so we can experience the
joy that comes with knowing the heavenly Father with all our heart, soul, mind, and
strength. Working through the book will renew love of the Father, joy in Jesus, and
peace through the Spirit."

—GERRY BRESHEARS, professor of theology, Western Seminary, Portland

"John Bishop has written a book that will bring healing, encouragement, and restoration to anyone who's wrestled to reconcile their earthly father with our heavenly Father.
This is a book that will breathe hope and life into your world."

—MARGARET FEINBERG (www.margaretfeinberg.com),
author of *Wonderstruck* and *Scouting the Divine*

"*God Distorted* provides insight to a hurting generation. John is very transparent in this
book, and if we had more Christian leaders this transparent talking about some of these

things, we would have a better church, community, and nation. We must acknowledge, accept, and work on these problems we carry within us. We must allow God to change us, and then we can help change others. I was with Pastor John Bishop and spoke at his church on Father's Day, and following the service we had a very quick lunch—the reason being that he needed to rush off so he could spend time with his son. That was John's priority, and it made a strong impression on me."

—NICKY CRUZ, evangelist and author

"The message of *God Distorted* is simple but profound: No matter how good or bad your earthly father was, you haven't truly found home until you're in the arms of your heavenly Father. John Bishop's message is one of hope, healing, and restoration."

—JIM DALY, president, Focus on the Family and author
of *ReFocus: Living a Life that Reflects God's Heart*

"John Bishop is passionate about helping us let go of our distorted image of God and embrace Him as our perfect Father. John's transparency about his experience as a son, a father, and a pastor will encourage you as you seek to replace broken paradigms with biblical faith."

—STEVEN FURTICK, lead pastor, Elevation Church, Charlotte,
and author of the *New York Times* bestseller *Greater*

"*God Distorted* challenges your view of God. John Bishop helps you see God for who He is, not who you imagined Him to be."

—KERRY SHOOK, founding pastor of Woodlands Church, Houston,
and coauthor of the national bestsellers *One Month to Live*
and *Love at Last Sight*

"Everyone has a view of God, a perception of who He is and what He wants in our lives. Some see Him as a loving creator; others may see Him as a detached deity. In *God Distorted*, John Bishop helps readers peel back the layers of their past and discover the foundation of their perception of God—their experience with their earthly father. And through open, honest, and powerful examples, John helps readers discover what it takes to overcome the distortions and instead gain a clear image of God."

—ED YOUNG, pastor, Fellowship Church, Dallas/Fort Worth,
and author of *Outrageous, Contagious Joy*

GOD
DISTORTED

How Your Earthly Father
Affects Your Perception of God
and Why It Matters

John Bishop
Foreword by Ruth Graham

MULTNOMAH
BOOKS

GOD DISTORTED
PUBLISHED BY MULTNOMAH BOOKS
12265 Oracle Boulevard, Suite 200
Colorado Springs, Colorado 80921

All Scripture quotations, unless otherwise indicated, are taken from the Holy Bible, New Living Translation, copyright © 1996, 2004, 2007. Used by permission of Tyndale House Publishers Inc., Carol Stream, Illinois 60188. All rights reserved. Scripture quotations marked (God's Word) are taken from God's Word, a copyrighted work of God's Word to the Nations Bible Society. Quotations are used by permission. Copyright 1995 by God's Word to the Nations. All rights reserved. Scripture quotations marked (HCSB) are taken from The Holman Christian Standard Bible®, © copyright 1999, 2000, 2002, 2003 by Holman Bible Publishers. Used by permission. Scripture quotations marked (KJV) are taken from the King James Version. Scripture quotations marked (MSG) are taken from The Message by Eugene H. Peterson. Copyright © 1993, 1994, 1995, 1996, 2000, 2001, 2002. Used by permission of NavPress Publishing Group. All rights reserved. Scripture quotations marked (NASB) are taken from the New American Standard Bible®. © Copyright The Lockman Foundation 1960, 1962, 1963, 1968, 1971, 1972, 1973, 1975, 1977. Use by permission. (www.Lockman.org). Scripture quotations marked (NIV) are taken from the Holy Bible, New International Version®, NIV®. Copyright © 1973, 1978, 1984 by Biblica Inc.™ Used by permission of Zondervan. All rights reserved worldwide. www.zondervan.com.

Italics in Scripture quotations reflect the author's added emphasis.

Details in some anecdotes and stories have been changed to protect the identities of the persons involved.

Trade Paperback ISBN: 978-1-60142-485-3
eBook ISBN: 978-1-60142-486-0

Cover design by Mark D. Ford

Published in the United States by WaterBrook Multnomah, an imprint of the Crown Publishing Group, a division of Random House Inc., New York.

MULTNOMAH and its mountain colophon are registered trademarks of Random House Inc.

Library of Congress Cataloging-in-Publication Data
Bishop, John L.
    God distorted : how your earthly father affects your perception of God and why it matters / John L. Bishop.—
First Edition.
        pages cm
    Includes bibliographical references and index.
    ISBN 978-1-60142-485-3 (alk. paper)—ISBN 978-1-60142-486-0 (electronic : alk. paper)
    1. God (Christianity)—Fatherhood. I. Title.
    BT153.F3B39 2013
    231'.1—dc23

                                                    2012049986

Printed in the United States of America
2013—First Edition

10 9 8 7 6 5 4 3 2 1

SPECIAL SALES
Most WaterBrook Multnomah books are available at special quantity discounts when purchased in bulk by corporations, organizations, and special-interest groups. Custom imprinting or excerpting can also be done to fit special needs. For information, please e-mail SpecialMarkets@WaterBrookMultnomah.com or call 1-800-603-7051.

Yet to all who received him, to those who believed in his name, he gave the right to become children of God.

—JOHN 1:12, NIV

To David, my father. I wish I could know you, and I wish you could know me. We would have had so many memories, but on February 17, 1967, that all changed when you died. I forgive you, and I am sorry for all of the anger. What we missed out on, I have tried to give to my kids. My biggest hope is that you are in heaven and that we can catch up someday. Through all of the pain, I have discovered God's promises and presence. He promised to be the Father to the fatherless and has been to me.

~

To David, my only son. I love you so much. I believe in you, David. You were named after the grandpa you never knew, but you have a heart like King David. I am proud of you in more ways than I can explain. My heart is so full of joy and promise when I think of you. David, thanks for loving me even in the moments I didn't know how to be a dad. You have always loved me for who I am, in spite of who I am not.

~

To Katie, my lovely and beautiful daughter. Your conviction to strive for prayer and holiness is inspiring. Being a daddy in your life has not only been easy but also encouraging. You are always joyful, always prayerful; you always try to make the best right choice, and you have always shown me the grace I don't deserve. Never stop dreaming and being fully sold out to Jesus.

~

To Hannah-Jo, my baby girl. When I took you to Grandpa's grave for the first time and you walked over to hug me, is a moment that will be etched in my heart forever. You are so driven by purpose and are contagiously generous. I love that *you make me smile so much and you have such a heart for doing what is right—to love God and speak His truth unashamedly to this generation.*

~

To Pop. God provided, but I was blinded. I am sorry for not seeing your sacrifice and not saying thank you more. You were the best a kid could ask for in a grandpa and a dad. You did more for me than words can explain. The day you asked Jesus into your heart birthed a dream to start a church to reach people who didn't go to church. Pop, I simply want to say thanks for never making me feel like a burden, although I know I was. Thanks for being there, for loving me, and for being a great example as a husband. I will see you soon enough!

~

To the perfect Father, Yahweh. You are my God, You are my protector, You are the lifter of my head when I am tired or confused, and You are the lamp to my feet when I don't know which direction to walk in. By Your grace You allowed the pain in my life that both defined and redefined me, and now You are redeeming the pain to help so many who have a distorted view of You. I love You and welcome You to love me more, and more, and more.

CONTENTS

Part 3: OUR REFLECTION:
Experiencing Healing and Restoration

STUDY GUIDE: MY PROGRESSION:
Letting Go of Daddy Damage

FOREWORD

By Ruth Graham
Author of *In Every Pew Sits a Broken Heart*

I love God and I know He loves me. But in my life I have had a difficult time knowing He was always available to me. I thought He was off busy with someone else, caring for them—as my own father was.

Despite having an amazing man as my daddy, I have a closet called "fatherlessness" in my life. The closet door was shut and tightly locked. I passed by the door each day but was not really sure what was inside. At times it made me uneasy, sad, angry, insecure, and a host of other unhealthy things, but I was unwilling to open it. I was afraid of what I would find in there and afraid of the pain I would feel to face it directly. To most folks, it looked as if I came from the perfect Christian family with the perfect father. But the closet was there and very real. Every once in a while something would slip out from behind the door, but I cleaned it up and stuffed it back in before anyone saw it. Maybe they wouldn't notice the energy I used to keep it closed. Maybe I didn't know myself. But I do know I was weary and sad. In discouragement, I wanted to quit living this way, but I knew I couldn't and wouldn't. But did I have to continue feeling like I didn't belong?

There are many causes of fatherlessness. Death. Divorce. Abandonment. Abuse. Absence. I knew all about absence. My father, the Reverend Billy Graham, was gone so much as he traveled the globe preaching the Gospel. To my young heart it felt like abandonment. It wasn't. He was a unique man at a unique time in history doing what God had called him to do. But at home there was a little girl who desperately wanted her daddy. A girl whose little heart ached to have his attention and the security of his arms. When I needed him most, he seemed to be the farthest away. (Please understand I am not disparaging my father. He is my hero. But I am being real.) And I saw God that way as well. I had a distorted view of God.

The book you hold in your hands, written by my friend John Bishop, was a key for me to unlock the door and examine the contents of my closet. He has helped me sort things out and clean them up—although this will be a lifelong process. It was a comfort to know that John understands. He has done this himself. He knows the pain, the pitfalls, the emotions, and the weariness because he has his own closet of fatherlessness. He lets us peer into his closet and into the process of coming to grips with his loss.

John has given to all of us practical tools to help us identify our "stuff," examine it, deal with it, and then get rid of it. As you read the book and do the exercises in the back, my prayer for you is that you will be able to do the same. I pray there will be an "aha!" moment for you as you discover the symptoms of your fatherlessness and the cause; that you will be able to identify the longing of your heart and slowly you will recognize the true image of the God who is pursuing you. I pray you will see His heart and hear His voice more clearly, falling in love with the One who knows you best and loves you most.

Find the comfort, the joy, and the freedom to be yourself because you have the true image of God your heavenly Father. I pray you will finally be able to let go of the distorted view of God and realize your true potential as His beloved child.

ACKNOWLEDGMENTS

Carly Major: Carly, I want to express my deepest appreciation for all of the work you have poured into this project. Behind a good book and author, there is a team that makes it so much better than it would have been without help. Your ability to think, write, edit, and help on this project is an unspeakable gift to me and to a generation of people that needs God. Hopefully this book will help them in their journey of finding the greatest and only perfect Father. You won't know until heaven the full impact of your sacrifices. Thank you.

Teresa Petker: Teresa, simply, you make me look better than I am. This book is another example of your taking the vision and burden that God puts on my heart (just like preparing a message every weekend) and completely and sacrificially giving whatever you can to make it better. You see it, take it, and enhance it. Jesus said it best that the servants here will be the greatest there. Thank you for your hours upon hours of research to find the perfect quote to make each chapter so much better. I am thanking God that with your help, one of the deepest and most personal messages in my heart can become a resource for so many people. My prayer is they will find God as their perfect Father. Thank you.

David Kopp: I'm not sure what you saw in our initial meeting (maybe it was the sushi?), but I'm so glad you were willing to take a risk on me. I absolutely love working with the whole team at WaterBrook Multnomah. Thank you!

Susan Tjaden: Susan, thank you for making us feel like this book was the only project you were working on. Thank you for "getting" me as an author, for protecting my voice in the edits, and for believing in the message. Thank you most of all for always remembering to ask about my son; it matters more than you know, to both him and me. Beyond the work, we have become friends.

The sales and marketing team at WaterBrook Multnomah: Thank you for the prayers, for listening to the story, and for shedding tears with us. Your encouragement has been priceless. I am praying for God's favor in every conversation.

Echo Bennett: So much of what you do is unseen by all but your audience of One. Thank you for being vulnerable with your story and for the hours spent on the workbook. Your investment matters, Echo, and lives will be changed for all of eternity.

Stephanie, Sheila, Marlette, and all the Living Hope staff: Thank you for everything done behind the scenes to support the writing team. Thank you for releasing me and for encouraging me to get this message out there. I am so thankful to our staff for creating an environment where it's okay to not be okay, which has been me at times.

Mama: Raising two boys without a father is not the way it should be, and I know it wasn't easy, so thank you. Thanks for having the courage to say no that fateful day when my dad wanted to take me with him, which would be his last day on this earth. I can hardly comprehend how different things might have been. I love you.

Michelle: You did what you always have done: you dreamed with me, you encouraged me, you read and prayed for the project, and you loved me on "those days." Also, you have given me both space and grace to get this done. Thanks, love.

You, the reader: I want to say thank you up-front. Simply, you are the reason this book was written. I am praying for you as you take this journey with me. It takes courage to confront the past and pursue a better relationship with God. Thank you for taking a step that will give you hope and a better future.

INTRODUCTION

I am broken, just like many of you who by God's grace are reading this book about dads, children, and God. As much as I knew my earthly dads (yes, plural), I have learned to know God even better. By no stretch of the imagination or résumé am I an expert on parenting, or on the role of fathers in the lives of their children, or on the character of God as the perfect Father. However, having had four very different earthly fathers, being the father of three very different kids, and serving as a pastor for over twenty years, I at least have a broad, varied, and hopefully helpful perspective in being both child and father. I was the child dreaming of the perfect father, and I finally found him in the God who I now know was always there.

Writing this book has been an experience full of irony that isn't lost on me. Take today, for example. This morning I got a Father's Day card from my daughter Katie and son-in-law Jordan. I am sitting here staring at a card that says so much and ends with "I love you, Daddy. Forever and always—Katie Lee." But just moments ago I hung up the phone with my son, David, who is currently incarcerated at our local county jail. He had to end our call abruptly because he was being put in lockdown. Talk about emotional whiplash! *Honestly, God. Really?*

To hear David's voice and his words, "Dad, I love you and will call you when I can." Yeah, those words break the heart of a daddy. That's when the irony hurts. Who am I to write about fathers when I am mad at myself as a dad, aggravated by the residual issues from the fathers I had, and frustrated with God and others? I know David has made wrong choices. Lots of them. I get it in my head, but I really have a hard time being okay with it in my heart. But then God lets me know that this is exactly why He wants me to write this book. He has me right where I need to be, learning exactly what I need to learn, in order to share what He wants me to share.

In life—not just as a pastor, but as a dad—I have heard more stories than I can count about brokenness, pain, anger, resentment, and insecurity that are directly related to dysfunctional father relationships. I have plenty of my own! I don't have all the answers, but I have learned some things that have helped me both cope and become better at being a dad.

I can't explain every situation, but I can empathize with most. Whether you are fifteen or seventy-five, you are still the child of your dad. The wounds of a dad, admitted or not, can bring so much pain and confusion to the heart of a child.

I cannot change your past, but I am praying about your today and am hoping that the words in this book will help you walk toward a new future. Have you been broken and hurt? I have too. Have you felt controlled, abandoned, ignored, or rejected? I have too. I get it. I don't necessarily know more than anyone else, but I am willing to share with you my journey to healing, in the hopes it may benefit you in some way.

I am a child who was abused, abandoned, and left. I am a father who is trying to be a better father. But most importantly, I am a child of God who has learned to be healed and be a healer of others.

Why This Book? Why Now? Why Me?

It is my life's passion to help people meet the God who loves them so much He died for them. But often we have to begin by tearing down a wall of preconceived ideas and distorted images of God that have been created by the images projected by our earthly fathers.

I am a confessed accidental pastor who somehow by God's grace has been blessed to be part of a church that has seen over eight thousand people baptized in eight years and has seen tens of thousands changed by grace and for the glory of only God. We are in a part of America where people don't really want to go to church. In my life personally and in our lives corporately, God has been distorted into something that isn't right.

The God distortion needs to be changed. It needs to be different for our generation—a generation that has been broken by dad issues and needs to be restored and reclaimed by God. Fathers—and the lack of them—have in many cases tainted our view of God and prevented relationship with Him. I have dedicated my life as a pastor to knowing God and making Him known. I don't care what struggle you have or what God looks like in your mind, but I can say without hesitation that the God I have come to know is the answer to the deepest longing of your heart.

My intent is not to make fathers feel or look bad, but to help us as children identify the fears and insecurities we still carry as scars from our childhood. I have been challenged as a father while writing this book, and I am now determined—passionate, even—to do better as a result of what I have learned.

What Is This Book?

This book is split into three parts. In the first part, we identify eight different types of fathers. You are probably going to recognize yourself and your family members somewhere in here. It's not always easy reading about what goes on in the home, how children develop emotionally and relationally, and what impact that has on their God-image. Some of the stories are extreme examples, and you may see your father as a milder version of the one described. Or you may even see Dad as a combination of more than one description.

In part 2, we begin a journey of discovering who our heavenly Father truly is, as defined in God's Word. What aspect of His character specifically speaks to the wounds of our past? What does God promise that can heal the deep fears that drive our dysfunctional behaviors and steal our joy? This is where you meet a God who loves you more than anyone ever has, could, or will, in spite of the things you might hate about yourself.

Part 3 is where we get practical. It is my sincere hope that here you will experience healing and then bring restoration to the lives of those around you. Maybe you feel constantly discouraged by the Enemy and want to fight back. Perhaps you struggle to live differently, even as a child of God. When you learn, pray, and perhaps cry, and when hope is rebirthed in your heart, maybe you will see the need to forgive someone for hurting you. This section addresses all of these issues, and more, giving you all the tools you need to do better than you have before.

Following part 3 is a study guide to help you work through the fears that distort your view of God. That will be the opportunity for you to pray, read the Bible, and allow God to speak healing into your heart.

I pray that you will, by the end of these pages, see God more clearly and understand His unconditional love and acceptance of you, right as you are today.

Part 1

OUR
PERCEPTION

Understanding Different

Daddy Types

Image Distorted

The most dangerous untruths are
truths slightly distorted.

—GEORG C. LICHTENBERG

As a child I often imagined what it would be like to be raised by the perfect dad. He would be always encouraging, always there, always patient, always trying to make me laugh, and be with me when I cried. I imagined a dad who believed in and supported my dreams and was my biggest cheerleader. When I got hurt, he would be the first person I'd go to for comfort and guidance. He would never be too busy but would always be available to say just the right thing at just the right time. He would be a dad I could trust 100 percent.

I remember watching different dads on television shows, like Andy Taylor giving great advice to his son, Opie, on *The Andy Griffith Show.* Then there was Cliff Huxtable on *The Cosby Show*—arguably the most popular TV dad—who was played by Bill Cosby in the '80s and '90s. How could you not love Cliff Huxtable? He was so funny and his family seemed to be perfect. He was a doctor, his wife was a lawyer, but still *family* was the most important thing. Cliff was the kind of dad anyone would want. He was perfect.

But Andy and Cliff aren't real. Writers made them up. I never had a dad like that. I'm betting you didn't either.

Real Dads

If you were to describe what a real dad is like—or more importantly, what your own dad was really like—chances are he would bear little resemblance to Cliff (unless you were really fortunate!). Cliff is more make-believe than believable, more heavenly than human.

Our perceptions of what a father is really like are colored by our experiences. Some of us might describe our dad as demanding or abusive or distracted. Some might say he was controlling or impossible to please. Some of us didn't even have a father in the house. But thankfully, a few lucky ones would describe Dad as a kind, caring, loving man.

No matter what was normal in your house, there are some reasonable expectations of what a father is—or should be. I think we can safely say he's a male parent. He might not be a birth parent; rather he might be a stepfather or an adoptive father or some other male figure who is in some way responsible for your care.

A dictionary might define *father* simply as "a man who provides and protects." Yet in reality he is so much more. What the dictionary cannot possibly explain is the emotional impact a father has on a child. According to sociologist Dr. David Popenoe, "Fathers are far more than just 'second adults' in the home." He said that involved fathers "bring positive benefits to their children that no other person is as likely to bring."[1]

A father is not just a sperm donor or a physical provider; he is the one who speaks significance into our lives. He teaches us to love and how to treat people right. He affirms our existence and helps us grow toward our potential. Or at least, that's the way it should be.

I know people who have incredibly blessed relationships with their fathers. But sadly, in my experience, they are the minority. Mostly I hear stories of people who feel abandoned, devalued, criticized, and unable to measure up. I have heard stories of horrible abuse and of dads who were there but never really "there." Yet, as important as a dad is, many children in America and throughout Western civilization are living without a father, or they bear the scars of an abusive, demanding, uninvolved father. The statistics are frightening:

- 63 percent of youth suicide victims are from fatherless homes.
- 90 percent of all homeless and runaway children are from fatherless homes.
- 80 percent of rapists with anger problems come from fatherless homes.
- 71 percent of all high-school dropouts come from fatherless homes.
- Children living in two-parent households with a poor relationship with their father are 68 percent more likely to smoke, drink, or use drugs, compared to all teens in two-parent households.

- Children with fathers who are involved are 40 percent less likely to repeat a grade in school.
- Adolescent girls raised in two-parent homes with involved fathers are significantly less likely to be sexually active than girls raised without involved fathers.[2]

These statistics point to an epidemic rather than just a problem, and they cannot be ignored. No group of people is immune to the effects—not the church or even the White House. In a recent online article titled "Why Do So Many Politicians Have Daddy Issues?" author Barron YoungSmith made an interesting point about the correlation between politicians and dysfunctional fathers:

American politics is overflowing with stories of absent fathers, alcoholic fathers, neglectful fathers, and untimely deceased ones. Indeed, one of the more interesting questions raised by [Paul] Ryan's biography is: Why do so many of our politicians have daddy issues?

The list is surprisingly long. Take Ronald Reagan, who was haunted by a moment when he discovered his alcoholic father on the front porch "drunk, dead to the world," his hair filled with snow. The 11-year-old Reagan had to drag him indoors. Or Bill Clinton, whose biological father drowned in a car crash, and who remembered standing up to his alcoholic stepfather and demanding that he never beat Clinton's mother again. Gerald Ford's father, an alcoholic, was found guilty of extreme cruelty to his family, and refused to pay child support when Ford's mother left him. George W. Bush's relationship with his father was less lurid, but infamously resentful: He spent his entire life, including his presidency, careening between attempts to live up to H.W.'s impossible expectations and efforts to garishly repudiate them. And it hardly bears recounting that President Obama built his political persona around a search for his absent dad.

The author proposes a number of reasons why such a childhood would propel a man into politics. Some may have developed a high sensitivity to the emotions of others and have strong coping mechanisms, while others probably had to take on a leadership role very early in life. He finished with this thought:

Of course, there is the hunger for attention and the gaping psychological need to be loved. It's often been observed that electoral politics is so demanding and unpleasant that no normal person would endure the indignities required to become a successful politician. In that sense, anyone who is willing to fundraise, glad-hand, and defend their smallest gaffes for months must derive some additional psychological benefit from politicking. Many of the people willing to keep going must be, in some sense, broken inside and driven to salve their emotional pain by courting the adulation of voters.[3]

Father Effects

Good or bad, present or passive, Dad defines us. He shapes what we become, how we think, how we act, how we feel about ourselves, and how we respond to others. Our first emotions and feelings are formed so much by his words.

Your relationship with your own father defines you far more than you realize. It shapes you in almost every conceivable way—how you treat people, how you handle money, how you treat your children or spouse, and even how you view yourself.

In the book *The Transformation of a Man's Heart,* contributor Gordon Dalbey stated, "When a man abdicates his calling as a father, the world suffers the effects. The father not only defines a boy's past…but also stands at the gateway to his destiny." Dalbey told this story:

Julian Lennon, son of the late Beatles pop idol John Lennon, is a classic example. In his early twenties, Julian made his musical debut with a best-selling album. Then, to everyone's shock, he suddenly stopped recording altogether. Seven years later, when he finally released a second album, he talked with a reporter about struggling to find his calling.

Julian's mother and father had divorced when he was five, and after that he saw his father, John, perhaps a dozen times. "He walked out the bloody door and was never around," Julian snapped. "I'd admire him on TV—listen to his words and opinions. But for someone who was praised for peace and love and wasn't able to keep that at home, that's hypocrisy."

As the reporter notes, "Julian became a self-taught musician. His father never gave him a music lesson." In the son's words, "We sat down once and maybe he played five chords—that was that.… The only thing he ever taught me was how not to be a father."

His hate for his father blinded Julian Lennon to his own calling, and the world suffered the loss of his talent for seven years.[4]

Thinking About Father God

The ways your father behaved toward you—what he said to you, how he treated you, everything he did and didn't do—had an impact on you in some way. Depending on how you were treated, mistreated, or just plain ignored, you have come up with your own ideas of what a father is like. Because of this, I am quite certain that how you see and perceive your heavenly Father, God, has also been impacted—distorted even—by your relationship with your earthly dad.

When I became a Christ-follower, I struggled a bit with the Trinity. Mind you, I had no issues with Jesus or the Holy Spirit, but I struggled to see God as "Father." Having only my personal experience as a reference point, I wondered if God would be like a bigger version of my dad. Would He leave me when I failed? Punish me for not measuring up? For years I wrestled with the concept of God as Father.

Then sometime later I read a quote from the brilliant theologian A. W. Tozer that literally changed my life. He said, "What comes into our minds when we think about God is the most important thing about us."[5] Why? Because how we see God determines how we relate to God, and how we relate to God determines everything else about us. After hearing those words, and determining them to be true, I realized I would never become all I was intended to be until I could see God for who He is, not whom I imagined Him to be.

Stop here for a minute. Try it—think about God right now. What comes into your mind? What feelings or images come to you? What does He "look" like to you? How do you think He feels about you? Be honest here—don't give some churchy answer that you think you're supposed to give if that's not what you really feel deep inside.

So now let me ask, when you think of your *earthly* father, what is the first thing that comes into your mind? Provider? Teacher? Generous? Funny? Or, perhaps like me, you think of abandonment, abuse, or neglect? Maybe you think passive or uninterested? Controlling and judgmental? Some of you will be thinking of a dad who expected more than you could ever give or more than you could ever be. I have friends—successful businessmen and church leaders—who to this day are still trying to please that kind of father. Perhaps your father loved you but never disciplined you. Or maybe your dad was loving and amazing!

Regardless of your answer, I think that whatever comes to mind when you think about your father, there is a good chance that you attribute similar characteristics to your image of your heavenly Father. Simply put, your image of God has been formed and shaped by the father figures in your life, as explained by mental-health nurse Juanita Ryan:

> Long before we were old enough to think in words, we thought in pictures or images. These images are loaded with emotion. From the first days of life we began storing memories of our emotional experiences. Images of our mother's face when she was distressed and when she was pleased, or of our father's face when he was angry or when he was laughing—all are stored in our memory. These images became linked with the soothing we felt or with the increased fear we felt in interacting with these important faces and voices. All of our experiences, from our earliest days, have been stored in our minds, some of them as emotionally laden images. These emotionally laden images of parents or of other early caretakers form the basic foundation of our expectations in relationships with all other people, including God.[6]

So many of us have drawn a picture of Dad in our minds, and that image has been transferred to how we see and relate to God. But guess what? That image of God is inaccurate. And if there's one thing I want you to hear me say, it's that *God is not a bigger version of your earthly father.*

Looking Through a Distorted Lens

The distortion of how we see God ultimately comes from what the Bible refers to as our Enemy or the devil: Satan. Satan is a liar who wants to distort, discredit, and deceive you about God the Father. Satan isn't just a liar but "the father of lies" (John 8:44), and his number-one goal is to deceive you by making God out to be less than He is. Deception, in fact, is the primary tool Satan uses to misdirect your attention away from a God who is massively in love with you and died in your place so that you have the opportunity to live with Him in heaven forever.

If Satan can distort your image of God, he can destroy your life. You will be unable to relate to the father heart of God, and you will never experience the intimacy, love, and complete acceptance that await you. Through his misdirection, you'll miss the best relationship possible this side of heaven.

Too often we believe the lies, and in doing so, we miss the full nature, character, and goodness of God. We won't approach God as the perfect Father that He is, but instead try to gain His love through performance, thinking we are bad and He is mad at us. So many who already know Jesus spend time worrying they will lose their salvation (which they never *earned* to start with). That is one of Satan's biggest lies! Others see God as a policeman, or as passively uninvolved, unconcerned, and too busy running the universe to possibly care about the details of their lives.

You May Have Given Up on God, but He Hasn't Given Up on You

Some of you would say you have no desire for a relationship with God. Your image of God may be so distorted you have nixed the possibility of forming any kind of connection with Him. I hope you will continue to read. The ultimate goal of this book is not that our minds would be informed but that our hearts would be transformed. It is my hope that your image of God would be clearer and brighter tomorrow than it is today and that your relationship with Him would be stronger.

If you are reading this book but couldn't care less about God, the truth is, there is a part of you that really does care; and although you have stopped thinking about engaging in a relationship with Him, He has never stopped pursuing you. God has revealed Himself through His creation, and you can see evidence of Him all around. He has also revealed Himself in each of our hearts. The Bible tells us in Ecclesiastes 3:11, "Yet God has made everything beautiful for its own time. He has planted eternity in the human heart, but even so, people cannot see the whole scope of God's work from beginning to end."

God Is God, Not Your Earthly Dad

I'm going to say this over and over again: God is not a bigger version of your earthly father. These words may bring tears to your eyes because you so want this to be true. You have resisted God because you wanted nothing to do with a heavenly Father who could possibly be a bigger version of the dad you experienced as a child. Neither did I. After I came to Christ and heard about God being a father to me, I wanted to turn in my salvation at the neighborhood Goodwill store. I did not want another father, and certainly not if He was the kind of father I'd already had. (I'll tell you more about my dad experiences in the next chapter, and then you'll understand why I felt this way.)

I had to know God was different, so I spent countless hours studying, thinking, talking with professors, and asking pastors and friends about the character of God the Father. I was soon convinced that our heavenly Father is like no father I had ever known! We will talk much more in a later chapter about the perfect father, but for now please open your mind and heart to the possibility of a Father unlike your own...a Father unlike any other.

I love this verse: "See how very much our Father loves us, *for he calls us his children, and that is what we are!* But the people who belong to this world don't recognize that we are God's children because they don't know him" (1 John 3:1).

I pray that through the pages of this book, the distorted image you have of God can be realigned with the truth, and that you can walk in the full joy and understanding of what it means to be a child of the most high God. It is only when we face reality that we can change things. It is only through brokenness we can truly be made whole. Sometimes, in order to move forward toward healing, we have to go backward a little first. We may have to reopen a wound so it can heal properly.

I am so glad that God recycles our pain. He really does use for good the things that Satan means for harm (see Genesis 50:20). I found this to be so true in my own life. In the next chapter, you'll read my own dad story. I hope my story, my life, and the things I have learned can bring hope to you and to anyone who may be hurt, broken, or stuck because of father wounds.

My Daddy Story

It doesn't matter who my father
was; it matters who I remember
he was.

—ANNE SEXTON

A s I sit here and stare at a blinking cursor, I am not sure where to start, to be honest. (I can hear you wondering how on earth I can write a whole book when I'm struggling to find words already!) Telling my story, even after all these years, still stirs emotions and memories that I usually prefer to leave alone.

Mine is actually not a story about just my father; rather it is a journey with my different fathers. There have been a few in my life.

I guess the beginning is as good as any place to start.

My biological father was David Bishop. I have one picture of him, and that is it. I have no real or tangible memories. Mostly I think of him in regard to what could have been and what wasn't. I know he was a truck driver, I know he spent time in the army serving our country, and I know he died just two days after I turned four. He was with his best friend at the time, out driving in his Corvair, when he lost control and hit a tree. Both men died on impact. Dad died drinking and driving. In fact, police found over twenty empty beer cans in the car while investigating the accident.

My parents had divorced not long before the accident, and earlier that day Dad had come by the house wanting to take me with him for the day. My mom said no, and to this day I thank God for giving her the courage and wisdom to do the right thing. How different things could have been.

As a young boy, I didn't know the right words to describe my feelings, but I know now I felt abandoned by him. Abandonment, which we will deal with extensively in another chapter, carries with it horrible wounds and insecurity. It leaves you feeling unwanted and unloved. Growing up I was an angry teenager, but underneath the anger was simply a little boy who never dealt with the pain of losing his daddy. I remember wishing I could go camping with my dad as I watched my neighborhood friend leave to go camping with his. I remember being aware of fathers and sons. I always noticed other kids working on cars or playing ball with their dads. Looking back, I guess the best word I can come up with is *conflicted*. I understood that my dad had died and wasn't coming home, but how is a young child supposed to deal with those emotions? It took twenty-five years after his death for me to finally begin the process of healing and forgiveness.

I have learned that if we don't deal with pain, we can be certain it will eventually deal with us. Pain becomes like a bag of garbage we carry around, and our memories become our best friend. Our pain will follow us and, ultimately, define us. In my life, abandonment became my identity, and to this day I struggle with loss. Being fatherless defined me.

Dad Number Two

Eighteen months after my dad died, my mom remarried. I soon found out what it meant to have a physically, emotionally, and verbally abusive stepdad. Despite wishing the memory would go away, I still remember watching him throw my mom on the ground like she wasn't even human. I remember the yelling—so *much* yelling—and living in a totally unpredictable environment. I haven't seen my stepdad since I was eight years old, and as I type these words, I can say I finally have found peace. Though I can now pray for him, he will always be the one who taught me how being abused creates fear in a young heart. Abuse became part of the baggage I carried around, and once again I was being defined by the actions of a father. Being abused also defined me.

In later chapters, I will deal more with the trauma of abuse, and I will share my path toward finding healing and wholeness after the violent treatment I received and witnessed from my stepfather. There is hope and wholeness beyond abuse, but it is a process, and not an easy one. I hope as we walk together we can learn about the true nature of our heavenly Father, let go of the pain, and live with a new sense of joy, peace, and freedom.

"Dad" Number Three

One of the most sobering things about pain is how it robs you of your current blessings. I believe we can focus either on what was lost or on what is left. When you are constantly living in the past and are consumed by your hurt, you cannot see what God has provided for you in the present. What did I lose? My childhood, my father, and in some ways my ability to feel secure and protected. I grieve for the absent memories of a dad at sporting events or on a special camping trip, or having a father to show me how to change the oil or how to love my wife. So much was lost, but the biggest loss was my ability to see what was left in my life. I was so focused on what I didn't have that I missed what was right in front of me.

In the wake of two failed marriages, riddled with abuse and abandonment, my mom, brother, and I moved into her parents' house, where my grandpa became the new father figure to my brother and me. We affectionately called him "Pop" or "Papa." My grandpa was consistently dependable, always available, and he never hurt us in any way. At that point in my life, he was everything I had never experienced in a dad. He provided for my needs and protected me.

I miss my Pop more than words could express. To be honest, I only wish I could have seen God's provision while he was still alive. I realized too late that He had given me a great "dad" in Pop, a man I could look up to and learn from, both as a child and as a future parent to my own kids. With Pop, finally, being accepted defined me.

Dad Number Four

My fourth father, Gregg, didn't enter my life until my late teens. Although he has not had to play a father role in my life, it has given me peace as a son to know my mother is now well loved and cared for. She deserves nothing less, and I am grateful to him for accepting my brother and me as his own.

Passing the Pain to the Next Generation

As I type these words, my only son—who has struggled for years with drug addiction—is in jail. We named him David, after the father I never knew. I can't help but play questions over and over in my mind: *What did I do wrong? What could I have done better? How did I fail?*

My thoughts taunt me, but David is twenty-seven years old and has made choices for himself. I pray, hope, and believe for David, but I also want to find healing in how I view myself as a father. I want to better understand my role in his life and not blame myself for everything that happens with him. The insecurity that I feel in my relationship with my son and my efforts to protect him from the consequences of his own actions are directly connected to my own past and wanting to help him avoid the pain I knew as a child.

The Journey Begins

When we come to Christ, we are God's adopted sons and daughters. We can live without condemnation and with confidence. We do not have to live in fear, because we are unconditionally loved. I love what Paul wrote to the churches in the region of Galatia: "Because you are sons, God sent the Spirit of his Son into our hearts, the Spirit who calls out, '*Abba,* Father.' So you are no longer a slave, but a son; and since you are a son, God has made you also an heir" (Galatians 4:6–7, NIV). You're part of the family, and nothing can ever change that!

We all have a daddy story. I shared mine, and I hope it heartens you to know you are not alone. God does have a plan, and together we can learn to live better, not bitter. Sometimes learning begins with unlearning. I am now defined by what God says about me, not what my fathers said. God can restore our hope and redeem our pain; I can personally guarantee this.

Let's journey on toward wholeness, healing, and peace.

The Father Who Wasn't There

The Absent Father

Not long ago I read a story about an initiative to provide inmates with cards to send out for Mother's Day. All they had to do was request the card and postage. The results were astounding; almost 90 percent of inmates asked for cards for their moms. The demand was far greater than expected, and the project was such a success that plans were made to offer the same service for Father's Day. Again, all the inmates had to do was make the request, and the card and postage would be provided to them. The results again were astounding and beyond expectation—except in this case *none* of the inmates asked for a card.[1] As it turned out, most of the inmates did not know their father or have any kind of relationship with him, or he had already passed. While the statistics indicate that inmates have higher rates of fatherlessness than most, this is still indicative of the current crisis.

According to statistics, 43 percent of children live without their fathers. About 40 percent of children in father-absent homes have not seen their fathers at all during the past year, 26 percent of absent fathers live in a different state than their children, and 50 percent of children absent from their fathers have never set foot in their fathers' homes.[2]

Sitting, Waiting, Wishing, Hoping

When my son, David, went to jail for drug abuse, I suddenly found myself with unexpected opportunities to talk and pray with other inmates. I met Shannon there, and before long he became the first inmate I led to Christ. Since that day Shannon has been writing me, and through those pages I am hearing a story that only too well demonstrates the impact of an absent father. Here is an excerpt from one of Shannon's letters:

> I come from a family line of drug addicts and alcoholics.... My whole life has been anger, hate, and disappointment—with a failed marriage and two kids I haven't seen in years. For as long as I can remember, I've felt like my life never mattered, and I have contemplated suicide more than I can recall. All this stems from a broken family, a broken home, and nobody to ever be there or care. I grew up on my own and never had a chance in the world at a normal life. As of today, my dad passed away last year of cancer, my mother is a bad drug addict/alcoholic, [and I have] a severe alcoholic brother and a sister on her way to prison for drugs.

Shannon was just like so many of us with absent fathers: sitting on a curb, hoping, waiting, longing, and desperately discouraged by what should have been. For so many, that confusion and discouragement turns to anger and a sense of constantly being alone, even when surrounded by people. This is my story too. I can relate to those struggling with the fear of being left.

As I shared previously, my dad died just two days after my fourth birthday. I simply never knew him. All I know of him has been learned through stories shared by his brothers and sisters, and though I tried hard to learn all I could about him, people either had nothing good or nothing at all to say. You can imagine what kind of hole a "missing" dad creates in the heart of a child. No matter how nurturing a mother we may have, there is still significant need for a father in all of us. This is especially important when it comes to meeting the four basic emotional needs all humans have, as defined by Jack Frost in his book *Experiencing Father's Embrace:* the need for unconditional expressed love, the need to feel secure and comforted, the need for praise and affirmation, and the need for a purpose in life.[3]

Without a father to meet these needs, I could hardly imagine how God could be a Father to me. Did I even need a father? My image of God the Father and His role in my life was completely distorted.

Maybe your father died like mine, or perhaps he is alive but left your family. Maybe you see him on special occasions, or perhaps you never see him at all. Whatever the circumstances, abandonment affects children in significant ways.

Donald Miller, author of *Father Fiction,* described the effect of his abandonment this way:

> There have been times in my life when I didn't know exactly how to be. I mean, there were feelings, sometimes anger, sometimes depression, sometimes raging lust, and I was never sure what any of it was about. I just felt like killing somebody or sleeping with some girl or decking a guy in a bar, and I didn't know what to do with any of these feelings. Life was a confusing series of emotions rubbing against events. I wasn't sure how to manage myself, how to talk to a woman, how to build a career, how to—well, be a man.
>
> To me, life was something you had to stumble through alone. It wasn't something you enjoyed or conquered, it was something that happened to you, and you didn't have a whole lot of say about the way it turned out. You just acted out your feelings and hoped you'd never get caught.[4]

I spent a large portion of my young life trying to please a dad who wasn't there. It sounds obvious, but it's hard to get the approval of a dad who isn't even alive. I found myself serving our country in the US Air Force, just like my dad. I was married, had a son, was working on a bachelor's degree, and actively working (in my spare time) at two different businesses. I was also by default wrecking my marriage of less than three years. I just wanted to be worthy of Dad's love, and yet I could never receive it. As a result, my abandonment led to a deep insecurity and fear of rejection that I projected onto other relationships.

In hindsight, the abandonment I felt when my father died was nothing compared to the pain of abandonment and rejection I experienced several years later at the hands of my stepfather, Dean. He was abusive in nearly every way—physically, mentally, verbally—up till the day he left forever. Despite the abuse, his leaving created a gaping hole in my young heart. We were sitting at the dinner table at what was soon to become the last time I would ever see or talk to him. I don't remember what set him off, but I clearly remember his anger as he picked up the table and dumped all of the dinner, plates, silverware, and glassware on my mom, grandpa, grandma, younger brother, and me. We sat, shocked and speechless, as he proceeded to yell at each of us—using words I can't repeat—before he finally left. I was just a young child—confused, lonely, wanting so desperately to have a dad in my life—and yet here I was again, watching another dad leave me. I ran after him as fast as I could, catching him just as he reached his car, and yelled, "Dad, please don't leave me!" He glanced at me and, without hesitating, put his hand on my chest, shoved me to the ground, and said, "You are not my kid. You never were, and I am not your dad. Get over it." I sat on my driveway and watched as his car drove away for the last time. *Another father gone.* I hated him.

It is incredible how vividly we can remember those moments. In fact, we couldn't forget them if we tried. How painful intentional abandonment is! Who would have thought the grief over my deceased father would turn out to be less painful than the purposeful rejection Dean chose that day? His actions imbedded a deep insecurity in my young heart, along with the belief that I was unworthy, unloved, and unwanted.

The Fear of Abandonment and the Striving for Approval

Insecurity creates instability in a heart and also in a family home. For me, it proved itself early in my marriage. Because I was so afraid that my wife, Michelle, would leave me as my fathers had, I thought I had to literally buy my way to her continued acceptance. I bought her what I thought I needed to so she would continue to love me. Unfortunately I was acting from a posture of fear and not love. I couldn't understand real love in a marriage, so everything was basically self-centered love. I loved so I could be loved in return. I bought so she would not leave me. Don't get me wrong: doing things for another isn't wrong in itself, but the reason can be wrong and the motives can be skewed; and when they are, eventual relational destruction is inevitable. It is a cycle of brokenness that affects most other relationships.

The absent-father imprint transfers to every human relationship. As you build friendships later in life, you may be guarded and afraid to trust, believing friends will leave you. Alternatively, you're the friend who wants to hang out all the time and who will be there "forever." When you find people you love and can trust, you're afraid to let them go. When you become a parent, you might be the hovering mom or helicopter dad, staying close to feed your codependency. You may find yourself enabling your children out of fear that they will not love you or will leave you too soon. It's funny how we often become the opposite kind of parent from the ones who raised us. I always wanted to be the dad I never had, but you'll see in later chapters how I swung the pendulum too far in my parenting, until I became codependent in my relationship with my son.

My friend David—abandoned by his father before birth—was also fearful people would eventually leave him. However, he had a completely different approach to relationships:

> My biological father left before I was born, and I can attest to the anger and destructiveness that comes from abandonment. I grew up a very angry and violent kid. I used to get into fights all the time, was sent to see the principal and the school counselor often, and was suspended from school multiple times a year. I even hit a teacher in the face while he was talking to me about how I had gone after a kid with a baseball bat in PE. The same teacher I hit showed me so much love and compassion at the time, but I just didn't realize it. I was very self-destructive as well. I remember one time in sixth grade when we were making model rockets, one of the kids made me mad, and my reaction was to destroy my own rocket.
>
> As I grew up, I realized that I really wanted relationships and to be liked by people, and that I wouldn't be able to have those things if I continued to go through life being externally angry and violent. But I never really dealt with the past hurt and pain so I didn't get past being angry; I just learned how to stuff it, hide it, and to be passive-aggressive.
>
> Obviously being abandoned by my father left me constantly fearing abandonment and rejection, which meant remaining distant in my relationships…coupled with constant people-pleasing and being fake so that people would like me. I was so distanced from my wife when we got married, partly because I secretly thought "this too shall pass." I didn't want to get too attached so I wouldn't get hurt. We struggled in this for a while and I'm really just now letting her in fully. It only took about six years!"

Insecurity from abandonment becomes a scar in your heart that challenges relationships and affects every aspect of life, including the way you see your heavenly Father. If you are anything like me, you find yourself asking, *"Is God going to leave me? Can I trust Him? Does He care about me? Do I really matter?"* As I grew up, I worked hard to cultivate friendships. I was a great friend, but it was often for the wrong reasons. I loved so I wouldn't be left. Now I have learned that humans can and will leave, but God never will. Ever. The Bible says in Hebrews 13:5, "For God has said, 'I will never fail you. I will never abandon you.'"

Your dad may have already left you, or may yet leave you, but the truth is, God never will. I lived under a fear that God would eventually leave me, but after coming to Christ, I learned through the Bible and through life with Christ that God's promises are true—always.

Look at what it means for Shannon:

Until I met you [John], I hardly had hope or a dream. But today my face has a smile. Today I stand with my hands in the air like I have my whole life… but now my hands are not raised for the police, but for Jesus!!! Today my biological father may be gone, but my Father in heaven stepped to my side and so did you, John. I still have a long way to go in life's journey, but I know as long as Jesus is in my heart and leading my life—and as long as you will accept the challenge to turn an ex-con full of morbid flaws into a testimony of the Most High—I am already on the path and I definitely need lots of help, encouragement, and faith, guidance, and something I hardly felt before…LOVE. My mission is to continually let the Lord into my heart and to make my life's decisions.

If you have felt forgotten, rejected, or left behind, take this promise to heart: God will never, ever, ever, ever, ever leave you.

The Father Who Was There, but Not "There"

The Passive Father

If you ask people what the opposite of love is, they will usually respond with the obvious: hate. But I'm not convinced that's really correct. Author and Holocaust survivor Elie Wiesel once said, "The opposite of love is not hate but indifference," and I believe that to be true.

Both hate and love have passion at their core, but indifference is the absence of passion. So while it's easy to identify an abusive or controlling father, the effects of an indifferent or passive father may be harder to pinpoint.

Think of this dad as the guy who is sitting with his child, yet whose nose is buried in the newspaper. I know many of you remember this scene from your own childhood. This dad is present in body, but not in mind or emotion. Though he is not physically absent, he is absent in a different way. He is there, but not available to his family. He resides in the home, does not physically abuse, yell, scream, or control, but he is uninvolved and unengaged as a parent. He is a great guy who is liked by others, and while he provides shelter, food, sometimes even rules and guidelines, his children cannot connect with him emotionally. He may be too busy with work or hobbies to interact with his children, or he has simply not enough energy to give more than a cursory answer. Sometimes this dad buys lavish gifts to make up for the lack of his time and attention, doing the only thing he knows to show his love. The passive father may be stressed, overwhelmed, or depressed, and struggles to show emotion. He was possibly raised to be "seen and not heard," and while happy when his children do well, he does not know how to see them as individuals with dreams, hopes, and fears.

Most of you are probably familiar with the story of serial killer Jeffrey Dahmer. He is notoriously known for not only murdering seventeen people but also for performing unspeakable acts of dismemberment and cannibalism. Dahmer was sentenced to 975 years in prison, but he was murdered by a fellow inmate about two years into his incarceration. After Jeffrey's death, his father, Lionel, began to explore his own life and his son's childhood for any signs or clues about what might have turned his baby boy into the monster he later became. He wrote a book called *A Father's Story,* which described the home life of Jeffrey as a child. Jeffrey's mother, Joyce, was often ill and was mentally unable to give her son the attention he needed. Lionel and Joyce had a difficult marriage, and there was a lot of tension in the home. Lionel admits to being a father consumed with his own graduate work rather than being attentive to his son.

I saw him in glimpses, a boy shooting around the room or eating at the dinner table. I felt him in snatches, a quick hug on the way in or out. I spoke to him in brief hellos, in good-byes tossed over my shoulder as I left the room. The Ph.D. loomed before me like an enormous mountain. Everything else seemed small.

Lionel Dahmer summed up raising his son with these words:

And so I wasn't there to see him as he began to sink into himself. I wasn't there to sense, even if I could have sensed it, that he might be drifting toward that unimaginable realm of fantasy and isolation that it would take me nearly thirty years to recognize. And yet, it may have been happening even then, while I gulped down my dinner and bolted past him for the door.

I want to make it clear that I am not in any way suggesting Lionel Dahmer is responsible for his son's behavior, or that any kind of parenting would result in someone becoming a serial murderer. But it is worth noting that Lionel himself acknowledges he was not there to see the early indications of his son's downward spiral. The warning signs were there, but his own busyness kept him from recognizing the depth of his son's problems. Dahmer ends his book in profound simplicity:

Fatherhood remains, at last, a grave enigma, and when I contemplate that my other son may one day be a father, I can only say to him, as I must to every father after me, "Take care, take care, take care."[1]

I can hardly begin to imagine the emotions, the horror, and the regret of Lionel Dahmer as a father when he looks back at what he could have done differently, knowing all the while he cannot change what has already been done. We can at least do our best to learn from his mistakes. What seems like the most simple of advice, in fact, requires determined intentionality. It is not enough to simply be there. We must do everything in our power to take care of our children, take care of their relationships, and take care of their emotional well-being. We are the ones God has entrusted to take care of His most precious possessions: His children.

The Alcoholic Father

Another type of passive father who may still live in the home but is absent from his parental role is the dad who is lost to drug and/or alcohol addiction. According to the Substance Abuse and Mental Health Services Administration, "7.5 million children under age 18 (10.5 percent of this population) lived with a parent who has experienced an alcohol use disorder in the past year."[2] That figure does not include drug, gambling, and other addictions that leave the adult unable to parent in any normal way. Children in an alcoholic's home are at much greater risk for behavioral, health, and mental problems, and they are more likely than any other group of children to become addicts themselves.[3] In addition, the children of an alcoholic or drug addict often have to function within extremely rigid family roles in order to survive the chaos. These roles enable them to create an illusion of normalcy but come at a great price. According to psychotherapist Chloe Sekouri, children of addicts will take on a variety of roles including "the little parent, the hero, the family scapegoat, the chief enabler, and the lost child."[4] These children are really not allowed to be children at all, having to take on responsibilities and problems far beyond their years.

Even Negative Attention Is Better than None at All

The present but uninvolved father can leave his children starved for affection and deeply hurt by his lack of interest. The children cannot grieve for a father who is still there, but some will feel loss just the same, questioning their own worth, purpose, and significance. They feel invisible and will commonly act out, desperate to get attention. Any attention. To an attention-starved child, even negative attention from a dad is better than none at all.

The repercussions are heartbreaking. Daughters with a passive father will sometimes dress inappropriately in an effort to be noticed by men, or pursue sexual relationships at a young age to fulfill their desire to feel loved. Adolescent girls raised without involved fathers are significantly more likely to be sexually active than girls raised in two-parent homes with involved fathers.[5] Children from the passive home become fiercely independent, and due to the lack of emotional response and love they receive as children, they often find it hard to form attachments later in life, experiencing loneliness even when surrounded by friends.[6]

If you are a parent, you might ask yourself these questions: When did I last give my child uninterrupted attention? Do I ask my children to wait till the commercials come on before they can talk to me? Do I allow my hobbies, work, or addictions to keep me from spending time in the home? Do my children know without a doubt that I love, care about, and value them?

Real Connections Don't Come Easy

Author and clinical psychiatrist Dr. Stephan Poulter estimates "40 percent of people are raised with a passive dad,"[7] and researchers seem to agree that this style of parenting is potentially the most damaging to children. According to Dene Garvin Klinzing, professor of individual and family studies at the University of Delaware, these children "have the most problems dealing with the world. They have little emotional control and often have trouble forming attachments. They are easily frustrated. They have more academic problems and delinquency issues."[8]

If you are a child from this kind of home, I would expect your image of God to be significantly distorted, although it likely happened in a subtle way. Due to your father's distance, you may see God as also being way off in the distance, too busy running the universe to care about the details of your life. You see Him as the Creator, but you probably struggle to believe He wants to connect intimately with you or that He cares deeply about your hopes and dreams. Your approach to God is often more intellectual than personal; you believe God is loving, but you do not open your heart to Him easily. You are probably uncomfortable when people refer to God as "Daddy," but you may secretly desire to experience that kind of relationship. You have learned from your earthly father to be independent and not to bother him, so consequently you see God as disinterested. You probably try to handle things on your own, rather than take your concerns and problems to your heavenly Father. You love God but often wonder if God really wants a relationship with you. You ask, "Can He see me? Can He hear me? Do I matter?" Your deep loneliness and fear of rejection distorts the truth, so while you function in life, you never experience the fullness of the relationship with God.

My friend Kay wrote of her experience:

I can't really remember what it was like when I was super young. I don't remember my dad ever seeking me out for a hug or a kiss on the cheek. I know he was physically there. But he was definitely not emotionally present. The only time he really interacted was for discipline. As a teenager, I was starved for that kind of love a daughter needs from her father. My tank was empty and my parents' marriage was falling apart, creating anxiety in the home. I began to search for "love" elsewhere. I tried to find it in guys, my job, anything that would put a Band-Aid on the hurt. That is when my dad would interact and call me names—horrible, degrading names that no man should ever call his daughter.

From the depth of my heart I truly had no idea of what love looked like, let alone that God loved me. I really thought that I was what my dad said I was, and in turn I assumed that was what God thought of me. I was this unclean, unimportant, unworthy girl that was not fit to be loved by my dad and God. I didn't feel I was fit to walk in a church either. I spent a great deal of my life (minus the last few years) having, at best, a very far-away relationship with my dad, and with God. I knew they existed, but because of my perception of myself, and believing the lies about myself, I just kind of thought, *This is it. This is what it is like to have God in my life. He judges, looks down on me, and disciplines me.* I wasted so much time feeling this way! It is still an enigma to me sometimes…so many mixed emotions…even now as tears fall from my face, I get saddened that I didn't know God could love me as He does.

What Kay is learning now, and what I want you to know, is that the same God who created the universe sees you. He not only placed the stars in the sky but also numbered the hairs on your head. He knows you the best and loves you the most. Look at what the Bible says in Psalm 139:1–4:

> O LORD, you have examined my heart
>> and know everything about me.
> You know when I sit down or stand up.
>> You know my thoughts even when I'm far away.
> You see me when I travel
>> and when I rest at home.
>> You know everything I do.
> You know what I am going to say
>> even before I say it, LORD.

It is my prayer that as we look closer at the nature of God, you will see that He truly does care about the details of your everyday life. I hope you will realize He longs for intimacy and closeness with you, and that through a clearer image of God, you will experience the father relationship you were always meant to have.

5

The Father Who Expects Perfection

The Demanding Father

I think we would all agree that from your deepest area of brokenness will come your greatest strength and—in most cases—your biggest weakness. Trying to please a father who wasn't there (an impossible task) turned me into an overachiever in almost everything I did, including my role as a first-time parent. Because I had a deep-seated—and completely unrealistic—belief that my father always expected more from me than I could ever deliver, I then in turn set a very high level of expectation for my own son, who for the longest time could never please me.

The first time this became outwardly apparent was when we lived on five acres out in the country near Mount Saint Helens in Washington State. We were the proud owners of a new ride-on lawn mower, and my son at the impressionable age of ten or eleven would watch in awe as I mowed the yard. Eventually the day came when he asked if he could mow.

Every father's dream is to sit on the front porch, ice-cold beverage in hand, and proudly watch his son mow, right? While that may be true, it's *not* a child's dream to be observed by a father who expects only mistakes and failure. My son wanted praise, and instead, I pointed out all the things he had done wrong. Looking back, I can see the hopeful look on his face after working for hours, trying so hard to please me—a boy just wanting to be like his dad. But I didn't see him then. I didn't see what he had accomplished as a young boy trying to do his best. I didn't see what he needed from me because I was so focused on his shortcomings, like the corners he missed by the flower beds. I remember—and so does he—that I said not a single positive comment in response to his efforts.

I would do anything to be able to go back in time and do it all differently, to affirm him and let him know he was loved. But I can't. The damage was done.

Impossible Expectations

My brokenness and desire to perform was being passed on in a different form to my son, who just wanted to please his daddy. David has never said a word about it, but in some ways that day shaped him. I was setting a standard he would never be able to measure up to. I was not just criticizing his work; I was effectively criticizing *him*. According to author Jack Frost, "Dr. James Dobson, founder of Focus on the Family, has stated that it takes at least forty words of praise to counteract the impact of just one word of criticism in a child's heart."[1] If that's true, I think I owe David a *whole lot* of praise to make up for the times I let him down in that way.

I am not suggesting that we never say a word to correct or instruct; I don't believe that to be true at all. But it usually isn't *what* we say; it's when, why, and how we say it. Correction given in love is completely different from correction for the sake of perfection, and I wasn't doing for David what God did for me.

We often see this scenario of impossible expectations played out when it comes to school and grades. Children need our approval, and we should be proud when they do good things. Our society rewards people who perform well, but so many of us grew up being praised *only* when we excelled. That creates an unhealthy belief that love is based on performance. It creates a relationship based solely on how good the child is and how the child is meeting expectations.

The demanding father values and requires obedience to his very high standards. He wants his children to succeed, so he rewards when his expectations are met and shows disapproval and disappointment when they are not, thus creating the belief that his love is conditional and has to be earned. This father is concerned about how the children's behavior reflects on him, so he also expects them to behave as if they are older than they are.

Children raised by demanding fathers will find their value in what they do rather than who they are, so they are constantly striving to succeed. They are often more concerned with looking good on the outside and putting on a front, believing only their best will impress. This kind of childhood is one of the root causes of adult depression. It's interesting to note that 80 percent of pastors' kids have been treated for depression.[2]

Why? Because pastors' kids usually carry the weight of not only their parents' expectations but the whole church's as well. They live their lives under a spotlight and feel they have to be perfect at everything, all the time.

Many children from this type of home will grow to formulate unrealistic expectations and require the same high level of performance from others around them. If you were raised this way, you may find yourself demanding your spouse or children to continually do better and "get it right." We are all wired to perform, and this style of parenting exacerbates what is already inside of us. It creates an unpredictable environment and produces insecure children who believe they have to earn love.

God Does Not Expect You to Earn His Love

The necessity to earn love is never more untrue than when it comes to the relationship with our heavenly Father. If you were the child of a dad who expected perfection, you probably struggle to understand God's unconditional love. You imagine God to be unrealistically demanding, critical, and accepting only of your successes. You're afraid of disapproval, and believe that God's love is a prize to be earned through performance. He may seem out of reach and impossible to please. You have probably asked God, *"Am I good enough? Can You accept me? Are You happy with me?"* Your picture of God has been distorted by a father who loved imperfectly.

Look at how constant expectation affected Andrew:

> My father was too expecting. However, rather than expecting me to succeed, he expected me to fail. He frequently said to me that I was not smart enough to do well in school, not coordinated enough to play sports, not sensible enough to make good decisions. Subsequently, when I look at God, I tend to see Him as disappointed with me, as someone whom I can never please. Then my tendency is to fade into depression, wanting a relationship with Him but never feeling able to have one.

Andrew's story is like so many of ours. We see God through the eyes of our experiences with our earthly father and consequently respond to Him in the same way. The problem with the story I shared about my son earlier is that while he knew he was loved, protected, and provided for, he didn't know yet that no matter how good or bad he performed a job, he was still accepted. Over time I learned that the job is never more important than the person, and I am willing to admit that the longer I am a parent, the less I know about being a parent. Unfortunately, we often learn the hard way with our firstborn.

One of the things that helps me as a child of God and as a father of children is to see how God views His own Son. Look at what God said about His Son at the time of His baptism: "And a voice from heaven said, 'This is my Son, whom I love; with him I am well pleased'" (Matthew 3:17, NIV). Before a single miracle had been performed, before Jesus healed even one person, before He fed thousands, and before He completed the ultimate task of dying for the whole world, God was "well pleased" with Jesus, and so He is with us. When I could see God more clearly as a father, I could see myself more completely, and I was able to see my role in the lives of my children more appropriately. It helped me to realize that what I do for God is not about earning His love but is *a result of* my love for Him. It helped me sincerely rest as a child, and therefore I was able to speak words of life, encouragement, and adoration into my daughters, and my son as well.

As hard as it may be to stop listening to the lies and start believing the truth, please know that God accepts you just where you are. He loves you more than anyone has, could, or will, and nothing you do will make Him love you less or more. Our goal is not perfection but progression. When you can learn to live at that address, you will see results that are insanely personal. Allow this realization to settle in your heart, and then your children, spouse, and friends will begin to receive it in their lives.

6

The Father Who Rescues

The Enabling Father

I have been putting off this chapter for days, and now as I write it, I am beginning to see more of the reality of my brokenness. I'm seeing clearly how the "dad wounds" in my own life have affected not just me, but my wife, my children, and even those who are close to me at work and in life. That's a long introduction to simply say, "I am a father who enables." Yes, even as I type that, I want to hit the Delete key—to delete it from the page as well as from my life. It was bad enough to admit in the last chapter that I expected perfection from my son. Now writing all these new words is like revealing more dysfunction to the world. But I know that revealing is the beginning of healing, and healing is the goal.

The reality is that I can't ask you to be real about your life if I can't be real with myself about my own. We are on a journey of discovering what is true—not to feel guilt, not for condemnation, but so that you can change yourself and subsequently help those affected by you. By God's grace and providence, you will find the true you—the person you are made to be.

It seems we so often get locked in our own prison and then throw away the key, even though God wants to free us from the past. It is only when we allow the wounds of our past to be reopened that the pain can be identified and healed. If we allow it, these moments of self-revelation can become hinge points that begin the long process of changing our future.

By now you are familiar with my story. Having a dad die when I was so young caused some abandonment issues for sure, but being abused and living in a "be seen and not heard" environment made me feel worthless. I guess you could say I was provided for but not pursued. I longed to be loved, noticed, hugged, and cared about. So I learned—as most children will—that behaving badly got attention, as we talked about in a previous chapter. Even though it was the wrong kind of attention, at least I was being noticed. As a result, I got in a lot of trouble, was suspended from both middle school and high school for bad behavior, and even had to stay a few nights in juvenile detention hall. Although I regret my stupid choices, if nothing else, it made me determined to be the kind of father I never had. Unfortunately the pendulum swung a little too far.

From an Ignored Child to an Enabling Father

For every active wound in our hearts, there is a reactive consequence in our homes. In my case, not wanting my son to feel the unworthiness I experienced as a child, I went overboard in a different direction. I rescued my son, David, from every situation he got himself into. He never had to experience negative consequences of his behavior because I always intervened and protected him from the pain and the penalties he really should have endured. As a result, I never allowed David to find his own path, learn from his mistakes, or learn to make good choices on his own for the right reasons. I couldn't shield him from an addiction to heroin. I couldn't protect him from the law. I couldn't save him from jail. And sadly, he couldn't spare himself either, because he had never learned about the consequences of poor choices when he was growing up. Although I can't be sure, I wonder if different choices on my part would have resulted in a different outcome for David. My heart breaks every day as I picture my son in jail. He is facing possible time in prison, multiple felonies, and a lot of change to overcome this whole thing called *addiction*.

David calls me every day from jail. He is my only son, and we have a deep love for each other. He loves God and loves people. He is gregarious, funny, and so smart. David has so much potential, and I know God has a massive plan for his life. I just wish I knew how to love him like God loves him. I wish I could make every decision out of concern for his wholeness and not as an outcome of my woundedness. I just wanted for him what I didn't have for myself. My lack of receiving attention led me to give too much attention to my son. My own deficit of protection caused me to overprotect my boy. My own sense of worthlessness propelled me to cause overconfidence in David's life. The lack of a dependable father in my own life drove me to become the person David could depend on for everything—and unfortunately, he depended on me rather than on God.

I know now that I stepped in to rescue David instead of allowing God to work. I literally pushed God out of the way in my efforts to minimize David's pain. Stupid? Maybe. Helpful? Not in the long run. Every opportunity I took to fix David's problems was an opportunity I took from God to fix David's life.

Disabling the Enabler

An enabler is someone who intentionally or even unintentionally promotes a specific behavior or action in another person. The term *enabler* is most often associated with people who allow loved ones to behave in ways that are destructive to themselves and to others in the family.

When confronted with our actions, enabling parents will probably spend countless hours in guilt and shame, reliving and regretting the choices we thought were right but maybe weren't the best. Chances are, enablers are rescuing and protecting their children because they weren't rescued or protected when they were children. Some enablers are afraid their children won't like them or will leave, and others—like me—want to save them from the life we had, where instead of being able to trust your parents for protection, you learned to depend on yourself and ultimately protect yourself. I simply wanted to be for my precious son the dad that I never had in my own life.

I believed I was giving David opportunities to do better, but in fact I was removing David from the consequences of his own bad choices. He never felt the pain from his choices, so he never learned from them. I taught him that he can live above the rules and that consequences can always be figured out, minimized, or avoided altogether. As an enabler you put your head in the sand and hope your kids will figure it out, while you run around to pay their fines, fix their cars, write notes for school absences so they don't get suspended, and pay bills they owe with money you don't have.

I still struggle to identify the difference between enabling and helping. In essence, enabling is offering the wrong kind of help. The Bible gives some insight: "Do not be deceived: God cannot be mocked. A man reaps what he sows. The one who sows to please his sinful nature, from that nature will reap destruction; the one who sows to please the Spirit, from the Spirit will reap eternal life" (Galatians 6:7–8, NIV).

I have now realized that when I step in the way of David's consequences, I am mocking God. What I have interpreted as loving him is really a dysfunctional way of doing so. Sin always causes destruction. There is no safe way to sin and no easy way out. It is the simple law of the harvest. If you sow, you will reap. I was like so many parents who cannot stand idle and watch their children suffer pain from bad decisions, so we talk to our kids, who nod in agreement, and then we rescue them from the consequences.

Where Is God in This?

The enabled child can best be identified by an attitude of entitlement. They may be sorry for their actions but lack an authentic sense of repentance. It is a vicious cycle in which they end up even more disappointed than other children who receive less favor, because enabled/entitled children expect more to begin with. When looking at God they may see an ATM machine in the sky who will bless their every move and make all the hard things in life go away. Some may misunderstand grace as complete freedom to do what they wish. They have a tendency to blame God when things go wrong in their lives, becoming disillusioned and disappointed when everything doesn't go their way. They will struggle with the "unfairness" of life and ask God, *"Why did You let this happen to me? Why aren't You blessing me? Why aren't You answering my prayers?"*

My son, David, has a relationship with God, but I think he would agree he has a distorted image of Him. He never had to fully depend on God because Dad was always there. I understand now that although the things we do for our children are motivated by love, we still may be hindering their ability to trust God for His protection, for His provision, for His intimacy. God is able and can be trusted with our kids—they're really His kids anyway. Letting them go means letting them fail. We'll be there to hug, to love, and to listen when needed, but we'll allow God to be God in their lives and their choices.

If you have a tendency to enable, most likely you are afraid to trust God with the person you love so much. For me, it finally meant laying David at God's feet, releasing him to the One who created him and loves him even more than I do. I long more than anything to have my son back. Heroin has stolen so much from our family, and now I am choosing to wait *for God* to bring him home.

Sometimes we have to step out of the way in order for our kids to make their own way to God. I am learning this even now as I wait for my son to call from jail. You could say God has put us both in a corner—so I can deal with my brokenness and so David can learn again about a God who is able to meet his every need and has his best in mind. The ugliness of brokenness is heavy, but the beauty on the other side is priceless.

One day we will celebrate, and so will you. Wait on God. Trust God. Believe for and anticipate that day.

7

The Father Who Is Always Right

The Controlling Father

I grew up reading Dr. Seuss books and can think of no better story to illustrate a controller than *Yertle the Turtle*. Let me give you a quick recap of the story if you are not familiar with it or in case it's been a few years since you've read it.

Yertle the Turtle is the king of his own pond, and he rules over all that he can see. When Yertle becomes unsatisfied with the little stone that serves as his throne, he commands the other turtles to stack themselves beneath him so that he can see farther and thus expand his kingdom. The higher he is and the more he can see, the more he rules and the happier he becomes.

At the very bottom of the pile is a turtle named Mack, who obviously suffers the most under the weight of the others. Mack asks Yertle for a break to get some relief, but instead of allowing a break, the king yells for Mack to shut up. Unfortunately, Yertle is still not satisfied and decides to expand his kingdom even further, commanding more and more turtles to add to his throne. Mack makes a second request for a break because the increased weight is now causing extreme pain to the turtles at the bottom of the pile. Again Yertle yells at Mack to shut up and announces proudly, "There is nothing, no nothing, that's higher than me."

Then Yertle notices the moon rising above him as the night approaches. Furious that something "dared to be higher than Yertle the King," he decides to call for even more turtles in an attempt to rise above the moon. But before he could give the command, Mack decides he has had enough. He lets out a loud burp, shaking the stack of turtles and tossing Yertle off into the mud, leaving him "King of the Mud," and freeing the other turtles.[1]

The Effect of the Controller

As cute as this children's story is, it's a pretty good illustration of how some homes are ruled by a father who sees himself as "the king of the castle." He rules his kingdom with little regard for the wants and needs of others. His way is always right, and he can make overarching decisions as he sees fit. He makes the rules and can change the rules whenever he wants, and no one else's opinion matters. What he says, goes!

Think of a father who not only expects performance out of his kids but also demands obedience. His unrealistic expectations create fear and intimidation in the hearts of his children. The king is selfish and does not see the uniqueness of each child. He loves them...but on his terms. His love is conditional on whether or not his children do what he says. In other words, his children are viewed as servants, and their lives revolve around his needs and goals.

The controlling father cares about being right more than being in a relationship. His children feel quenched and unimportant; they are afraid to disagree or have their own opinions. This dad is a legalistic authoritarian, with lists of often extreme rules that must be followed exactly. He believes strict adherence to his ideals will set his children up for future success, and he sees no room for emotion. While it is not wrong for parents to create boundaries and rules, the king fails to explain why, and when asked replies, "Because I said so!"

When asked to identify the line between healthy and unhealthy parental control, family therapist and author Dr. Dan Neuharth said this:

> First of all, you have to exert control over children as a parent. You have to tell them, "The stove is hot, don't touch," and "Don't play in traffic." The litmus test I suggest for parents to tell when they have crossed the line is to ask themselves this: Are the rules and roles in your family designed for optimal growth of your child as well as all family members...or are your family's rules and roles designed primarily to protect you, the parent, from some personal fears or serve your personal needs, yet are not in the best interests of your children?

In the same interview he explains how to identify controlling parents:

Controlling parents micromanage their children's lives. I interviewed a number of people for my book and one woman I interviewed recalled that when she was five, her mother put a sign on her daughter's back whenever the girl was out in public. The sign read: "Do not feed me." You can imagine the horror that young girl felt. It was her mother's agenda. The girl was of normal weight but her mother was concerned that she not become overweight. That is an extreme example. One man I interviewed had to say, "Father, may I speak?" or "Mother, may I speak?" before every sentence, or his parents would ignore him. Another woman I interviewed told me how she would get the love letters she sent to her father back with the spelling and grammar corrected. Parents send double messages sometimes, such as the father who says to his son, "Be a man—but don't ever challenge my authority." Or the mother who sends signals to her daughter that the daughter should be smart, poised, and attractive but then treats her in ways that undermine her daughter's confidence.[2]

Children from this home may experience a range of long-term emotional consequences, from low self-esteem to anger and anxiety. The statistics are very revealing when it comes to how overcontrolling affects children when they become adults. In survey results from a questionnaire of forty adults ages twenty-three to fifty-eight who grew up with unhealthy control, an overwhelming percentage still experienced anxiety and fear when dealing with their parents. Statistically, 82 percent "feel perfectionistic, driven, or rarely satisfied." A full 96 percent "worry or ruminate over confrontations," and 91 percent "feel extra-sensitive to criticism." In retrospect, 100 percent of their parents "seemed unwilling to admit it when they were wrong," 100 percent "seemed unaware of the pain they caused others," and only 5 percent had "encouraged their children to express feelings."[3]

Psychologist Matthew J. Miller describes it this way:

Children growing up in an authoritarian home, like growing up under an authoritarian regime, experience a loss of control over their own lives. When we come to believe that no matter what we do, we cannot gain actual control of our own life, eventually a sense of helplessness ensues. This "learned helplessness" is a major component in the development of depression. This sense of powerlessness does not leave us when we leave the authoritarian parent. Instead, this becomes a deeply entrenched view of ourselves that can take years to overcome and can impact all future relationships including marital and parenting relationships. Along with a loss of control, children who grow up with authoritarian parents often experience anger at how they are being treated. However, their anger is not typically allowed to be expressed.[4]

Angie, who attends Living Hope Church, told me her story:

One of my earliest recollections as a child of a controlling father was that I was never good enough. I couldn't live up to his expectations. I was taught that God was everywhere and knew everything. However, the emphasis was always on anything bad we did. There was no nurturing or caring. By the time I was a teenager, I didn't think God cared, and if He did, He didn't think much of me.

My distorted thinking sent me through a long journey of broken relationships and struggling to find what was missing. I heard that God is love. That took me a very long time to process! Through a series of events and years of on and off again counseling, and more broken relationships, I found myself trying out different churches. I was very emotional when I accepted a "relationship" with Jesus. God really did love me! Yet I had no real understanding.

To this day, I still struggle with feelings and the ability to show them or talk about them. I am able to converse with God, but do not think of Him as Father. That concept is especially difficult. My brothers have accepted Jesus and now refer to "God, the Father" in conversation, and I find that strange. Why is it that they can say that and I cannot? I still have some distorted thinking to resolve.

Putting God Above the Controller

If you were raised in a controlling environment, your view of God is quite possibly distorted. A strict upbringing devoid of freedom can lead you to see God as a fearful dictator who wants only to be obeyed. You might see His commandments as yet more rules telling you what to do, and at the same time you may be unable to see the love behind them. You comply with God's laws, but it's obedience motivated by fear, not as a response to His love. You are afraid to fail, believing He is constantly disappointed with you. People raised by a dad who is always right have a tendency as Christians to become judgmental, with little tolerance for "wrong thinking" by others. They look at others with the same high expectations they have come to see as normal and want others to work like them. It's possible you will feel anger toward God as the ultimate authority figure.

Submission is a word that's so abused and misunderstood in our generation, but in the context of a healthy marriage or family, it fosters so much health, if understood. Mutual submission in a family—as seen in the book of Ephesians—will be a hard concept to comprehend. You will have a tendency to see God as a King, but a distant, controlling one, and you will probably relate to Him in an unhealthy fear, if you relate to Him at all. You believe God is in complete and total control, but you fail to see how He could care about you, listen to you, or help you when you're in need. You may ask yourself, *"Does God care about my dreams? Does He believe in me? Do I really have a purpose?"*

One thing I know for sure is that you were uniquely created by a God who wants to clear up the distortion and begin the process of redefining your image of a father. He wants you to see yourself as created for a destiny. He formed you with a plan and purpose that only you can fill. He sees your potential and wants to make your dreams come true. Look at Psalm 37:4: "Take delight in the LORD, and he will give you your heart's desires." God wants to bless your life beyond your imagination! Who wouldn't want to have a relationship with a God like that? When your heart is open to clearly see God, the perfect Father, you can boldly approach His throne without fear. He is in perfect control. He is the Father you have always wanted.

The Father Who Hurts Others

The Abusive Father

I s there a proper or an easy way to talk about abuse? How do you describe an abusive father? Is there any way to adequately represent the emotions and fears of an abused child?

When considering the abusive father, I think of words like *horrible, unpredictable, hurtful, selfish, demented*…but these are just words and can never really do justice to the truth of what a child feels.

Of all the things a father can do, abuse leaves the deepest wounds. When the person you trust the most hurts you, it robs you of the basic safety and security that is the birthright of any child. It turns your world upside down when the "protector" becomes the perpetrator. All sense of security and safety is gone, and the child finds himself or herself in an environment of constant instability and unpredictability.

I wouldn't understand it if I hadn't lived it. Thinking about abuse brings back memories. I remember being a kid cowering in fear of someone I should have been able to trust. I learned to sit still and shut up. To this day I wrestle with God about it. Sometimes I am (strangely) grateful for the experience I had to grow through, and at other times I am angry that my heavenly Father allowed me to be physically, emotionally, and mentally abused, leaving me with scars that have in so many ways defined my life as a person, as a child of God, and as a parent.

Living with an Abusive Monster

Let me first say that my mom is awesome and has always been helpful to me, and she has a heart of pure gold. Unfortunately, after my father died, she married an abusive monster in a rebound situation. Dean frequently hit and screamed at my mom, me, and others. He kept loaded guns sitting around, and he loved to fight. He took pleasure in infuriating and scaring people. I have no idea what caused him to be so mean.

When you live with an abuser, there are some experiences that become imprinted on your soul that you can never forget—like the memory of watching Dean strike my mom, then feeling his hands grab me and throw me across the bathroom.

But there was one particular incident that really solidified my fear of my stepdad and set up my fear of any father figure, which at that time included God. Because of a near-drowning experience when I was five, I was terrified of water. Knowing that, my mom would take care washing my hair to avoid getting water on my face. Admittedly, Mom would sometimes go over the top in caring for my brother and me, probably in an attempt to fill the father void after our birth father died. My stepdad was jealous and didn't like the attention she gave us, and I guess one particular afternoon he decided it was time to teach us a lesson.

My mom was carefully washing my hair as usual, when all of a sudden Dean busted open the door of our bathroom, grabbed my mom, and threw her in the hallway. He then shoved my face and head into the toilet. I can still hear the words he shouted and my mom's screams as she tried to help me. She was pushing on the door, pleading with him to stop and to let me go, but he held it closed with his foot, yelling at her to shut her mouth or he would shut it for her. He shouted, "I'm tired of you giving this little b------ more attention than you give me!"

That is the defining moment when Dean taught me that fathers were to be feared and when my mental image and concept of "father" instantaneously twisted. That incident would define how I responded to God's love and shape my future relationships with others.

The Staggering Reach of Abuse

So many children like me experience abuse instead of love and cruel punishment instead of discipline and guidance. According to the U.S. Department of Health and Human Services, in 2011 there were over 676,000 victims of child abuse and neglect, and over 80 percent of perpetrators are the parents.[1] What a tragedy that a child needs to be protected *from* the very man trusted for his or her protection. Whether it is verbal, physical, mental, or sexual abuse, an abused child instinctively feels unlovable and terrified at the unpredictability of the father's actions. I never felt safe in my own home or in Dean's presence. I learned quickly not to talk unless I was spoken to and not do anything unless I was told to.

By God's grace, I was never sexually abused, but I meet people every week who were and who years later still feel the pain of it. If you were sexually abused, my heart goes out to you. Maybe your father didn't hurt you, but he didn't intervene when he knew someone else was. Either way, the protector has now become the perpetrator. My friend Echo experienced this. She allowed me to share some of her story with you:

I was six years old when my father put his hands on me in ways no father should ever touch his daughter. It started out as touching, but as years passed, it turned incestuous. I cowered in fear every time I heard footsteps pause outside my door. At first, it was just my father…then it was my uncle…then it was men I didn't even know, some faces are still etched in my memory…my father was aware of it all. I lived in a constant state of fear and terror of any and all men. It wrecked my identity as a woman and as a human being. I was a thing to be used and discarded, not good enough to be loved. No matter how I tried, no matter what I accomplished or achieved, I could not win my father's heart. I was never good enough, not worth anything more than satisfying a sinful desire. He never said "I love you," mostly didn't even look me in the eye or acknowledge my presence.

I was fifteen years old when I finally accepted Jesus into my life. The abuse stopped, but the damage of nine years had still been done physically, mentally, and emotionally. I surrendered my life to God but lived in fear and dread of Him. I fell into religion and legalism because, in my mind, with a set of rules and regulations to follow, I could hopefully do everything right and please God and thus avoid punishment. When bad things happened, I blamed myself, rationalizing I failed as a daughter, now I was failing as a Christian. I didn't think God loved me…how could He? I was wretched and worthless…a thing to be used, not a person to be loved.

I couldn't see God as a loving Father because my own father abused his rights as a parent. He didn't protect me as a father should, he didn't love me, he didn't cherish me. I had no clue how to be a daughter, much less receive love from a father. Honestly, I still struggle with it to some degree. I don't always ask God for blessings or the desires of my heart because I do not feel worthy of such tenderness or affection. I didn't receive good gifts from my dad, so why would I expect to receive good things from a heavenly Father who is perfect in every way? The thought that the Creator of the Universe would adopt me as His child and love me unconditionally escaped my understanding for most of my life. I was living in a victim mentality, expecting bad things rather than blessings, hatred rather than love.

Without question, abuse can cause massive wounds in the life of a child and distort a right image of God. If you were abused, you probably see Him as a harsh, mean God who will hurt you for no good reason. The thought of God as a father may be upsetting and incite fear in your heart if you believe Him to be easily angered and demanding. When considering God the Father, you ask, *"Am I safe? Can I trust Him? Will He protect me?"* Echo struggled with all of these.

Echo is now one of the most dedicated people on staff at the church where I pastor, Living Hope Church. She has a heart to please others and also grow in her relationship with God. But Echo is also afraid. She told me recently during some job restructuring that she was preparing herself to be hurt and abandoned. She is a great friend to so many, but I can see the effects of the abuse in her past. She still struggles with the fear of being hurt. She is learning to trust men in positions of authority again, but it has taken years for her to be able to see beyond the pain of punishment and horrifying abuse to now see a God who is massively in love with her, who doesn't want to hurt her, and who has a plan for her. Recently we got to see her speak in front of hundreds at a crusade in Nicaragua. What a great day! Seeing God redeem and recycle the pain in Echo's life is worth all of the investment.

God Redeems the Abused

God wants us to see Him as completely safe, approachable, and accepting. He wants to be seen as a refuge—someone we can run toward, not run from. Psalm 9:9 says, "The LORD is a shelter for the oppressed, a refuge in times of trouble." He is a shelter in times of trouble, but so many victims of abuse struggle to believe in a God who would allow such things to happen to them.

If you were abused, you have probably experienced anger and might even direct it at God. I get it. I've been there, done that, and got the T-shirt for it. You might need to tell God how unfair it has been. You might want to cry out to Him and let Him know you're mad at Him for allowing the ugliness of abuse in your life. Most of the psalms in the Bible are psalms of lament. To *lament* means "to complain."

But it's not about complaining to other people. When we complain to God, we open our hearts for Him to heal. When we complain to others, we never fix the problem because we are not talking to the God who allowed the evil. You're thinking, *Wait, He allowed it?* Unfair? Most definitely. But as we will learn later, fairness ended when sin entered the world. It doesn't make it okay; it just makes it part of life. So tell Him…tell God how you truly feel, then give it over to Him.

Here is what I can promise for every child who has experienced childhood abuse: God is not the author of abuse. Every single person who hurt you made his or her own choice to do so, and God grieves for your pain. Please know that God wants you to live free from guilt or shame. You are worthy, you do matter, and God wants to heal the wounds that keep you from entering a full relationship with Him. In part 2 of the book, we will deal extensively with God's character as the perfect Father, and although no one can adequately answer the "why" question, we can talk about the other big questions: What now? How do I deal with it all? What does forgiveness look like?

To those who were abused like me, like Echo, and like so many others, I want to encourage you to begin to look forward. There is so much promise for the future. In no way do I want to minimize the unthinkable pain of abuse, but I do want you to consider what direction you are looking. One of the most simple but helpful illustrations for me personally was the rearview mirror. I have learned, over time, not to look back at the ways I have been hurt and not to relive the times I have been hit, but to look forward to something much more promising: the future God has for me. If I spend my time looking in the rearview mirror, not only can I not go forward, but my viewpoint is so much smaller than what it should be. It might seem too simple and even cliché, but it helped me refocus my attention throughout the healing process.

I want to simply pray for you here:

Heavenly Father, tears are flowing down my face as I go "back," and I know there are tears in the lives of so many right now. God, only You can heal. Only You can redeem; only You can begin to make a message out of the mess. Jesus, I pray that You would wrap Your loving, strong, and tender arms around them. Help them to let go and know You are safe. You are a refuge, and You will protect them. Please help them in their journey to heal and be healed, to forgive, and to trust You. God, I don't know the details of each life, but I know You. I don't know the path and the horrifying moments people have gone through, but I know You. I know when I came to the end of my own anger, hatred, and frustrations, I found my perfect Father. I found a Father full of compassion, safe in every way, and always there for me. Help us run into Your arms in our pain, loneliness, and fear. Help us to live as Your children, not as orphans. I pray these things in the mighty name of Jesus. Amen.

I hope these words can become the beginning of healing in your life. I pray together we will learn, heal, and find God's path of forgiveness. I am so sorry for what has been in your life, but I am so excited for what will be in the days ahead.

The Father Who Blames

The Accusing Father

I t is all your fault."

"Your brother is the way he is because of you."

"If you wouldn't have done it, our family wouldn't be where we are now."

"I trusted you, and you let me down."

"If you hadn't been born, things would have been so much better."

"You are making me angry."

"Mom left our family because of you."

Reckless words of blame that cause shame and destroy lives. Do any of these statements sound familiar to you? Do they bring back painful memories?

I think one of the most ridiculous sayings ever is "Sticks and stones may break my bones, but words will never hurt me." Anyone who's ever been mocked, ridiculed, blamed, accused, teased, or taunted can tell you exactly how hurtful words are. I think I'd rather have a broken bone than feel the weight of someone else's accusations. Haven't we all felt the effects of words? We can remember in great detail every negative thing said about us, and one negative comment can undo and erase a hundred positive ones. Words come at us like rocks, damaging our self-esteem and breaking our hearts, causing doubt, fear, shame, and insecurity. Negative words from a parent—even if they aren't true—can become part of our belief system, shaping how we see ourselves.

Our worth is intrinsically tied to words that will either build up or tear down. So how much more effect does blame or accusation have when it is false?

The Victim: the Scapegoat

Some accusing fathers not only judge and point fingers at their children, but they often pick on one child in particular, making him or her the family scapegoat. Scapegoating is the practice of singling out one person for unmerited negative treatment or blame. While it may begin with a parent, it becomes a system by which the whole family operates. Before long, the father, mother, and siblings will target one child to accuse and blame for everything bad.

The Bible teaches that originally the scapegoat was set apart to atone for the sins of the people. One goat was sacrificed, and the other—the scapegoat—was released but made to bear the iniquities of Israel. The scapegoat was not chosen to be guilty and condemned, but rather to represent how God forgives and forgets sins. Over time the concept has been twisted. It is no longer about forgiveness and atonement for sins, but it is a way for dysfunctional families to place the consequences for all wrongdoing on one person. I love this explanation from LightsHouse.org:

> The Scapegoat is the one who assuages the narcissistic parent's (and ultimately, the whole dysfunctional family's) guilt, shame, and feelings of inadequacy. The Scapegoat is the shock absorber, the buffer against the harsh reality that there is something wrong with the family picture altogether—the trash bin into which all unwanted matter is cast. The scapegoat role facilitates the existence of family denial.[1]

If you grew up as a victim of blame, you probably live in constant guilt and shame and are most likely critical of yourself. Negative dads create negative kids. Guilty people guilt other people.

Accusing dads are habitual blamers who have become judges in their homes instead of fathers. They are master manipulators who expect the scapegoats to obey their unwritten rules. They cannot be questioned, never accept responsibility, and believe they can do no wrong. They have little respect for boundaries and think they are helping by pointing out what they see as flaws and mistakes in the children. The accusing father expects everything to be done his way because his child's behavior reflects on him. However, his judgment and consequent punishments are unjust and have no bearing on the actual "crime."

A child raised by blaming parents will feel distressed, anxious, guilty, and incompetent. If this was your reality, you may believe you are a terrible person who can do nothing right. You are constantly afraid of not being accepted. As an adult you may struggle in relationships and employment, and you may have trust issues. The effects of this upbringing will be significant and far reaching. This child develops a deep level of insecurity and eventually becomes angry, but anger is only a surface emotion hiding the devastating pain, frustration, fear, and condemnation.

A Scapegoat's Story

One Sunday in June of 2012, we were honored to have Nicky Cruz speak at our church. Nicky is a former warlord, whose life story was told in the movie *The Cross and the Switchblade* and the best-selling book *Run, Baby, Run*. The horrors of his upbringing are beyond comprehension, and it is a miracle he is alive today. Nicky was the eighth of eighteen children and singled out by his parents (and especially by his mother) to be the family scapegoat. He said, "Now, out of all those children, why she chose to go after me? Why I was the one? That's hard for me to explain. I don't know why she didn't go after her other children, but she aimed straight towards me. The things that went on were the most painful types of things a child could go through."

For some unknown reason, Nicky received the brunt of his parents' savage anger, being beaten and tortured in unspeakable ways. He said,

But through all these things, do you know what hurt? The words. I think words can be so strong that they can really, really damage you. I was immune to the physical pain; you could shoot me and I didn't feel any pain, you could step on me and I would feel nothing—my mother was a good teacher; she taught me how to deal with physical pain. But [her words were] the one thing that put a dagger in my heart; the thing that completely destroyed me psychologically and emotionally. When my mother grabbed me by my two little arms and told me, "Get out of my life, you are not my son! I've never loved you and I curse the day that you was born. You have failed; you are good for nothing!" Here I am as a little boy listening to all of this. Now, you should see the way I was breathing and the pain that was welling up inside. I couldn't believe it! I didn't express the pain I was feeling with screaming,

but with tears. Silent tears—running and running and running down my
face. It taught me so much pain; listening to those words of rejection and
to my mother telling me that I was a son of the devil and that I was ugly.

At the age of nine he tried to end his own life and, not surprisingly, grew into a
troubled youth. He explained it this way:

> I know how to be in the pits of hell. I know that loneliness that eats at your
> heart early in the morning when you cannot sleep. I would be smoking, my
> mind trying to deal with all the memories. I hurt a lot of people. I left long
> lines of blood. I was in a cage with myself.... You see, I died when I was nine
> years old; when I hated the guts of my mother. When I said to myself, "I
> never will love again; I will never cry again." I died that day when I buried
> little Nicky inside of me. I promised him that I would defend him, that I
> would fight for him, that I would kill for him; and with my two little arms
> and my two little hands, I dried those tears and hatred became the power and
> force in my life.

When Nicky was fifteen, his father sent him to New York to live with his brother,
and by sixteen, Cruz was the leader of the Mau Mau gang.

> I left home. I ran away, but it got worse and I hit the bottom of nothingness.
> I didn't believe in anything; I was brutal and cruel. I didn't have any mercy
> for others because I knew I would be leaving my life; I knew I was going to
> die before I was twenty-one years old. I accepted death because I knew I was
> a garbage can, and through all these things I joined a gang thinking that it
> was my family.... I went wild. We burned the city; we went into territory
> and fought all the other gangs. I was literally possessed by evil. I had no fear;
> I could care less about the electric chair; I felt immortal. I used every power
> I believed my mother had cursed me with.
>
> I had been in jail so many times that the Criminal Court of Brooklyn
> gave me a psychiatrist for six months so I could hear this man tell me, "Nicky,
> you are doomed; you are finished. You are walking straight to jail; to the
> electric chair, and to hell. There's no hope for you."[2]

Nicky's life changed dramatically upon meeting street preacher David Wilkerson, and he became a powerful testimony to God's redemptive grace. But what a perfect picture of the devastating effects of scapegoating. His is an extreme case, but it speaks to the hopelessness and shame that mark the life of a scapegoat. Having borne the brunt of accusation and punishment for his siblings, he was incapable of love and seemed determined to fulfill his parents' words about him.

Although many of us will deal with some degree of guilt, the scapegoat sinks far beyond that, developing a deep sense of shame. On the surface, guilt and shame may seem quite similar, but there are some important distinctions. In his book *Bradshaw On: The Family,* John Bradshaw explains the difference: "Guilt says I've *done* something wrong; shame says there *is* something wrong with me. Guilt says I've *made* a mistake; shame says I *am* a mistake. Guilt says what I *did* was not good; shame says I *am* no good."[3] Shame is the absence of self-esteem, a dark despair in which a person believes himself or herself to be without worth on this planet. Shamed individuals often feel lonely, hopeless, and inadequate.

In the scapegoat's attempt to wipe out the worthlessness, different compulsory behaviors, such as drug abuse or anorexia, take over. Whether such a person is working too much, eating too much, eating too little, or trying too hard, the goal is the same: to fix what's wrong and gain approval.

God Bestows Grace upon the Blamed

If you were raised by an accusing father, you probably see a God in heaven pointing His finger, just waiting for you to fail so He can dish out punishment. You may believe you are a hopeless case, destined to fail, and responsible for everything bad that happens around you. You may love God but feel ashamed in His presence. You come to God saying, *"I don't deserve grace; I am unworthy of Your love; how can You possibly forgive me?"*

A woman from my church told me how it is for her:

I have the lowest self-esteem. I take blame for things that are not my fault. When stuck in old patterns of behavior, I am constantly apologizing to the Lord. God must always be angry with me, because He loves me so much and I always let him down. God must be punishing me, because my husband struggles with drugs. He didn't save me to give me an awesome life, but a crappy one, because I'm not good enough. Or maybe He wanted to give me a good life but I screwed it all up. Yep, that must be it. I will just try harder. I yell at my own daughter without intending to. I try to fix my husband, thinking, "If only I didn't mess up all the time, then he wouldn't do drugs." If I just pray enough, speak only kind words, exercise, eat right, everything will be okay. God will bring him home if I do it right. God loves me. I adore Him, but I feel ashamed in His presence.

God wants to remove your shame and guilt. He wants you to know He approves of you exactly how you are. He sent His Son, Jesus, as the ultimate scapegoat to take all the blame so that we can be free from condemnation. My prayer is that together we can learn what God says about us, and that we can learn to live not as orphans but as adopted sons and daughters of God. My hope for our generation is that the lies would be exposed, the distortion would be cleared up, and that God's words would matter more than any other person's.

The Father Who Is Good

Good Is Still Not God

I f you're reading this chapter, I imagine it is for one of two reasons: Either (1) you can't believe there is such a thing as a good dad and are curious to see if he really exists, or (2) you scanned the table of contents, confident you wouldn't see a need to read this book until you got to chapter 10—and there was your dad, the father who is good.

The truth is, there are some really great dads. There are dads who encourage their children, spend time with them, and speak life into their hearts. This dad believes in his kids and prays for them, doing all he can to help them succeed. Sure, he's got flaws, but he has always been there physically, emotionally, and in many cases, spiritually. If this was your dad, you know that he listens to you and makes time for you, and you know you matter to him. He is the dad that you can call day or night, and he'll be there to help. He is safe and you adore him. He's a good dad, your friends love him too, and you couldn't imagine better.

Sounds perfect, doesn't he?

The thing is, he's not perfect; no earthly father can be. He's good, but he's still not God. There is an infinite and eternal difference between good and God. While I sincerely wish everyone could have this kind of dad, there's a chance that, if you did have this kind of father, it may have left you unaware of your need for a heavenly Father. You may come to God without fear or distortion, but having your emotional needs well met by your own father may have kept you from fully pursuing a deep relationship with God. Children raised by a good father might have, as adults, an overdependence on their earthly father to meet their physical and emotional needs. Daughters might struggle to let go of Dad as their main protector and provider. If you are the daughter of a good dad, you will have a tendency to compare your husband to your dad, and rarely will your spouse measure up. Other times, these children develop such high expectations of their fathers that they are overly disappointed when he cannot fix or prevent their problems. My daughter Katie, who was married in 2011, had some of these issues. We have been able to walk through it, and she is very happily married to a godly man named Jordan.

Relating to God When You Already Have a Great Father

Christian children raised in good homes may become pastors because they see God as someone to serve, rather than someone to develop an intimate relationship with. They love God and want to serve Him, but they miss out on the full blessing of being His child, because they are simply unaware of their need for Father God. My friend Carly is a great example of this:

> I am blessed to have been raised in a Christian home, with a loving, encouraging father. He was present, kind, fair with his boundaries, and he disciplined in love. (I even remember him crying one time because he had to spank me!) He adopted and embraced the three boys from my mother's first marriage and made our family a complete unit. But better than all that, he taught me to love, to worship, and to serve God with my whole life. I'm not going to try to spin a negative here; I know I am one of the lucky ones. My father was a great man with a humble heart, and I couldn't have asked for more. As a result I have spent my life in the church. I gave my heart to Christ when I was only five years old, and I didn't come with brokenness or an awareness of my need for a heavenly Father. When I think of God, I imagine a King on a throne, worthy of my adoration and serving. That's not a bad image; it's just not a complete one. I am now a pastor and devoted as ever, but I never really see myself as His "daughter." I relate to God as a Master, a King, a Savior. These are all good things, but I feel like there is something missing. I don't know how to move from being His servant to being His family. I love Him but don't necessarily feel intimate with Him. I struggle with unconditional acceptance—constantly working for, instead of relating to, God. Sometimes I worry that I will stand on Judgment Day and hear Him say those awful words: "I never knew you."

Talking to Carly has made me realize how easy it is to be insecurely in love with God. Serving should be an extension of loving God, not an attempt to gain His love. We have to be careful not to replace worshiping God with working for God. He is always more interested in who you are than in what you can do. Put knowing Him ahead of serving Him, and rest in a right relationship with Jesus. His love for you would not change even if you couldn't do another thing *for* Him. He just longs to know you more! Give Him your heart as well as your hands.

I want to encourage good dads to keep making their children a priority. What you do matters so much. Your love, support, and provision will set your children up to reach their potential, no matter what choices they make. Simply do the best you can to lead them to Christ, and allow Him to be their ultimate source. You have done well!

If you had the blessing of a loving, involved, encouraging father, I hope you will take the time to thank your dad if he is still alive. Good dads are just trying their best and are well aware of their failures. Although I made many mistakes, I have tried hard to be a good father to my children. I want their picture of a future spouse to be formed by how much I love and protect them. I still get it wrong, and no dad ever "arrives" or does it all perfectly except for God, the only perfect Father. No matter how good you think your dad was, he could still rattle off a list of how he could have done more, made more time, provided better, or something else. So bring honor to your father. The Bible is so clear that we are to honor our parents. Honor isn't just what you *do* but also what you *say*. Take the time to send the card, to write the e-mail, to visit him and tell him. It matters so much to fathers to hear your words of encouragement back to them. I love what the Bible says about this: "We always thank God for all of you and pray for you constantly. As we pray to our God and Father about you, we think of your faithful work, your loving deeds, and the enduring hope you have because of our Lord Jesus Christ" (1 Thessalonians 1:2–3).

I would also encourage you to tell God how grateful you are that He allowed you, in all of His sovereignty, to be raised in a home that was safe, stable, encouraging, and filled with love. It is still a small minority of kids who would say they were raised by a great father. So thank God for the father He gave you.

Moving Forward

As we finish up this section on the different father types, I am more convinced than ever that A. W. Tozer is profoundly correct in his statement that what comes into your mind when you think about God is the most important thing about you. We've learned on this journey so far that even the best dad can distort your image of God the Father. I am so acutely aware now of the role I play in my children's lives, and I can see so clearly the wounds that have been left in others by their dads. Beyond all that, I am strongly reminded of how desperately we need a heavenly Father who is perfect in every way, with a love that will heal all wounds.

In the next section, we will search out the promises of God that answer the secret fears we bear as a result of our upbringing. We'll see that His love is perfect and His grace is sufficient. We'll discover that He is all we need, and we'll learn to depend on Him. We'll find practical answers for the questions that keep us from fully embracing a relationship with God.

Before we proceed, please pause to consider your own life. Your honest answers to these questions will give you a platform from which to approach the next section. It is only in acknowledging what is true that you can really begin the journey of healing. Take a moment to establish your current reality:

- What father type(s) did you have?
- Can you identify any fears or emotions you struggle with?
- Can you identify how your experience has distorted your God image? What comes to your mind when you think about God? How do you see Him?
- What is the biggest hindrance to your ability to having a deeper relationship with God?

No matter how great your father was or how hurtful he may have been, I pray you can step away from the distorted image in your mind just long enough for God to speak to you. It is my hope as we uncover the true nature of God that you will clearly see the perfect Father and begin to experience the most incredible relationship you can imagine. This is the relationship you were created for. He is desperately in love with you, and He wants to make right all that is wrong. I am praying you will find the Father you always wanted, in the God you never knew.

Part 2

GOD'S PERFECTION

Discovering the True Heavenly Father

The Perfect Father

How great is the love the Father
has lavished on us, that we
should be called children of God!
And that is what we are!

—1 JOHN 3:1, NIV

How we see God matters more than any other thing about our lives. And yet, as we have already learned, that image is intrinsically tied to our imperfect fathers. It has been shaped by our experiences, memories, wounds, relationships—both good and bad—with our dads. Stated simply: we cannot see God clearly if we see Him as a bigger version of our fathers. That is a twisted, distorted view. Remember what I said in part 1: *God is not a bigger version of your earthly father.* As good as your father is or was, God is infinitely better. As difficult as things were for you, God can change the father-image you have and, through that, change your destiny. My hope is that having identified our distorted God-image in the previous chapters, we can now begin to replace that twisted image with the truth.

What's True About You

I think it's fair to say that our life experiences, our childhood, and our "daddy issues" have left most of us damaged to some degree. Many of us struggle with certain behaviors and emotions we simply cannot control, try as we might. We don't know why we cling desperately to doomed relationships or obsess over tiny details, or why we give too much freedom to a child who needs boundaries. Many of us are plagued by depression, addictive behavior, and self-destruction we don't understand. *Why am I like this? What is wrong with me? What is my damage?*

The answer is *fear.* Each of the eight father types we have discussed leaves a child with an underlying fear that becomes the foundation for future behavior. Some people struggle with the fear of being abandoned, some know the fear of rejection or of not measuring up, and some fear being hurt again. You may not consciously identify your fear, but I'm sure you deal with the fruit of it in your everyday life.

There is a difference between healthy fears that keep us safe from harm by enabling us to handle threats or certain problems in life, and unhealthy fears, or phobias, that can be debilitating, harmful, paralyzing, and destructive.

The word *fear* is used more than 440 times in the Bible, and *afraid* almost 200 times. The words *tremble, terror,* and *terrified* appear over 120 times. People are simply affected by fear. I have fear and you have fear. It is the human condition.

These fears cause reactions. Fear makes you self-protect and doubt things around you. Fear keeps you from making healthy change. Fear is the reason you feel stuck. It is the wall, the anchor, the barrier between your current reality and the full life you were destined for. When you live in fear from your past, you don't walk toward what could be. You won't look at the future that God has promised.

Authors Dan Allender and Tremper Longman III said it this way: "Fear distorts our perception of ourselves so that we seem weaker than we really are. It distorts the size of our problems so that they seem huge and undefeatable. But perhaps most significantly, *fear distorts our picture of God.* God seems weak, uninvolved, or uncaring in the midst of our troubles."[2]

When our fear becomes bigger than God, we become immobilized. We need to see differently in order to be different. God could not be the perfect Father we profess Him to be if He were weak, uninvolved, and uncaring. Thankfully, God is none of those things. Neither is He passive, absent, abusive, enabling, controlling, or demanding. The Bible says simply and profoundly, *God is love.*

What's Love Got to Do with It?

The best antidote for fear is the presence of love. The Bible says, "Such love has no fear, because perfect love expels all fear. If we are afraid, it is for fear of punishment, and this shows that we have not fully experienced his perfect love" (1 John 4:18).

Children grow up believing that whatever version of love they receive from their parents reveals how God will love them. A demanding father teaches you that God will love you based on what you do. A controlling father will teach you that God's love is for those who follow the rules and don't make mistakes. A passive father will leave you convinced God's love is distant and intangible.

In reality, God's love is unlike anything we know. It's not the love we have for french fries or football or even our spouses. Rather, God's love is *perfect love* that can only come from a perfect Father. The Bible doesn't just say *God loves*—although He does—but it clearly states that *God is love.* "But anyone who does not love does not know God, for God is love" (1 John 4:8).

There are four words for "love" in the Greek language. The first is *philia,* which is where we get our English word *philanthropy* and means "brotherly love or affection." It is used primarily when talking about friendship. The second word is *eros.* Eros was the Greek god of love, and that's where we get our English word *erotic.* It is romantic love. The third love word is *storge,* which means "affection." Its primary context is love within a family. The word used to describe God's love is *agape.* Agape love is mentioned 106 times in the New Testament and is the same word for "charity" or "benevolence." It is a love that you cannot earn and is not dependent on relationship or response. David Nelmes explained it this way:

Agape love [is] unconditional love that is always giving and impossible to take or be a taker. It devotes total commitment to seek your highest best no matter how anyone may respond. This form of love is totally selfless and does not change whether the love given is returned or not. This is the original and only true form of love.

Nelmes also explained how our distorted view of love allows fear to rule in our lives:

Having built walls between ourselves and our creator, we have distanced ourselves from sensing God's love, and the world we see around us is a reflection of living without real love. This environment breeds calamity and destruction since that is the result of life based upon fear instead of love. If accepting perfect love can cast out fear, then likewise, accepting fear removes our ability to sense perfect love.[2]

So what does perfect love look like? Ask anyone familiar with the Bible, and they will point you to the thirteenth chapter of 1 Corinthians. It is well known to Christians as the "love chapter." It's used at weddings and printed on wall plaques as a daily reminder of what love really is and what we should strive to achieve. But no matter how hard we try to emulate or show this kind of love, it is beyond our human ability. The love we read about here is the perfect love exampled only by God Himself.

We could, in fact, read 1 Corinthians 13:4–8 this way: "God is patient, God is kind. God does not envy, God does not boast, God is not proud. God is not rude, He is not self-seeking, He is not easily angered, He keeps no record of wrongs. God does not delight in evil but rejoices with the truth. God always protects, always trusts, always hopes, always perseveres. God never fails!" (see NIV).

Love That Makes All the Difference

Fortunately for all of us, God never withholds His perfect love but gives it freely. First John 3:1 begins "How great is the [agape] love the Father has lavished on us" (NIV). The writer could have chosen so many other words: God *shares* His love, or God *sprinkles* His love, but he doesn't. He uses a word that personifies the heart of the perfect Father. He has *lavished* His love on each of us. He bestows His love in generous, extravagant quantities. His love is not earned or fought for, but unconditionally poured out—more than enough to heal even the hardest of hearts.

Remember Nicky Cruz from chapter 9? Take a look at the rest of his story:

Summertime was coming and something strange happened in our neighborhood: a strange man came walking onto our turf. He was a preacher, a minister by the name of David Wilkerson. So we ran over there, then just like that, I got close enough to this guy to hear his voice say, "God has the power to change your life right now!"

I said, "You go to hell! There is no God! Who do you think you are? Shut up! Don't open your mouth and don't mention God because you are a dead man!" So Wilkerson didn't say anything.

Nicky proceeded to humiliate the speaker, spitting in his face and threatening to kill anyone who defended him. Wilkerson, shaken but standing firm, continued to speak:

"Nicky, I came over here to give you a message from heaven. Nicky, Jesus loves you."

I said, "What?"

He said, "Jesus loves you."

I pulled back a little bit, to psych him out because he confused me. Then he got brave. He said in such a loud voice, that everybody heard him, "Kill me! Go ahead, kill me! If that's going to make you feel good in front of all these people, go ahead! Do it! Nicky, you can kill me and cut me into a thousand pieces, and you can throw them right there on the street—but every little piece will cry out that Jesus loves you, Nicky. Let me tell you another thing: You can never, never, never kill love because God is love. He's going to hunt you every place that you go. You are lonely, but He loves you!"

Nicky left the meeting as fast as he could, but for the next two weeks his mind was filled with the words "Jesus loves you." Nicky said,

I was going crazy. When we were stealing and mugging, "Jesus loves you!" Getting stoned, getting high, "Jesus loves you!" In the park, in the train, in the bus, fighting, "Jesus loves you! Jesus loves you!" My brain was going to explode with it.

When Nicky went back to hear the preacher again, he took seventy-five of his gang members with him, and they heard the simple message of Jesus for the first time.

I had never heard the story of my sweet Jesus of the Bible before that night. It was like it came from another planet. You know what really touched me? The crucifixion of Jesus Christ. He painted a picture so strong that I could see it. I can see it in my mind and I remember, it really took me on a journey to the cross—it was so vivid. I could smell the blood, I could see the people scream-ing, I could see the cross; all these things. I felt like I was right there, and I was getting upset! I said, "That's not right! He's a good man, He deserves to live. I'm bad, I deserve the electric chair. He's beautiful but I'm ugly."

Then the preacher challenged us. It took me a little time but I opened up. I was honest and I said, "Oh God, I don't know who You are. This man says that Jesus Christ loves me." I was honest, I said, "I don't love You at all, Jesus Christ. I don't love You. I don't!" Then I was silent. I waited because I was scared. I was going to open my mouth and say something that had bothered me for years, and this was the moment. I thought He would reject me and I didn't want to be rejected like my mother rejected me. I became vulnerable in a way I never did. That question was one that would make all the difference because I didn't want to be rejected. It would be my suicide ticket straight to hell but I asked Him, "Do You love me, Jesus Christ? Do You?" Then I felt Him. I didn't hear Him, I felt Him. He gave me the approval, "Yes, I do love you. I do." I collapsed in surrender. And my shame? There was no more shame. I collapsed in His arms, He kissed my pain and my past, and He gave me a new heart. A heart of flesh to love Him and have Him forgive me. There is the miracle.

After that day everything changed. Nicky is now a world-class evangelist and author, with a ministry to the streets he came from. He shares his newfound joy:

I went to Puerto Rico when my mother was dying, to forgive her; and my mother gave her heart to Jesus Christ. Not only that, but the curse was broken and my mother brought my father to Jesus, and my father died praising the name of Jesus Christ. Thirteen of my seventeen brothers were converted, and three of them are now ministers of the Gospel of Jesus Christ. I am a blessed child of God![3]

How you see yourself matters because it determines how you will see and respond to the people around you. Imagine how much would change if you could see yourself as God's child.

I lived fatherless on this earth for years, all the while searching for the perfect father. Until I surrendered my life to Jesus and became a child of God, I lived as an orphan. My reality was fatherlessness both here on earth and for eternity. Nicky Cruz was living as an orphan, having been rejected by his own parents and unaware of a heavenly Father who loved him perfectly. Just like Nicky, orphans struggle to find their worth because they have no father to speak words of life and show them how much they matter. But unlike a physical orphan, you have a choice. A spiritual orphan is one who, having encountered the perfect Father, still chooses to live away from Him.

You can choose to live as an orphan, never feeling completely secure or truly loved, feeling empty, lonely, and unsatisfied by your constant separation from God the Father. Alternatively, you can choose to surrender your life to Jesus and begin to live as God's child, no longer fatherless but adopted into His family. It is only then that you will truly be able to rest, feeling secure and safe. Your distorted image of God can be changed in a moment by faith.

Your Most Important Moment

I will never forget the day I recognized and responded to God's love and surrendered my life to Him. It was the moment He ceased to be merely a concept and became my perfect heavenly Father. I remember thinking, *Is that all there is? I just pray a prayer, and believe Jesus died, then rose from the grave for me?* It seemed too simple.

The Bible says in Romans 10:9, "If you confess with your mouth that Jesus is Lord and believe in your heart that God raised him from the dead, you will be saved." It doesn't say, then go to a class or work really hard. It simply says to pray (confess with your mouth) and believe in your heart. Believing is not merely intellectual acceptance; it is much more. The word *believe* used in this verse is more than simply believing something to be true, as in agreeing with a statement or fact; rather, it is believing *on,* depending *on.* It is considering something to be true and worthy of your trust. Seeing a chair and believing it to be a chair is one thing, but until I sit in that chair, I am not depending on it to be a chair. So often we want Jesus, but not enough to completely trust and depend on Him. That was my story, until I almost died in a kickboxing accident at the age of twenty-five and was faced with my most important moment: eternity with or without God.

What about you? You picked up a book called *God Distorted* because you want to know more about who God really is. In your heart you know there is a God, and you don't want to be an orphan anymore. If you never have before, now is the time to respond to Him, just as I did, as my friend Nicky did, and as so many others have. We all have had our moment and made our choice to become part of God's family. Now is your moment. This is your opportunity to cease being an orphan and be adopted into God's family. "But to all who believed him and accepted him, he gave the right to become children of God" (John 1:12).

Believe, Receive, Become

When you believe Christ is the Savior and receive Him as Lord of your life, you become something—or rather someone—you weren't. You become God's child, and you begin the most incredible journey of following Him. He died for you personally and wants desperately to be your perfect heavenly Father. Having a relationship with God is the beginning of God's image changing you. If you are ready, and you want to surrender your life to Jesus and become God's son or daughter, please pray the same prayer I prayed:

> Dear Jesus, I believe the story is true. I believe You really died on a cross for me, and I believe You rose from the grave after three days. Jesus, here I am. I confess I have sinned and I want to give my life to You. I want a new start. I want a perfect Father. Please forgive me. Right now in this moment I invite You into my heart to be my Savior and my Father in heaven. From this day on I will follow You and I will walk with You. You are my God and I am Your child. I pray this in Your name, amen.

Welcome to God's family! You are no longer an orphan in search of a perfect father, but in this moment you are a child of God. "See how very much our Father loves us, for he calls us his children, and that is what we are!" (1 John 3:1).

What Now?

As a child of God you can go forward with confidence that He will not—in fact *cannot*—let you down. You may have been lied to before, but your heavenly Father cannot lie. His Word (the Bible) is full of promises that you can trust in and rely on. Look at this verse:

> God also bound himself with an oath, so that those who received the promise could be perfectly sure that he would never change his mind. So God has

given both his promise and his oath. These two things are unchangeable because it is impossible for God to lie. Therefore, we who have fled to him for refuge can have great confidence as we hold to the hope that lies before us. (Hebrews 6:17–18)

I pray this confidence will be yours as we begin to look at the promises of God and how they speak to the fears of our hearts. All fear comes from not being confident of God's love, but God can be trusted. Fear that has been learned can, over time, be unlearned as well. His promises are true, and they are for you.

In the rest of this section, we will see God's heart and hopefully begin to grasp the fullness of His love. It is my prayer that these words will be more than just information, but that through your response they will cause life transformation as your mind is renewed.

His perfect love is enough for you.

God Is Always with You

> The Lord is close to the broken-hearted; he rescues those whose spirits are crushed.
>
> —Psalm 34:18

Who can forget "Achy Breaky Heart," the song that made Billy Ray Cyrus famous? Look it up online if you're not familiar with it.

I love hearing the story behind a song. This one wasn't written or originally performed by Cyrus, although it became his signature song. Don Von Tress wrote the song in 1990 with the thought that perhaps a broken relationship would hurt less if there was some way to stop the heart from knowing. The song essentially became a humorous way of looking at a broken heart.[1]

Although there is nothing funny about a broken heart, the popularity of this song is a good indicator of the human desire to dull the pain of one. "Achy Breaky Heart" became an overnight hit, propelling Cyrus to fame, selling over 20 million copies worldwide, and fueling the craze for line dancing in the nineties.[2] So what made this song such a huge success? Is it the catchy lyrical style of the song, or the fact that people can identify with the heartbreak of being left by someone they love?

Think back for a moment. What broke *your* heart? A boyfriend or girlfriend? Divorce? A spouse dying? Or maybe, like me, you were abandoned as a child. Of all of the ways to cause heartbreak and heartache, abandonment is surely one of the most powerful. I would say that in some cases it leaves the heart shattered. There is nothing quite as devastating as being left, feeling rejected and unloved, with little hope that the situation will ever change. Abandonment leaves deep wounds and easy triggers. Psychotherapist and author Susan Anderson describes the five universal stages of abandonment as shattering, withdrawal, internalizing, rage, and lifting.[3] *Rage* is a good word for a stage! I can say from my own experience that pain becomes fuel to an anger that can be hard to control and that marks our behavior and relationships.

Anger is a powerful emotion that can, at the right times, be productive for you. It triggers the fight-or-flight response and can stir us to take action for justice when needed. On the other hand, it can be extremely counterproductive. In my earlier life, I used anger to cover up the real issues I didn't want anyone to see. The Bible never says anger is a sin; it's what we do with our anger that becomes a problem. But anger is a strong master and reveals itself inappropriately, usually directed at the wrong people for seemingly no reason at all. It is a form of control that makes people deal with us on our terms. Anderson said it this way: "The abandonment wound, stored deep within the limbic brain, is easily triggered. You feel its raw nerve twinge when you fail to get recognition at work, a friend forgets to invite you to a party, or a date you thought was special did not call back. When being left is the trigger, core abandonment fears erupt."[4]

Anger can, and so often does, rule your life. Look at this story of former middleweight boxing champ James Toney:

The son hates the father, and it is a coursing, relentless hatred born of blood and abandonment. The father was a big and violent man; he and the mother tore at each other in reckless rage until one night the father took out a gun and shot the mother, leaving a bullet in her leg. The father left a short while later, just up and split when the boy was seven months old. Today the son is 23, a middleweight champion of the world, and as he talks about the hatred, he works his knuckles in the way that some people spin the cylinder of a gun, as if he is trying to get in touch with something powerful just below the skin or at least trying to keep it at bay.

"I fight with anger," explains James Toney Jr. "My dad, he did my mom wrong. He left us, he beat my mother up all the time. He shot my mom, left her with a mark on her leg. He made my mom work two jobs, and he just left his responsibilities behind. I can never forgive that. Why should I? I know where he is. I hope he reads this, because if he ever decides to come out of the woodwork, I'll be ready for him. I'll have some fun then.

"Everything is about that. I look at my opponent and I see my dad, so I have to take him out. I have to kill him. I'll do anything I have to do to get him out of there."[5]

Toney's lifetime of wounds had created an anger that was now a physical force inside him. With every fight, he dressed himself in anger and a hatred that consumed him. When he entered the ring, he wore a hunger for revenge.

Undressing Abandonment

The fear of abandonment and our God distortion cause us to dress in protective clothing. We clothe ourselves in frustration, fear, cynicism, judgment. It is heavy armor to wear that in reality hurts others more than it protects us. Only when I undressed my abandonment could I more effectively deal with the real wounds inside.

In my heart I clothed my emotions with distrust. Abandonment and rejection taught me to not trust people and to build walls around my heart. It was my way to self-protect. I wish I could have seen much earlier how much my issues crippled me in other relationships. Trust is undoubtedly one of the most valuable commodities in any relationship, and because of my damage, people have had to work hard (almost inappropriately) to earn my trust. I was my own worst enemy. God would bring great people into my life, but I would keep them at arm's length, and in doing so, I failed to build relationships where I could learn to trust. It was a fear that reproduced itself over and over.

In my attitude I clothed my thoughts with cynicism. Having now grown so much in this area, I can look back and see how I guarded myself, keeping most everyone at a distance. The lack of trust in my heart created a sort of conspiracy theory in my mind, so I began each relationship with a posture of defeat, convinced "they will eventually leave anyway." I had to learn to stop generalizing and thinking that in every situation someone would leave. I played mental gymnastics and had to learn to trust God and allow myself to be vulnerable with family, friends, and coworkers. It's only when you are willing to be vulnerable (which means risking being hurt) that you will see what God might be trying to do in your life. Loving people can cause pain—because people can and will leave—but not loving others and always protecting yourself is so much more painful in the end.

In my relationships I clothed my reactions with insecurity. It was hard for me to let people get close, but when I did, those friends became like family to me. I would develop a codependency from the fear they would leave. I became a people pleaser and often cared too much about the opinions or thoughts of others. I wanted to make everyone happy so they would always stay with me. When I first got married, I smothered my wife, Michelle. Wherever she was, I was there too, like a little puppy following her around. She finally told me she needed space, and I couldn't understand it. I wanted to keep her close at all times. The problem is that insecurity creates a desire to control, which so often pushes people further away. Your insecurity may be working like a shield for you, keeping people out instead of keeping you safe.

New Clothes

The Bible is clear that as people of God we are to dress ourselves differently. Check out what the apostle Paul tells the church in Colossae: "Since God chose you to be the holy people he loves, you must clothe yourselves with tenderhearted mercy, kindness, humility, gentleness, and patience" (Colossians 3:12). That sounds like the opposite of anger, doesn't it? But anger is like a comfortable sweater or favorite jacket that over time has come to fit us well. We don't want to get rid of it, no matter how bad it smells or how ugly it looks. It has provided protection and warmth and has become part of our identity. So how do we take off anger and put on mercy, kindness, humility, gentleness, and patience? How do we let go of bitterness and rage and start dressing better?

When I think about stories of abandonment and heartache, I am instantly reminded of the biblical story of Joseph. Here is a young man who experienced abandonment over and over. He was the eleventh of twelve sons, and the Bible tells us he was favored by his father.

The story starts in Genesis 37:3: "Jacob loved Joseph more than any of his other children because Joseph had been born to him in his old age. So one day Jacob had a special gift made for Joseph—a beautiful robe." Joseph's new coat was long sleeved and not practical for working. It was a sign that this son was set apart and not expected to work as hard as the others. Some theologians believe it signified that the privileges of birthright, which usually belonged to the firstborn, had now been passed to Joseph. It showed others who he was in the family and that he was his father's favored son. As you can imagine, his older brothers were extremely jealous, and over time his brothers grew to hate him. Joseph didn't exactly help matters. He reported their bad deeds to their father, and he shared with his brothers his dreams that they would someday bow down to him. The Bible tells us that they couldn't say a kind word about him. One day the brothers had finally had enough, and they plotted to kill Joseph:

> When Joseph's brothers saw him coming, they recognized him in the distance. As he approached, they made plans to kill him. "Here comes the dreamer!" they said. "Come on, let's kill him and throw him into one of these cisterns. We can tell our father, 'A wild animal has eaten him.' Then we'll see what becomes of his dreams!"…
>
> So when Joseph arrived, his brothers ripped off the beautiful robe he was wearing. Then they grabbed him and threw him into the cistern. Now the cistern was empty; there was no water in it. (Genesis 37:18–20, 23–24)

Pit Theology

Like Joseph, we never choose to be in a pit. You don't wake up one morning and say, "Today is the day I will jump into a pit." You are pushed into it by someone close to you. The pit is a shock; it takes you by surprise. You weren't expecting it, hadn't planned it; you never thought it would happen to you. The pit is the place where you find yourself alone, thinking, *I will never trust again.* Joseph was just seventeen years old when his brothers put him in the pit and left him to die. Can you imagine what he was feeling? Anger, disbelief, fear, anxiety, hopelessness. I'm sure he asked the same questions we all ask the day we land in the pit: *Why me? Where's God? What now?* As we are going to find out, God was very close to Joseph, but there is still more to his story. From that day until he was in his late thirties, Joseph was abandoned over and over.

His brothers were not done yet; having taken his birthright robe, they decide to sell him as a slave rather than kill him. Joseph then travels with the slave traders and is sold to Potiphar, an officer in the house of Pharaoh, the king of Egypt. Joseph works hard and the Lord blesses his work, which earns him favor: "Potiphar noticed this and realized that the LORD was with Joseph, giving him success in everything he did. This pleased Potiphar, so he soon made Joseph his personal attendant. He put him in charge of his entire household and everything he owned" (Genesis 39:3–4).

Joseph had gone from zero to hero in Potiphar's house, now in charge of everything, and the Bible says the only thing he had to worry about was what to eat! If this were the end of the story, it would be great, but it gets worse before it gets better. The Bible describes Joseph as being a very handsome and well-built young man, and soon Potiphar's wife wanted to sleep with him. Joseph refused, but in her anger she accused him of trying to rape her. Of course Potiphar was furious, and Joseph was thrown into prison.

Now Joseph is in prison with two of Pharaoh's key leaders. They begin to have dreams, which Joseph is able to interpret, and all he asks is that they would not forget him when they got out. Unbelievably, Joseph is abandoned again. Genesis 40:23 tells us that "Pharaoh's chief cup-bearer, however, forgot all about Joseph, never giving him another thought." Joseph sits in prison for another two years before his opportunity comes around.

At this point, Joseph has now been undressed physically by his brothers, undressed emotionally by his abandonment—not once but four times—and has spent a total of twelve years in prison undeservedly. I think we would all agree he has reason to be angry. If it were me, I'd be dressing myself up in rage and cynicism. But Joseph wasn't like that. Through all the years, pain, and trials, we don't hear him utter a single word of contempt. I love that Joseph remained faithful to God, even when it appeared that God had abandoned him as well. You have to wonder what kept him so strong. Chapter 39 of Genesis gives us a pretty good clue. Four times in one chapter we see these words: "The LORD was with him." Even while in prison Joseph knew the presence of God: "But the LORD was with Joseph in the prison and showed him his faithful love. And the LORD made Joseph a favorite with the prison warden" (verse 21).

When I first became a believer, I needed to know that this verse was true for me too. My fear that God would leave me was so real it was disabling. I would never allow myself to open up or get close to Him for fear He would leave, just as my father did. I soon learned that the best antidote for fear is the promise of God's unwavering presence.

God Is with You Too

The central theological promise in the Bible is not that God *loves* you—although He does. It is not that God is *for* you—although He is. The central promise is that God is *with* you. He is always with you. He was with Joseph and worked His plan out in Joseph's life. Joseph started his journey alone and afraid in a pit, and eventually he became the ruler of all Egypt, second only to Pharaoh! God promises He is always with us and will never leave us.

One of the verses I studied over and over when first becoming a believer is in Hebrews. It was written to a church filled with Christians disabled by fear. They had forgotten the promise so central to faith and foundational to the life of a Christ-follower: "I will never fail you. I will never abandon you" (Hebrews 13:5).

When I first read that verse, it was a bit surreal to me. *Never* is a big word. Was it really true that God would never leave me or abandon me? When I studied the original Greek a bit further, I discovered that putting "never" twice in one statement is a double emphatic, which in English would mean "never, ever, ever, ever, ever!" God will never, ever, ever, ever abandon you. That one tiny verse written two thousand years ago to the earliest believers helped me more than I can explain. This verse became an anchor of hope in my life as a new follower of Jesus, and as a man trying to heal from childhood wounds and bitterness. It created in me a passion to live as if it were true. I thought, *If I can trust God for a heaven I have never seen, I can certainly trust that His promise is true too.*

There are many other scriptures that affirm this promise of God. Deuteronomy 31:8: "Do not be afraid or discouraged, for the LORD will personally go ahead of you. He will be with you; he will neither fail you nor abandon you." We need not fear anymore. Have you read Psalm 118:6? I love this so much: "The LORD is for me, so I will have no fear. What can mere people do to me?" Once this truth is settled in your heart, man can do nothing to separate you from the presence of God. He loves you, He is with you and *nothing* can ever change that.

Learning to Have 50/20 Vision

Joseph had what we like to call "50/20 vision." Secure in the fact that God was always with him, he could see God working out His plan, even when it seemed hopeless. Joseph learned that God would use everything for His good purposes. Look at Genesis 50:20 (hence the phrase *50/20 vision*): "You intended to harm me, but God intended it all for good. He brought me to this position so I could save the lives of many people." What great sight he had to see through all the abandonment, despair, and loneliness to the greater plan that God had in place. Joseph was now married with two children, one of whom he named Ephraim, which means "God has made me fruitful in this land of my suffering." I think this is one of the most difficult but important things for us to learn. The fruit of our lives comes through suffering. As a pastor, I cannot begin to count the times I have watched people living in the land of suffering. They misinterpret circumstance, blame others, walk away from God, and then quit before God is done and before the purpose of the suffering and its resulting fruit can be experienced. We have to see our lives through 50/20 vision: *God will turn into good what others meant for evil.* This principle doesn't just apply to Joseph's story from thousands of years ago in the land of Egypt, but Paul talks about this in the book of Romans as well: "And we know that God causes everything to work together for the good of those who love God and are called according to his purpose for them" (Romans 8:28). This is God's promise to all of us.

Joseph's story is still not quite finished. He has now single-handedly saved the nation from famine and, aside from Pharaoh, is the most powerful man in the land. He finds himself in an unexpected position when his brothers come to Egypt after two years of famine, begging to buy food. They do not recognize him, but he is shaken by their arrival. The very people who abandoned and betrayed him are now at his mercy. Joseph had a choice to make. He could hurt or help. What would you do?

To Play God or to Trust God?

It is interesting how often the very ones who hurt you will eventually need help from you. You'll also have a choice to make: To hurt or to help? To play God or to trust God? Again Joseph is our example in this matter. Look at what he does: "Then he broke down and wept. He wept so loudly the Egyptians could hear him, and word of it quickly carried to Pharaoh's palace. 'I am Joseph!' he said to his brothers. 'Is my father still alive?' But his brothers were speechless! They were stunned to realize that Joseph was standing there in front of them" (Genesis 45:2–3).

Can you imagine that moment? The ultimate "it stinks to be me" moment? His brothers are terrified, knowing he could lock them in prison or kill them on the spot. I'm sure they were experiencing immense regret, wishing they could undo everything they did and certain their lives were about to be changed. But look at the grace the 50/20 vision produced in Joseph's heart: " 'Please, come closer,' he said to them. So they came closer. And he said again, 'I am Joseph, your brother, whom you sold into slavery in Egypt. But don't be upset, and don't be angry with yourselves for selling me to this place. *It was God who sent me here* ahead of you to preserve your lives'" (verses 4–5).

Joseph's assurance of God's continuous presence had set him free from anger and enabled him to forgive the ones who had hurt him. His pain had now become his platform.

You Get to Choose

For years I lived in anger at a father I never knew, and that anger was beginning to affect my family. My son was barely a teenager and needed me to be whole. I wanted something different for my faithful wife, Michelle, and for all my children. I also wanted something different for me. I can say honestly now that the abandonment I experienced as a child, and as a man, has been used by God to save me.

In your situation, you have a choice: bitter or better. Will you look back at those who hurt you, or look up at the God who heals you? Will you bless them or curse them? Will you choose to continue living in anger, or will you live in faith? Will you hold on to the lie—seeing God distorted—or will you believe He is the Father who will never leave your side?

My friend David tells of the choice he had to make:

Growing up I didn't have much of a view of God. Like my father, God was just absent and I didn't really know any different. As I got older I actually had a lot of Christian friends who would tell me that God loved me, but I didn't believe them. I wanted to, I just couldn't seem to. I remember telling a friend that I wished I could have the faith to believe like they did, but I guess I just didn't have that in me.

Later, when I first became a Christian, everything was great; I had that mountaintop/honeymoon experience where everything was peachy-keen and rose-colored for a while, but after a few months I started doubting, first myself and then God. I had spent so much time being fake in order to get people to like me that I began to wrestle with thoughts like *"David, who are you kidding? You're such a phony. You're a Christian now? How long is this gonna last? Until they get to know you, find out about your past? Then what?"* Then I began to question if God really loved me and whether or not He would ever leave or give up on me. No one else in my life had ever loved me like that, especially my father, so why would God?

So I actually spent a couple of months trying to prove that God wouldn't really live up to His promise. I tested Him by going back to certain activities and making choices I knew He "wouldn't like." I would go out and get drunk and party Friday and Saturday, then show up to church and wear the "everything's great" mask on Sunday. It wasn't until I came to the end of myself that the words of a friend made sense. She told me that I would have to choose what I was going to believe about God. I had to choose to believe that God's Word is true, that He promises to love me and never leave me, and in the end I did.

David is now the pastor of the recovery and restoration ministry at our church. I'm so glad he made the choice to believe God could be trusted.

That central promise of the Bible was true for me, was true for David, and is true for you today as well. The pit will happen, but God is there. Divorce may happen, but God is there. Death will happen, but God is there. Heartbreak will surely happen, but God will be there.

If you have been undressed by abandonment, allow God to clothe you in something better. Trust Him for something beyond what you can see.

God Is Up Close and Personal

Loneliness and the feeling of
being unwanted is the most
terrible poverty.

—MOTHER TERESA

C an you imagine the very first problem in the beginning of time? God has just created the entire universe: spoken the stars into existence and created millions of animals, birds, fish, and insects. He formed every fruit, vegetable, plant, and flower, and each day as He surveyed His creation, He saw it was good (quite the understatement). He was pleased with His creation. On the sixth day God created man in His own image from dust, and on the seventh day He rested. Then He noticed a problem, the first problem the world had ever known. God recognized that Adam had no one to relate to. "The LORD God said, 'It is not good for the man to be alone. I will make a helper suitable for him'" (Genesis 2:18, NIV).

If God said it, it must be true: it isn't good for people to be alone. We were created for relationship. God's design is perfect, and we were made to do life together. He implanted connection in our DNA. Think about how much this matters, that even before sin entered the world and while Adam enjoyed a perfect relationship with his Creator and Father, he still needed a companion. Adam was the first man on earth, and he lived alone for an unknown period of time. He had no parents, no family, and no friends. The first problem ever in the history of the world is still a huge problem today: loneliness.

In his book *Traveling Light,* Max Lucado said, "Loneliness is not the absence of faces. It is the absence of intimacy. Loneliness doesn't come from being alone; it comes from feeling alone."[1]

Loneliness is a devastating emotion that doesn't develop overnight. It takes many years, many people, and a myriad of circumstances to shape and reshape us. Do you remember the passive father? His children are not abandoned, just unnoticed. He is in the room but not engaged. He is present but not "with you." The child is left feeling invisible, rejected, and unwanted. These are deep hurts formed through lack of intimacy with the ones who are supposed to love us the most. Loneliness is separation, isolation, or distance in human relationships, and aptly described by Christian psychologist Henry Cloud as a "sickness of the soul."[2] It is an unbearable feeling of separateness, emptiness, and hopelessness at a very deep level. Lonely people are commonly devoid of intimacy, and in many cases have never developed the skills to be intimate or have close relationships. Often they believe they are unworthy of being known. Although desperately longing to feel loved, they may cut themselves off from others for fear of further rejection and hurt. Lonely people suffer from the unmet desire for significance, the need in all of us to be seen and valued.

Even with the current saturation of social media and social networking, it can be argued that we are now lonelier than ever. Simply stated, social networking is a great tool to connect with others, but it has created a false sense of community, hallmarked by surface friendships that exist only through what information we choose to share. God did not design us to poke people on Facebook, smile only in texts, and send hugs via e-mail. While we are more socially connected than any previous generation, we are missing actual intimacy with God and with others. We are not supposed to do life with people through Twitter. We were made to love and be loved.

Whatever the cause, most people will experience a season of loneliness. It is not exclusive to those who are physically alone. I know many people who are lonely in marriage or while working and interacting with people all day. Sometimes even the outgoing and popular ones—those with many friends—are in fact secretly suffering with the burden of loneliness. One of the most critical groups affected is our teenagers and young adults. The void of intimacy in their childhood leaves them sad, depressed, and unable to build meaningful relationships. They are surrounded by friends, teachers, and fellow students, yet are lonely in the crowd. The need to be accepted and the desire to belong matters to everyone, but combined with the emotional immaturity of a teenager, it becomes a perfect storm of rejection in which they attempt to fill the void in inappropriate ways. Depending on their personality, they may excessively give themselves to others in sexual promiscuity or retreat into dangerous isolation, which in extreme cases can result in suicide. Through our own brokenness as parents, we are raising a generation of wounded kids, working out their insecurity in destructive ways.

I can relate to other groups who feel lonely but are less likely to admit it. Many pastors, business leaders, CEOs, and executives experience untold bouts of depression that come fundamentally from being lonely. They bear the weight of making difficult decisions alone and often have to separate themselves in order to get the job done. In some cases they are rejected for the decisions they must make, or worse, they are betrayed by those closest to them. As they say, "It's lonely at the top."

Misery Seeks Company

If you feel lonely, you are in good company. Remember Elijah, who killed 450 false prophets, called down fire from heaven, then started the rain again—but after receiving a threat of death, ran away in fear? The hero was now isolated and lonely. First Kings 19:4 says, "Then he went on alone into the wilderness, traveling all day. He sat down under a solitary broom tree and prayed that he might die. 'I have had enough, LORD,' he said. 'Take my life, for I am no better than my ancestors who have already died.'" And let's not forget Moses, who experienced the burden and loneliness of leadership. He eventually asked God to take his life: "I can't carry all these people by myself! The load is far too heavy! If this is how you intend to treat me, just go ahead and kill me. Do me a favor and spare me this misery!" (Numbers 11:14–15).

But few people have more reason to feel lonely than Jeremiah, the prophet who wrote the book of Lamentations. Jeremiah belonged to a priestly family that had been rejected from the religious and royal establishment. As a prophet, his ministry was marked by his enemy's attempts to silence him by means of arrests, trials, beatings, imprisonments, and even assassination plots. The prophet also endured great personal sacrifice for his calling, in that he was not allowed to have a wife or children. Being unmarried was so unusual among the Jews that the Old Testament had no word for *bachelor*. To make matters worse, he was also instructed to refrain from attending social events such as funerals and weddings. Completely devoid of family and friends, and seeing no fruit—not one single conversion in his ministry—Jeremiah lamented to God and earned himself the title "the weeping prophet."

You Never Think It Will Happen to You

Some years ago I experienced a season of betrayal that left me broken in so many ways. Our church was growing exponentially, we were running six services a weekend in just one location, and we had a weekly attendance of five thousand people. It was time for me as the senior leader to raise some of my most trusted staff—some of whom were also my closest friends—into a higher level of responsibility. I communicated our priorities, felt confident they would protect our DNA, and we began the process of delegating and redistributing responsibility. I was still the senior leader, but I felt freedom to focus more on preaching, writing, and vision, and was even able to accept some speaking opportunities overseas.

It was on one of these speaking engagements that my world changed. I was flying to Australia to speak to a group of nearly fifteen thousand people from over three hundred churches in Perth. It was something I had committed to many months earlier, and I was excited to go. But while waiting at the airport, I received a call to say that if I went to Australia, the very people I had trusted would leave to start another church, and they would do it while I was gone. It felt like someone took a baseball bat and hit me in the stomach.

My wife assured me it was still right to go, but as I got on the plane for that eighteen-hour flight, I felt as if I was entering a type of cave—lonely, dark, depressing, and hopeless. Even on a good day I don't like to be alone. My childhood abandonment issues have left me with a strong attachment to friends, and I like to do everything with a group. So to be traveling alone was very unusual for me anyway, and with the fresh sting of betrayal, I felt a loneliness I had never experienced before. I was overwhelmed with the feeling that no one cared, and it seemed like God was silent. I found myself confronted with the pain of separation once again and could do nothing but cry for hours. I didn't know whom I could trust or if anyone was still on my team. I felt so stupid and embarrassed that the flight attendants had to keep bringing me Kleenex, but it was by God's design that I was alone. Without distractions and no voices to listen to but God's, He became my refuge. With nowhere else to turn, I looked to the Bible, to the lives of my heroes, and learned a great lesson from the life of King David, who spent many years in an actual cave.

David is one of the unexpected heroes of the Old Testament. He failed in epic ways but had such a broken heart and bold courage. He is the only person in the Bible called "a man after [God's] own heart" (Acts 13:22). Once renowned as the hero who killed Goliath, he then became the one that stirred an ill-fated jealousy in the heart of King Saul (Israel's first king). First Samuel 18:9 says, "Saul kept a jealous eye on David."

Saul's jealousy caused David to run till he ended up in a cave in a place called Adullum. He lost everything he knew: his home, family, country, friends, position, and reputation. He was loved then hated, blessed then betrayed. He went from hero to zero in no time at all, hunted by the very people he had led and served. His own life was on the line. During one of the most difficult seasons of his life, the same cave that provided escape from potential hurt was also a place of isolation that left David lonely and discouraged.

We don't know how long exactly, but scholars believe that David was in the wilderness and in the caves for about ten or twelve years. Can you imagine the loneliness he felt during that time? We get a glimpse of his emotional condition from the psalms he wrote in the cave. "I look for someone to come and help me, but no one gives me a passing thought! No one will help me; no one cares a bit what happens to me" (Psalm 142:4). David is lonely in every sense of the word. Not just emotionally, not simply longing for deeper friendship, he is completely separated from people and devoid of a caring human bond.

Do you find yourself in that place? Confused, hurt, alone, maybe even mad at God for your situation? For me it was on the plane. That was my cave.

God allows things in our lives to teach us, to build our character, and to make us whole. Being whole means you have to let the cave teach you some things. I now know with certainty that long flight alone was the cave that God in His infinite wisdom sent me to. I am wired—like many of you—to control, to fix the problem, and to make everyone happy. With no one to call and no action I could take, that cave—my empty, lonely place—became a space for just Him and me and no one else.

Promises of the Cave

In the cave it's easy to believe God doesn't see us. Our loneliness distorts the truth and our image of God. We believe He doesn't care, that our issues aren't important. We're sure He is far too busy running the world to pay attention to our needs. We may even give up talking to God, believing He has more important things to do. We think, *Clearly He is there for everyone else, but not for me.*

Nothing could be further from the truth! Adullum—the place where David's cave was—actually means "refuge." God had led David, even in his running. David had lost everything and had every reason to question God's character. He could have given up completely, but instead he allowed the situation to strengthen his dependence on God. The Bible tells us, "but David encouraged himself in the LORD his God" (1 Samuel 30:6, KJV). I love that what seems initially to be a hopeless situation is actually an opportunity to depend only on God! The Hebrew word for "encouraged" in this verse is *chazak*. It means "to strengthen, to prevail, to become strong, to restore to strength or encourage." It is continuous—not a one-time thing, but something you are devoted to, a constant strengthening to be able to withstand something.

So how did David encourage himself, and how can we do that? To strengthen ourselves in God means we remind ourselves of what Scripture says about Him and His promises, and then we apply those truths to our current situation. It is an intentional act, not something that just happens. The Hebrew verb implies persistent and continuous effort. There is nothing passive about seeking out the Lord in times of despair.

I learned a little more each day that God was enough for me. In my cave, I took strength from His Word, His promises became a lifeline, and I discovered for myself that my heavenly Father is up close and personal.

Cave Promise 1: God is with you.

David had history with God, so he had a lot to draw from. He knew from experience that God was with him even in the darkness and despair. David said it best in Psalm 23:4: "Even when I walk through the darkest valley, I will not be afraid, for you are close beside me. Your rod and your staff protect and comfort me." This is not the picture of a God who is distant and uncaring. Whether your loneliness is the product of a passive father, a divorce, or a fractured friendship, please don't misinterpret your feelings of separateness for the absence of God. I learned that silence is not the absence of God, but the absence of activity in my heart. God might seem silent, but He is with you. He is for you. He is there and He knows your every thought. He is bound to His Word, which means you can trust His unfailing presence.

Cave Promise 2: God will defend you.

"Praise be to the LORD, for he has heard my cry for mercy. The LORD is my strength and my shield; my heart trusts in him, and I am helped. My heart leaps for joy and I will give thanks to him in song" (Psalm 28:6–7, NIV). What a great verse! He is our strength and our shield. In the cave you don't have strength to fight. It is a place of weakness and vulnerability. I am a fighter by nature, but in the cave I learned to wait on God. David didn't react, but instead waited for God to act. Everything inside me wanted to defend my name, to rebut the slander, and to let people know the things being said about me were lies. I could have taken things into my own hands and built a very strong case, but I felt God speak strongly to my heart that He would be my defender if I wouldn't try to defend myself. He would be my shield. I waited and trusted, and God acted. He did what I could not. Now I am better because of the cave.

Cave Promise 3: God has a purpose for you.

I love these words penned by David about the faithfulness of God: "Though I am surrounded by troubles, you will protect me from the anger of my enemies. You reach out your hand, and the power of your right hand saves me. The LORD will work out his plans for my life—for your faithful love, O LORD, endures forever. Don't abandon me, for you made me" (Psalm 138:7–8).

God can and will use our seasons of loneliness to build His character inside us. You might think that God isn't doing much with you in the cave, but when you get to the other side, you'll realize that He was doing so much *in* you. God meets us in the cave to prepare us for a better future. He did it for me, and for Kay too. (Remember Kay from chapter 4? Her relationship with her father left her feeling worthless and unlovable.) She has become a great testimony of God's redeeming power. Here is the rest of her story:

> I wasted so much time feeling this way! It is still an enigma to me sometimes…so many mixed emotions…even now as tears fall from my face, I get saddened that I didn't know God could love me as He does. Then on the flipside of the coin, I am in awe of Him and that He does love me. I am His precious daughter, and nothing can change that, not even my earthly father. I am a work in progress. I try to remember that He has been molding me my whole life, and He has plans for me—some of which I am walking out right now. And on the days when Satan tries to remind me of my past, I just try to remind him of his future, and start praying to God.

I can say I am grateful now for my time in the cave. Only through having to depend completely on God and no one else did I develop the security I know today. I am a better man, a stronger leader, and a more secure friend because of God's closeness through my emptiness. If you allow Him to, God will redeem your loneliness to be an unspeakable season of learning to trust and depend on Him alone. It will change you for the better and prepare you for even greater things. Don't quit in the cave—but don't stay there either.

God Is Intimately Involved

There is perhaps no greater need of the human soul than the longing for significance. Every person alive wants to believe they are noticed and valued by someone. How much more important is the assurance that the One who created us is deeply interested and actively involved in our daily lives. One of my favorite psalms of David is a powerful promise of intimacy with our heavenly Father. We can cling to these words in our loneliness. As you read these words, put your name in there. Apply this promise to your struggle, your problem, your pain and confusion. People and circumstances push us to caves, but it is in the cave you learn so much about yourself and God. He redeems these moments and brings us back to His loving arms. He isn't passive; He is involved. I pray that the words of David from thousands of years ago will be words that speak to you today. You are not alone; He knows your name.

Psalm 139: A Psalm of David

O LORD, you have searched me
   and you know me.
You know when I sit and when I rise;
   you perceive my thoughts from afar....

Where can I go from your Spirit?
   Where can I flee from your presence?
If I go up to the heavens, you are there;
   if I make my bed in the depths, you are there.
If I rise on the wings of the dawn,
   if I settle on the far side of the sea,
even there your hand will guide me,
   your right hand will hold me fast....

For you created my inmost being;
    you knit me together in my mother's womb.
I praise you because I am fearfully and wonderfully made;
    your works are wonderful,
      I know that full well.
My frame was not hidden from you
    when I was made in the secret place.
When I was woven together in the depths of the earth,
    your eyes saw my unformed body.
All the days ordained for me
    were written in your book
    before one of them came to be.

How precious to me are your thoughts, O God!
    How vast is the sum of them!
Were I to count them,
    they would outnumber the grains of sand.
When I awake,
    I am still with you. (Psalm 139:1–2, 7–10, 13–18, NIV)

God Is Fully Pleased

God puts something good and
loveable in every man His hands
create.

—MARK TWAIN, 1868

I will always remember Whitney Houston and her incomparable voice. According to
the *Guinness Book of World Records,* she is the most-awarded female recording artist of
all time, and her soundtrack from *The Bodyguard* reigned at number one on the bill-
board charts for twenty weeks.[1] Her gift to sing, perform, and act made an indelible
impact on the entertainment industry and in the lives of so many around the world. As
much as we remember her talent, I doubt anyone will forget hearing the shocking news
of her sudden death. As I sat with friends and family to watch her memorial service, I
felt as if I was there in person, seeing the tears and listening to the tributes that were,
appropriately, nothing short of epic. We were all so moved to hear her most famous song
once again as family and friends took her out to be laid to rest. In fact, after her untimely
death, downloads for that same song ("I Will Always Love You") were in the millions.
She was beautiful both inside and out. She seemed to have it all, and I imagined her to
be one of the happiest, most secure, confident people in the world.

But then her friend and costar Kevin Costner shared a story that touched my life in
a profound way. Costner recalled that when he asked her to star in *The Bodyguard,* she
had doubt at her audition:

> The day the test came and I went into her trailer after the hair and makeup
> people were done, Whitney was scared. Arguably, the biggest pop star in the
> world wasn't sure if she was good enough. She didn't think she looked right.

There were a thousand things to her that seemed wrong. I held her hand and told her that she looked beautiful. I told her that I would be with her every step of the way, that everyone there wanted her to succeed, but I could still feel the doubt.

Costner said that he wished he could have told her it was rigged, and that he had already made his decision but admits it wouldn't be fair to either Whitney or the studio to say that. Whitney asked for twenty minutes to collect herself, then came to the set. After only four lines they had to stop. They went back to the dressing room so Costner could show her what he had seen:

I turned her around so that she could see herself in the mirror and she gasped. All of the makeup on Whitney's face was running. It was streaking down her face and she was devastated. She didn't feel like the makeup we put on her was enough so she'd wiped it off and put on the makeup that she was used to wearing in her music videos. It was much thicker and the hot lights had melted it. She asked if anyone had seen… I said I didn't think so. It happened so quick. She seemed so small and sad at that moment, and I asked her why she did it? She said, "I just wanted to look my best."

Costner went on to say,

A half-hour later, she went back in to do her screen test and the studio fell in love with her. The Whitney I knew, despite her success and worldwide fame, still wondered *Am I good enough? Am I pretty enough? Will they like me?* It was the burden that made her great, and the part that caused her to stumble in the end.

I could hardly believe what I was hearing as he told this story. He clearly believed in her so much, while she had no confidence at all. Costner concluded:

Whitney, if you could hear me now, I would tell you, you weren't just good enough, you were great.… You weren't just pretty, you were as beautiful as a woman could be. People didn't just like you, Whitney. They loved you.[2]

As we watched that day in silence with tears streaming down our faces, we all wondered the same thing: How does Whitney Houston not feel good enough? Could it be that her most famous song was also the cry of her heart? Could all the talent and all the fame have hidden her need to be fully loved? To be secure in who she was? To know God would say, "I will always love you"? I could see in the eyes of those around me, and heard later in their conversations, that we all ask these same questions: Am I good enough? Do I measure up? Is God happy with me?

Picture a child showing his dad the A+ he got on a school test. He is hoping to hear a simple "Great job, son." He did well and his grade reflects that, but he still needs his father's affirmation. We all need that, don't we? We all want to make others happy. We find ourselves on a treadmill of constant performance, doing all we can to hear "Great job" from our dad, boss, spouse, friend, and even God. That desire for recognition causes an insatiable insecurity in relationships with both God and other people. That insecurity creates a lack of confidence in what we do, where we go, and what we say, and it begins to control our lives. We create a to-do list in our relationship with God, but the doing of it sucks the joy out of our lives. It seems a hopeless task anyway. After all, how could we possibly ever be good enough to please a perfect God?

Going Nowhere

I think insecurity leaves us confused and exhausted, as if we're on a virtual treadmill. Fitness centers are full of people frantically running, pedaling, rowing, climbing, but in spite of all their activity, they are going nowhere. They're totally exhausted, but there's no movement or direction. They are on the exercise equipment to nowhere. I am not knocking exercise, but I think it is a great analogy for our generation—we are a treadmill culture. We are busier than ever, more hurried than ever, caught up in so much activity, yet we seem to be going nowhere. We're just running around trying to impress people we don't know and get approval from people who don't know us. As a Christian you may find yourself volunteering on every team, at every service, doing every Bible study, and checking every box. But still you feel like it is never enough, and you are left exhausted and anxious and end up in despair.

This treadmill of activity isn't a relationship with God but rather a sick religious attempt to please God. It is a religious noise of dos and don'ts. It is surely not what Jesus had in mind when He hung bloodied, beaten, and unrecognizable on a cross so that we might be free. I love what A. W. Tozer said: "Religion has accepted the monstrous heresy that noise, size, activity and bluster make a man dear to God. But God says, 'Be still, and know that I am God'... as if He means to tell us that our strength and safety lie not in noise but in silence."

Our treadmill-based striving causes us to be tired, exhausted, and insecure. Insecurity is real and is something everyone faces. It is virtually impossible to be 100 percent free of doubt, to be 100 percent secure. Some will struggle with it for a lifetime. I don't mean to be bleak, but isn't it true? I often meet people who are mature, godly, and wise, but rarely do I find someone who has fully arrived at that address. Mostly we are like kids on a long drive, impatiently asking, "Are we there yet?" We wonder constantly, *Am I good enough?*

Signs of an Insecure Heart

Here are some signs that indicate you are probably not secure in a friendship or relationship. Are any of these familiar in your relationships?

- You are always defensive and hate to be evaluated or critiqued.
- You fear disapproval.
- You value consensus more than your own leadership.
- You are the life and laugh of the party.
- You love to talk about yourself, your family, your accomplishments, your goals.
- You are stupidly jealous.
- You stay in abusive relationships because you value acceptance more than safety for your own life.

Although this isn't an exhaustive list of the marks of insecurity, it is a starting place from which to ask yourself: *Am I that person? Could I be?* Here is the thing for me: I don't want just confidence; I want God-confidence—confidence that doesn't come from men or opinions but from God. Paul strived to have that kind of confidence, and you can see in the Bible Paul's heart to please only God: "Obviously, I'm not trying to win the approval of people, but of God. If pleasing people were my goal, I would not be Christ's servant" (Galatians 1:10).

Whom Are We Trying to Please?

Your strengths can also become your weaknesses in home, life, and work. For me, being a pastor means loving people, but the negative side of the equation is a tendency to seek approval from the people you love, and in the process not clearly hear the voice of God. You become so self-focused trying to be liked by others that you almost tune out God. The opinions of others, which are like waves in an ocean, become what you live your life by.

Trust me here. I've been there, done that. I struggled with wanting approval and seeking it almost to a point of idol worship. My heart, like yours and like Whitney's, craves to know I matter. I was constantly asking the question, "Have I arrived yet?" This was an issue for me as a leader because we would have meetings, agree on a plan, and then whoever had the loudest voice after the meeting would cause me to change directions. It brought discouragement to the other leaders and eroded over and over my own ability to decide. Pleasing isn't the issue here, because our lives will please someone. The question is, who? Will we please ourselves, our God, or others?

Pleasing yourself is simple. Your choices are based on what makes you feel good, with little regard for the effect on others. If you're happy, that's all that matters, right? But pleasing yourself is, in fact, self-destructive. If your thoughts and actions are always *about* yourself, you will eventually be all alone *by* yourself.

If your actions are about pleasing others, you will (like me) always be changing your mind based on what others think or want. It is what I call the "tail wags the dog" syndrome. My decisions were based on what others thought about me, because I so desperately wanted their approval. I cared more about the opinions of men whom I won't stand before in heaven, and who—by the way—didn't die for me, than I cared about the opinion of God who knows me best and loves me most. It is a sad but sick reality for people who constantly are trying to please others. They live with insecurity, striving to be liked, hoping for approval, believing their acceptance is conditional. That is drastically different from those who live knowing they are loved and are secure in the knowledge that God is pleased with them.

Learning to Please God

So how *do* you please God? It's not by running on a never-ending treadmill to His approval, in which you try to work harder, do more, do better, and strive more, because you think only then will God be happy with you—and only when He is happy can you rest. Phew! Exhausting, isn't it?

What if you could see God differently? What if you had a different view of a heavenly Father, one where He is already fully pleased with you? The verse that changed my life, that showed me *this* view of God, is when Jesus was baptized: "And a voice from heaven said, 'This is my dearly loved Son, who brings me great joy'" (Matthew 3:17).

These are the words God spoke to His Son when Jesus was thirty years old—just three-and-a-half short years before Jesus would die. The baptism symbolized the beginning of Jesus's ministry here on earth, so at this point there are no recorded miracles. This is before Jesus healed a single person, before He fed the multitudes, and before He gave His life for you and for me. Before His ministry had even begun, His perfect heavenly Father was already fully pleased with Him.

We are loved by God for who we are, not for what we do. As sons and daughters of God, He is fully pleased with us, as He was with His Son. I wish we could get this truth into our hearts. It would no doubt change our lives. Picture, if you can, a father so pleased with you, so proud of who you are. That is the image we need to get in our hearts and lives: God, the perfect heavenly Father, is fully pleased with you—His son or daughter. Think about that for a second. Please slow down long enough just to read these words from the mouth of the perfect Father. Read them word by word, and think about these words for you and to you. The perfect Father was fully pleased in His Son. Ponder it. Read it again. Breathe in those words. Believe it.

When Work Isn't Worship

One of my favorite stories in the Bible is in Luke chapter 10. It is the story of Jesus having dinner at the house of sisters, Mary and Martha. It is a well-known and often-referenced illustration, but I believe it is largely misinterpreted in a way that gives Martha a bad rap. Let's look at the passage a little more closely. Jesus and His disciples were on their way to Jerusalem when they received an invitation to the home of Martha. Worthy of notice is the fact that Jesus would even go—counterculturally—into the house of an unmarried woman. The invitation showed boldness on the part of Martha, even though she owned the house, and humbleness on the part of Jesus to spend time with Martha and Mary.

But Jesus was no ordinary houseguest. An invitation like this came with a lot of expectations and preparations, and Martha would have been very busy planning a big dinner for her guests. I imagine her to have a Type A, get-it-done personality. If this is you—and you love activity, you love the challenge of accomplishment, and you are very busy—then welcome to my club! If I were a girl, my middle name would probably be Martha. There are Marthas all around us: that person who is hospitable and who always thinks of everyone else. And Martha is doing a good thing by inviting Jesus into her home, so who could fault her for that?

So what is Mary doing? Scripture says, "Her sister, Mary, sat at the Lord's feet, listening to what he taught" (Luke 10:39). So, Martha is working for Jesus, and Mary is sitting with Jesus. Martha was wrapped up in making sure her guests were served and honored, but Mary was only interested in one thing.

The One Thing

But Martha was distracted by the big dinner she was preparing. She came to Jesus and said, "Lord, doesn't it seem unfair to you that my sister just sits here while I do all the work? Tell her to come and help me."

But the Lord said to her, "My dear Martha, you are worried and upset over all these details! There is only one thing worth being concerned about. Mary has discovered it, and it will not be taken away from her." (Luke 10:40–42)

Ouch. At first glance you would think Jesus is saying to Martha that everyone in the world should just sit around. (I have actually heard people justify their own laziness with this verse.) Frankly, I used to struggle with the fact that Martha seems to get a beating here, but we have to understand the context. I believe that Martha's self-worth came from what she did, not who she was—and not whose she was. I think Jesus is telling us that our work should be an extension of our worth, not to gain worth. The point here isn't that Mary was slacking from work, rather she was basking in worth. She did the one thing that mattered the most: she sat at the feet of her Jesus. Martha was worried and upset over all of these details—as so many of us are—and got distracted from the *one thing* she really needed to do.

Mary knew the one thing to be concerned about was sitting at the feet of her Rabbi, soon to be her Savior. This isn't some Mixed Martial Arts championship fight about which sister is better. Jesus loved both sisters and wanted to spend time with both of them. When we are so busy working to gain God's love, we miss simply experiencing God's love.

Look how gentle Jesus was with her: "My dear Martha…" Most translations say, "Martha, Martha," which is better translated and understood by us. Whenever Jesus said someone's name twice, it was to make sure He got their attention. Jesus wanted *time* with Mary and Martha, and the dinner wasn't His goal.

How many times do we exchange a God-thing for a good thing? Or how many times do we miss God's purpose because we have a plan? In every moment of every day there is only one thing that is the true God-thing. Yes, it will interrupt your plans, but God wants you to *stop doing* and *start being*. There are times to be Martha: to work, serve, sweat, and sacrifice. In fact, Jesus talks more about serving and sacrificing than He does about stopping, sitting, and resting. I think He knew that inside us is a little of Martha. There are also times to be Mary. We sometimes "do" to be loved, but Jesus would rather we "do" because we *are* loved. Let's choose what is better. Let's choose the presence of Jesus. Don't fault Martha or Mary. This isn't about that. It is about choosing to be so comfortable as God's son or daughter that you can rest in who you are because of whose you are.

Get Off the Treadmill

It can be a little scary to slow down and rest in who God says you are. Are you afraid to get off the treadmill? I want you to understand how futile it is to try to earn your approval through activity. Author Elyse Fitzpatrick wrote about the history of the treadmill:

In Victorian England,…treadmills weren't found in air-conditioned health clubs—they were found in prisons.

Treadmills, or treadwheels, as they were called, were used in penal servitude as a form of punishment. Some treadwheels were productive, grinding wheat or transporting water, but others were purely punitive in nature. Prisoners were punished by spending the bulk of their day walking up an inclined plane, knowing that all their hard labor was for nothing. The only hope the prisoner had was that, at some day in the future, he would have "paid his debt" to society and would be set free. He couldn't even look on his labor at the end of the day and know that, if nothing else, he'd been productive.[3]

How many more years will you and I seek the approval of people who will never be satisfied and who will never be able to satisfy us? How long will we stay in a prison of activity, when there is nothing we can do to make Him love us any more than He already does? I hope you will choose the rest of Jesus. When you come to Him, you will find the significance you need most. It won't come from a husband, and it won't come from a mom, and it most definitely won't come from your job. Sit in the presence of Jesus and find rest for your soul in the perfect, unwavering approval of the One who matters most. Only then will you get off the treadmill to nowhere.

For me, learning to please God first didn't come without wounds. It is the painful things in our lives that will shape and reshape us. We have to trust that we are loved by God no matter what and that He is fully pleased with us just as we are. I had to learn this the hard way. Choosing to please God sometimes meant displeasing people who mattered to me, but going through the pain of that rejection helped me learn to trust and depend on God first. When I finally got to the end of wanting to please everyone, I had actually grown closer to God and realized that nothing and no one could separate me from the love that is in Christ Jesus. I can say now that I have learned to thank God for allowing me to go through betrayal. Have I arrived? Not by a long shot. Am I making progress? Most definitely. Now what I do is not a reaction to gain God's love, but a response of love for what God has done for me. Once you get that He is fully pleased with you, you can then learn to rest. If you are tired or worn out, or burned out on religion, I pray you will drink in these words, that you will sit at the feet of Jesus, and that you will find rest for your soul and grace for your life. Read these words from the gospel of Matthew:

Are you tired? Worn out? Burned out on religion? Come to me. Get away with me and you'll recover your life. I'll show you how to take a real rest. Walk with me and work with me—watch how I do it. Learn the unforced rhythms of grace. I won't lay anything heavy or ill-fitting on you. Keep company with me and you'll learn to live freely and lightly. (Matthew 11:28–30, MSG)

When you come to Jesus, He promises one of two things. He will either remove the burden from you, or He will remove the weight of the burden as He walks with you. He will replace false confidence from people's opinions with God-confidence. This is truth, friend. You are the object of His affection. You are why He died. The burden He came for is the heaviness in your heart. Surrender to Him. Walk with Him. Find real rest, know peace beyond comprehension, and hear these words: "You are my dearly loved child, in whom I am fully pleased."

God Does Not Owe You

But seek ye first the kingdom of
God, and his righteousness; and
all these things shall be added
unto you.

—MATTHEW 6:33, KJV

Perhaps nothing can rob a person of joy faster than a sense of entitlement. It is the attitude that says, "I am owed something, I deserve something, and I have the right to whatever I want." A spirit of entitlement serves only the interests of its owner, but at the same time it creates a never-satisfied demand for more—more attention, more leniency, more stuff. While some entitlement can be the result of having an enabling parent, the truth is, we all live in a society that values self-satisfaction above almost every other thing. An enabling father may have kept you from the consequences of your bad choices, but our culture would have you believe you have a right to whatever suits your fancy. Nearly every advertisement, song, and television show idealizes the pursuit of our own happiness, even at the expense of others. We are encouraged to do what feels good, with little regard for the consequences. After all, we've earned it, right?

No one wakes up thinking, *I'm going to enable my child,* but sometimes we do it in a misdirected attempt to protect him or her. For me, not having a dad was a catalyzing reason and motivation that I would always be there for my own son, no matter what. I sadly realize that my attempts to love and protect my son have prevented him from learning valuable—and, yes, painful—life lessons. The intent of my heart was good, but the outworking of it created a spirit of entitlement in David. Did I want to do that? Of course not. In fact, my intentions were just the opposite. I tried to help him rely on God in every way, but whenever he would fail, I was always the net beneath him, cushioning the pain of the fall. I protected him from his own bad choices, and in doing so, I inadvertently protected him from the greater things God wanted to teach him. As I am writing this book, he has been in jail for over five months. We talk almost every day. I tell him how much I love him, and never has he questioned that. But now I am teaching him that he can no longer rely on me to get him out of situations. He is on his own—with God—and having to pay his debt to society.

I hope it doesn't take jail for all of us to make changes.

Today we have a generation age thirty-five and under that some call the "me generation." Many are immature narcissists who expect life to go their way and believe the world revolves around them. They defend their "rights" (which, in many cases, they have no "right" to) and believe their opinions should be considered equal with experts'. They are offended when required to earn their keep, and they think life is so unfair when things don't go their way. Dr. Jean Twenge, author of *Generation Me: Why Today's Young Americans Are More Confident, Assertive, Entitled—and More Miserable than Ever Before*, warns that narcissists lack empathy, overreact to criticism, and favor themselves over others. They are incapable of cheering anyone else's success. Ultimately, they lead miserable lives because they cannot form and maintain healthy relationships.[1]

Children who have been enabled will often guilt their parents into helping them, saying, "If you really loved me, you would…" Entitlement takes a gift and turns it into an expectation. Instead of receiving things with gratitude, the attitude of expectation says, "Of course you should have given this to me." It takes the joy from both the giver and the receiver.

But entitlement is not the sole domain of the teenager. It affects the rich and famous, the mature Christian, even the poor and homeless. We have noticed in our church that financial aid and benevolence is often received ungratefully, and many times more is expected. When talking to one of my leaders about this topic of entitlement, she admitted that even as a Christian for thirty years and having been in ministry for twenty years, she still sometimes gets mad at God, wondering why He doesn't "bless" her more. She said, "I catch myself thinking, *Surely, after all the years of service I've given, I deserve a house of my own or a bit more money. Don't I?* Before long I'm unhappy, discontented, and have completely lost sight of the purpose for which God created me."

Perhaps no story illustrates this better than the life of Tiger Woods. One of the greatest golfers of all time, Woods placed first or second in 60 percent of the tournaments he entered from 2007 to 2009 and earned over $26 million from tournaments alone in those three years. He was at the top of his game, enjoying fame, fortune, and unprecedented success, when it all fell apart at the end of 2009. A cocktail waitress came forward, claiming to have had an affair with Woods and backing up her story by supplying an incriminating voice message from Woods on her phone. After that, a dozen other women came forward, also claiming to have had affairs with him. It all went rapidly downhill from there. His wife divorced him, his sponsorships and endorsements dried up, and his golf game suffered tremendously. In a public statement on the issue, Tiger made a profound statement about his behavior:

> I stopped living by the core values that I was taught to believe in. I knew my actions were wrong, but I convinced myself that normal rules didn't apply. I never thought about who I was hurting. Instead, I thought only about myself.... I thought I could get away with whatever I wanted to. I felt that I had worked hard my entire life and deserved to enjoy all the temptations around me. I felt I was entitled.[2]

In 2010 and 2011 Tiger Woods entered twenty golf tournaments. He won none of them and finished second in none of them. He finished in the top ten in only two of them. And in his last tournament, the PGA Championship, he did not make the cut. It's an extreme but real example of how entitlement sets us up for ultimate failure. Without gratitude and humility we will find ourselves walking a dangerous path of bad behavior, without regard for consequences.

Our English word *entitlement* comes from a Latin word that means "the right to receive something or to do something." Of course it carries a lot more meaning than that. I think in the minds of some it also means "You owe me," "I deserve it," and "How dare anyone question me?"

There is a difference between actual entitlement and false entitlement. My employees are actually entitled to their wages. I do owe them, and they do deserve it. They have a right to receive their wages. But false entitlement is when people expect to receive what they have not earned and don't deserve. I have seen this attitude affect both staff and volunteers. For some, the more they serve, the more they feel they deserve. Over time they forget whom and why they are serving and start focusing on their work instead of their worship. It starts as a subtle shift away from gratitude and becomes an obvious shift in attitude. And although it has become an epidemic in our culture, it certainly isn't a new thing. Even Jesus dealt with those who felt entitled. His own disciples, who had seen unspeakable miracles—blind people healed with one touch, sickness healed, thousands fed—allowed pride to puff up their expectations: "Then they began to argue among themselves about who would be the greatest among them" (Luke 22:24).

The very people Jesus chose to serve alongside Him were actually arguing about who would be the greatest! We are not sure what caused the argument among the disciples; they simply viewed themselves as more important than they really were.

Entitled people can rarely see their own attitudes. They forget that any success they may have experienced has come because God allowed it. Instead of putting Jesus in the center, they are centered on themselves. Living a life surrendered to Christ is about emptying ourselves and being filled with Him. If we are filled with ourselves, we cannot be filled with Jesus; then His passion and purpose for our lives becomes diluted, and our image of God becomes distorted. We start to believe He will give us anything we want and that He exists to bless us. Jesus came to serve, not to be served, and He evidenced it to the disciples over and over again. They just never got what being fully emptied was about.

Jesus Turns Things Upside Down

Jesus told them, "In this world the kings and great men lord it over their people, yet they are called 'friends of the people.' But among you it will be different. Those who are the greatest among you should take the lowest rank, and the leader should be like a servant. Who is more important, the one who sits at the table or the one who serves? The one who sits at the table, of course. But not here! For I am among you as one who serves.

"You have stayed with me in my time of trial. And just as my Father has granted me a Kingdom, I now grant you the right to eat and drink at my table in my Kingdom." (Luke 22:25–30)

Jesus's response is both to help them understand their role as servants and also to set the record straight. Instead of fighting for first position, He calls us to humble ourselves to the lowest rank. He challenges all leaders to become like servants. He turns popular culture on its head. I love that instead of calling out their pride and putting the focus on them, He simply reminds them whom it is all about. Very gently, in the way only He can, Jesus makes three profound statements: these are *My* trials; it is *My* Father who has set us in place; and you are eating at *My* table in *My* kingdom. It is all about Him.

We should all consider what Jesus said to the disciples and be reminded today that any ministry we participate in or position we may achieve is possible only through Jesus Himself. We are entitled to, and owed, nothing. How easily we forget this and take for granted the freedoms for which He gave His life. Jesus, the most authentically entitled person who ever has or ever will walk on this planet, set it all aside so that He could help each of us find our way home to God. We deserve nothing. Or should I say, we deserve nothing more than an eternity without Jesus.

Believing Results in Behaving

Entitlement is a self-centered focus on "getting," while *faith* results in a Jesus-centered focus on "giving." We could all afford to do a check on our inner world: is your life about you or about others? The greatest detriment to relationships is self-centeredness. Instead of wanting to be reconciled, or to restore relationship, we want to be right. Selfish ambition and an attitude of entitlement are the by-products of pride, and pride is the ugliness that lies at the root of every other sin. Paul speaks about this to the church in Philippi. He begins with what should be our attitude to others: "Do nothing out of selfish ambition or vain conceit, but in humility consider others better than yourselves" (Philippians 2:3, NIV). Paul simply tells them to do nothing from a posture of self-centeredness. The word "consider" he uses here is an accounting term that means "to do the math." Add it up; do the balance sheet. Price people better than yourself. It doesn't say people are better than you but that you simply need to consider them and treat them better than yourself.

Can you imagine how it would be if we would actually live this way instead of in the self-centered approach that is so common today? What would our homes be like if we treated our family this way? What if a boss chose to see and serve his employees, instead of lording over people in the workplace?

When we see other people as valuable and having been made in the image of Christ, it will change how we respond to them. Our belief will always determine our behavior. Paul goes on in verse 4: "Each of you should look not only to your own interests, but also to the interests of others" (NIV). In every fight, someone wants their way to be the right way, but Paul tells us that the right way is to see others better and to look at what matters to them. The word here for "look" is *scopos,* and it means "to regard intently, or to fix one's eyes on and direct one's attention to." It is where we get our English words *microscope* and *telescope.* In each of these instruments, you can only focus on what you are looking at, not on yourself. It is not a quick glance but an intentional focus on what is important to others. It is a statement of intrinsic value: my eyes are off me and are on you.

Your attitude should be the same as that of Christ Jesus:

Who, being in very nature God,
   did not consider equality with God something to be grasped,
but made himself nothing,
   taking the very nature of a servant,
   being made in human likeness.
And being found in appearance as a man,
   he humbled himself
   and became obedient to death—even death on a cross!
      (Philippians 2:5–8, NIV)

Theologians refer to this passage as the kenosis passage. *Kenosis* comes from the root *kenoo,* which means "to empty, or to render void." Jesus "emptied Himself, taking the form of a bond-servant, and being made in the likeness of men" (verse 7, NASB). Jesus never ceased to be God during His earthly ministry, but He did set aside His independent authority. He added to Himself a human nature and humbled Himself. Jesus went from being the glory of glories in heaven to being a human being who was put to death on the cross. In the ultimate act of humility, the God of the universe became a human being and died for His creation. The kenosis, therefore, is Christ taking on a human nature with all of its limitations, except with no sin.

This is God emptying Himself and humbling Himself, serving in human likeness. It is Jesus willingly choosing to set aside His rights, deny Himself, humble Himself, and eventually die the most brutal, torturous way a person could possibly die: death on a cross. The most right and righteous person who has ever lived—the only One who was truly entitled—chose to deny Himself, empty Himself, and become a servant to the very people He created. Jesus could have said, "Come follow Me, I am the most right human ever," and yet He never did. He loved and served people. He focused not on

Himself but on the needs of others. He was an example for us to follow. Emptying ourselves and living in humility is dying, not on a cross, but to our own desires so that we can serve the needs of those around us.

My Pop

There are few people I can think of in my life who exemplified selflessness more than my grandfather, whom I called Pop. I wish I had appreciated him more when he was alive. He died in November 2008, in the midst of one of the worst times of my life. He was the daddy God had provided, but because of my anger, resentment, and pain, I couldn't see that. Pop was a true man in every sense of the word. He was proud to serve in the US Air Force when it was still called the Army Air Corps. He was close to retirement when my mother, brother, and I found ourselves once again abandoned and alone. I was a kid who just wanted to know what was wrong with me and why no one wanted me. Without hesitation my grandpa and grandma took our family in and raised us boys as their own children. For them, it wasn't a temporary thing; their attitude was simply, "We are family; this is the way we roll."

I remember other relatives saying how unfair it was that my grandparents were "stuck" with us. But I also remember my pop saying he wouldn't have it any other way. I was Pop's boy, and he affectionately referred to me as "John Boy." He believed in me, spoke encouraging words to me, and never made me feel for one second that I was an inconvenience. In fact, quite the opposite; he considered it a privilege to be the dad I never had.

Although he never did, Pop truly had a right to feel entitled. He served his country. He put in his years and retired from a job. He raised his daughter and he was owed his retirement. He deserved a motorhome and freedom to travel as he pleased. But now, here he was with two grandsons to love, raise, and care for. No one would have blamed him for being frustrated. Most people would be upset about the infringement on their right to be done raising kids, but my beautiful grandfather never claimed what he was rightfully entitled to. Instead, he was authentically happy to raise my brother and me. He never held it over us or hurried us to move out. He just embraced me and made me feel like I mattered. He protected me, he loved me, and he accepted me; he never hurt me, but he did appropriately discipline me. He was the father I always wanted, needed, and longed for. I miss him so much. He was the most incredible example of humility and selflessness, and it was my great joy to lead him to Jesus Christ in 1995. He became the inspiration for the church we started in 1996, and his legacy lives on in its success today.

Humility Before Honor

Therefore God exalted him to the highest place
    and gave him the name that is above every name,
that at the name of Jesus every knee should bow,
    in heaven and on earth and under the earth. (Philippians 2:9–10, NIV)

Whenever you see a "therefore" in Scripture, it is setting up the results of what has gone before. Because Jesus humbled and emptied Himself and willingly gave up His life, God exalted Him to the highest place of honor. It is always humility before honor.

When you give up your rights and let go of your entitlement, you may feel vulnerable, unnoticed, and even unappreciated. You'll wonder if anyone notices what you do, and there will be moments when you look around and think no one cares. You may even feel you want to quit. Being a servant to others is not glamorous, brings no glory, and means a long, hard road to the finish, often with little reward. At times all you can do is to keep your eyes on Jesus, remembering whom and why you serve.

When I was first serving as a youth pastor, I remember dealing with parents who felt that I wasn't the right guy for the job. They wondered why I was serving, they questioned whether or not I knew anything about the Bible as a new Christian, and so on. It was hard to keep going in the face of opposition. I felt I deserved better. And then I read a story that encouraged my heart. I learned from this story that life isn't fair, and sometimes it seems that God isn't either, but there will be a day when everything will be set straight. It touched my heart, and I hope it encourages you.

Ray Stedman wrote the story his father told him in the book *Talking with My Father: Jesus Teaches on Prayer:*

Many years ago, an elderly missionary couple returned from Africa to retire in New York City.... They had no pension.... Their health was broken. They were defeated, discouraged, and fearful about the future. And they couldn't help comparing their circumstances with those of a fellow passenger who also had boarded the ship in Africa—President Teddy Roosevelt, who was returning from one of his big-game hunting expeditions.

As the ship pulled into the harbor, past the great city and the Statue of Liberty... A huge crowd had gathered to welcome the returning president from his hunting trip.... The old missionary turned and said to his wife, "Dear, something is wrong. Why should we have given our lives in faithful service for God in Africa all these years? This man comes back from a big-game hunting expedition and everybody makes a big fuss over him, but nobody gives two hoots about us."

"Dear," his wife replied, "you shouldn't feel that way."...

"I just can't help it," he replied. "It's not right. After all, if God is running this world, why does He permit such injustice?"...

The mayor of New York City was on hand to greet the returning president,...but no one even noticed the missionary couple. They slipped off the ship and found a cheap flat on the East Side, hoping the next day to see what they could do to make a living in the city.

That night the man's spirit just broke. He said to his wife, "I can't take this! God is not fair!... If God is faithful, why doesn't He meet our need?"

"Why don't you ask Him?" said his wife....

He went into the bedroom and prayed for a while. Later, when he emerged...,he seemed completely changed.

"Dear, what happened?" asked his wife. "What has come over you?"

"Well," he said, "the Lord settled it with me.... I told Him how bitter I was that the president should receive this tremendous homecoming, when no one met us as we returned home. And when I finished, it seemed as though the Lord put His hand on my shoulder and simply said, 'But you're not home yet!'"[3]

You Are Not Home Yet

Instead of fighting to get what you think you deserve, trust the God who put breath in your body. You are an heir to the throne of grace, but this side of heaven you have to continue to have the same attitude that Jesus had. He consistently put the needs of others above Himself, always glorifying His perfect Father in heaven. Jesus is now in that place, sitting at the right side, the place of highest honor, next to His Father. When we decide to have the same attitude that Jesus had, we are expressing our gratitude to Him. In this world, we fight to receive, but in God's kingdom, giving is the measure of success. Keep considering others better than yourself. Keep having the same attitude that Jesus had. Look not to this day, but to that day when you will walk into the arms of the God who made you and the Savior who died for you. You are not home yet, friend.

God Is in Perfect Control

There are no failures—just
experiences and your reactions
to them.

—THOMAS KRAUSE

I love hearing about the image non-Christians have of God when they don't really know Him. When a conversation turns to God or faith, they will usually say that Christians are judgmental, narrow minded, legalistic, or hung up on rules. More than likely, they see God as controlling or critical. In fact, over 47 percent of Americans believe God to be authoritarian and judgmental.[1] They believe Him to be fixated on obedience, punishment, and creating fear in people. Not surprisingly, this distortion of God's nature can leave people with anxiety, a void of self-confidence, and a crippling fear of failure and consequent punishment.

Where has this image come from? More often than not, from a father or parent who exerted his authority as control. Healthy levels of control will create well-disciplined and responsible children, and eventually healthy adults. Authoritarian parents, while not intending to harm their children, go beyond normal guidelines to rigid, extreme expectations and boundaries, in which children are prevented from thinking for themselves or becoming who God created them to be. The controlling parents criticize the child and expect perfection, causing the child to become discouraged and fearful. Such children don't feel listened to, and because their personal desires don't matter, they believe they have little purpose outside their parents' wishes. Their fear of failure comes into their relationship with God, and their Christian walk can become bondage of religion rather than freedom of faith.

It is, in fact, quite the opposite with God. He is perfect and yet doesn't expect perfection from us, but He allows us to make choices and fail—and all the while He knows us completely and loves us perfectly. How I wish I could love my children the way God loves me. How I wish I could be that kind of father! But I also would like to be the kind of child who rests in knowing God, knowing He is in perfect control, and knowing He wants (as He does) what is best for me and my life.

It is my prayer that the words in this chapter will help all of us to see the God who holds the universe in His hands, and yet still allows us to have free will. He is not threatened by our thoughts or feelings, and He is unshaken by our failures! He is not a controlling king like Yertle the Turtle with his own good in mind. He is the King of kings, in perfect control, ensuring that the choices we make—even our mistakes—are used for His purpose and redeemed for our good. He is the perfect Father, the perfect King, and He is perfectly in control. I love what Ephesians says about approaching God: "Because of Christ and our faith in him, we can now come boldly and confidently into God's presence" (Ephesians 3:12).

Let's just get honest here: failing in a safe environment is both necessary and healthy for growth. When children are overly controlled during their formative years, they invariably grow up to be insecure adults. The rules and boundaries of a controlling parent ultimately protect the child from failure, but also make him or her unable to process or accept failure of any kind. This unpreparedness for life's reality leaves the child with a disabling lack of self-confidence—unable to make decisions, unaware of his own talent, and unsure of her worth in this world. On the other hand, having self-confidence is the measure of your beliefs about your own judgment, your skills, or your abilities. It is a healthy self-assuredness about what you think you can accomplish.

With God there is both perfect control and free will. There is safety in risking, choosing, and failing. The security that comes as a child of God gives you confidence to risk, and in risking, you will sometimes fail. It is in that environment you grow and can go forward. No one wakes up and says, "This is my day to fail," but failing in a safe environment is what creates safety to be real, to learn, and to grow. In a controlling home, you are raising your kids to rely on you, not on God. (I'm sorry if that hurts, but it is the truth.) I have witnessed this so often, especially with a firstborn child. These children often make the right choice to please the parent and avoid punishment, rather than making the good choice because it is the right thing to do. As a consequence they find themselves "out in the real world" and unable—or unwilling—to make proper choices on their own.

Here is the bottom line: in a controlling home, there is no safety in failing because there is usually punishment or shame afterward. To achieve the greatest success through failure, you have to embrace the lesson of failure. Failure is not failure itself. Failing to learn, grow, and do better the next time is true failure. If fear of failure keeps us from ever risking, we find ourselves stuck and unable to move forward to a better future and the destiny that God alone has planned.

Freedom to Fail

Many of the most successful people have experienced spectacular failure before becoming the household names they are today. Did you know John Grisham's first novel was originally rejected by many publishing houses? He is now the author of twenty-three best-selling books.[2] Most everyone has heard of baseball legend Babe Ruth, but not everyone knows he also struck out 1,330 times. Since then he has been named the greatest baseball player of all time by *The Sporting News* and the greatest baseball player of the twentieth century by *Sports Illustrated.* So successful was he that his 1920 Yankees jersey sold for $4.4 million![3]

Steven Spielberg, famous Hollywood moviemaker, was unsuccessful getting into top college film programs because of his low grades in high school. Spielberg went on to become one of Universal Studio's youngest television directors in the 1960s and won the Academy Award for directing *Schindler's List* and *Saving Private Ryan,* as well as directing blockbusters such as *Jurassic Park, E.T.: The Extra-Terrestrial,* and *Jaws.*[4] Beethoven, legendary musician and composer, was once told by his music teacher that he was a hopeless composer.[5] He went on to compose nine symphonies and become one of the world's most famous composers of all time. Henry Ford, who had two unsuccessful businesses before he began the Ford Motor Company[6], said, "Failure is the opportunity to begin again more intelligently." Can you imagine how different things would be if any one of these people had been too afraid to try again?

Author John Maxwell calls it *failing forward.* He says, "Failure is simply a price we pay to achieve success.... The only way you can get ahead is to fail early, fail often, and fail forward."[7] We have to learn to accept failure as part of successful living.

I love stories of triumph over failure and difficult circumstances, particularly in athletes who go on to break records. I was moved this year by the determination of Chinese Olympic hurdler Liu Xiang after disappointing his country four years earlier.

In the 2008 Beijing Olympics, Liu injured his right Achilles tendon during a qualifying heat of the 100-meter hurdles, forcing him to pull out of the event. The greatest basketball player in Chinese history, Yao Ming, knew how badly Liu was treated by the public after that failure, so he was compelled to talk with Liu before his event at the 2012 Olympics, to let him know that there is more to life than just winning games. Unfortunately, Liu was struck by the same injury he had in 2008. Yao talked about it, and what happened next, to *Sports Illustrated:*

> Liu crashed out of his 110m qualifying heat at Olympic Stadium after failing to clear the first hurdle, a victim of the same chronic Achilles injury that he suffered in 2008....
>
> Liu struck the first hurdle flat with his left heel; he tumbled to the track and grabbed his right Achilles, already taped for support. After sitting for a few seconds, then banging his head once on the track, Liu stood and, using only his left foot, hopped off the track and into the nearest stadium tunnel.
>
> His day, and perhaps Olympic career, looked as if it were ready to end on a miserable note. But then something remarkable happened: Liu changed his mind. Halfway down the tunnel he stopped, thought a moment and, still on one foot, turned 180-degrees back toward the track; Liu came hopping up the tunnel and back into view. With each hop, the cheering grew....
>
> Liu then hopped the entire length of the 110-meter race...veering into the middle to kiss the final Olympic hurdle, the one he hadn't crossed in eight years.[8]

What a powerful story of a true Olympian. Defeated by injury in 2008, he recovered strength and qualified again to compete against the world's best in 2012, only to fail once again. Yet he refused to quit, hopped on one foot to the finish line, and showed the world that to finish last is still better than not finishing at all.

Don't we all have a fear of failing, to one degree or another? When we fail, we feel disappointment in ourselves and vulnerable to judgment from others. Stumbling, falling, and failing create feelings of humiliation and embarrassment—we feel undone and almost undressed. If only we could see failure the way God does. Psalm 103:12 says, "He has removed our sins as far from us as the east is from the west." God doesn't record the defeats in our lives; instead, He turns them into a platform for our future achievements.

Jeremiah 29:11 says, "'For I know the plans I have for you,' says the LORD. 'They are plans for good and not for disaster, to give you a future and a hope.'"

Moments That Create Destinies

I love movies. I love the suspense, the storylines, the cinematography, and the endings. I love that there is usually a redemptive thread in every movie: good wins out over evil, the family gets back together, or the guy gets the girl. If I could pick a story from the Bible to be made into a movie, it would be the story of Peter in the gospel of John, chapter 21. Part of the reason for this unconventional choice is because when I was in seminary, my final thesis was on biblical restoration. As I studied, I was so surprised, encouraged, and blown away by how Jesus responded to Peter's failure that I needed to know more.

Let's look closer at this story. Peter is the one person Jesus said He would build His church upon. He is the first steward of all that would matter for thousands of years to come, trusted to look after the one thing Jesus started. He is also one of the closest friends Jesus had on earth. Imagine Peter leaving all he had ever known, planned on, and dreamed about. He left his family and the family fishing business and walked with Jesus for over three years. He was one of just twelve men that Jesus would call to be His followers.

Jesus called Peter when he was a fisherman. In Matthew 4:19, Jesus said to Peter and his brother Andrew, "Come, follow me,... and I will make you fishers of men" (NIV). Rabbis at that time would call a student whom they believed had what it takes by saying, "Come, follow me." This was the highest of honors for the young man and his parents. Jesus could see Peter's potential.

Don't we all want to be believed in? Don't we all want to make a difference? What was true for Peter is true for us; Jesus believes in you, more than you believe in yourself. He knows you the best and loves you the most. Can you begin to imagine that day? Jesus came from heaven as the one and only Son of God to die for the sin of all of humanity, and yet makes Himself fully available for Peter, with all of his questions, during his bouts with doubt, every day and in every way. Jesus calls him, walks with him, and knows him like no other person. He also knows something that will change his life.

Jesus sees who you can be and wants to make you something you are not. Jesus believes in you and is calling you, just as He called the disciples.

When Sift Happens, Jesus Prays

The defining moment in Peter's life came just hours before Jesus would be betrayed by Judas, then arrested, beaten, and abandoned by every disciple. Jesus and the disciples were sitting at the last Passover, but instead of a sacrificial lamb for God, Jesus will become the Lamb of God. The perfect Father sent His perfect Son to be the perfect sacrifice. Talk about a huge moment: this is the reason Jesus came to earth.

Peter, along with those first disciples, was positioned to do so much for God, and yet Jesus knew something that would rock his world. Jesus tells Peter that a test is coming. Peter was the name Jesus gave Simon. In the original language, Peter is *Petra,* which means "rock."

"Simon, Simon, Satan has asked to sift each of you like wheat. But I have pleaded in prayer for you, Simon, that your faith should not fail. So when you have repented and turned to me again, strengthen your brothers" (Luke 22:31–32). Jesus was referring to Simon being sifted till he becomes Peter—the unshakable rock, strong enough to be the foundation for an unstoppable church. To be sifted would imply pain. Satan has to ask permission to touch one of God's children, and God—at times—allows it because He is in perfect control, and He knows there is purpose in the pain. Sifting is a process that simply separates the wheat from the chaff. It means to separate what is valuable from what is not. It is a violent shaking process, but metaphorically speaking, it carries both a promise and a purpose for us. The purpose is to test our faith, grow our character, and remove baggage that slows us down. The promise is that Jesus will be praying for us, just as he did for Peter, and that He wants to do something with us out of it.

Denial Isn't Optional

Jesus told him what would happen, and Peter basically just opened his mouth and inserted his foot. Look at his response in verse 33: "Peter said, 'Lord, I am ready to go to prison with you, and even to die with you.'" Peter's mouth was bigger than his faith. Sound familiar? It's easy to make promises but much harder to walk them out. Look at the next words of Jesus: "But Jesus said, 'Peter, let me tell you something. Before the rooster crows tomorrow morning, you will deny three times that you even know me'" (verse 34).

We will either deny we know Jesus, or we will deny ourselves. The Greek word for "deny" is *arneomai* and a better, literal translation is "to disown." How powerful is that? How sobering is that? How many times do we choose ourselves over Jesus? The tension for every Christ-follower has to be one of continually and progressively denying ourselves. It is easy to flow with the crowd, to be popular, and then to miss what God wants to do through you. Sifting isn't optional, but giving up is. Will you choose to deny yourself or to deny Jesus? Peter's next defining moment in his relationship with Jesus comes after Jesus was seized and arrested.

> But when they had kindled a fire in the middle of the courtyard and had sat down together, Peter sat down with them. A servant girl saw him seated there in the firelight. She looked closely at him and said, "This man was with him."
>
> But he denied it. "Woman, I don't know him," he said.
>
> A little later someone else saw him and said, "You also are one of them."
>
> "Man, I am not!" Peter replied.
>
> About an hour later another asserted, "Certainly this fellow was with him, for he is a Galilean."
>
> Peter replied, "Man, I don't know what you're talking about!" Just as he was speaking, the rooster crowed. The Lord turned and looked straight at Peter. Then Peter remembered the word the Lord had spoken to him: "Before the rooster crows today, you will disown me three times." (Luke 22:55–61, NIV)

Imagine that moment: you see Jesus—bloodied, tired, alone—and His prophecy becomes your reality. You hear a rooster and then see the eyes of your Savior and your friend. The One who believed in you when no one else would. The One who was there for you when others weren't. I get choked up thinking about how many times I have chosen to disown Jesus instead of disowning my own desires. Those times when my actions said, "I love You Jesus, but I'm not going to forgive. I love You Jesus, but I am not going to give. I love You Jesus, but I don't have time in my busy schedule to stop and feed a homeless person. Jesus, I know that sex before marriage is wrong, but I am choosing to stay in a wrong relationship, and I am going to disown You in this relationship. Jesus, the reality is that though I love You, I just truthfully love me more." Peter said he would go to prison for Jesus, but when that moment came and Jesus needed Peter most, Peter disowned Jesus. Peter did what you and I and every human who has ever lived and breathed has done. He failed.

We all make promises to God and fail. But when we allow our failure to be like sifting, it can become a defining moment in our faith, our life, and our future. Just to be clear, when Jesus says Satan has asked to sift you, the "you" is plural in the Greek language, meaning we will all be sifted. Jesus is praying for you right now, so that your faith will be strong and that beyond the sifting you will strengthen others around you. The last verse is Peter's moment of utter brokenness, where his faith would now be based on Jesus's working in him, loving him, and restoring his life. It wasn't about his talk, but his walk. Check out Peter's heart: "And Peter left the courtyard, weeping bitterly" (Luke 22:62). Peter was authentically broken and repentant. In the original language, "weeping bitterly" means he cried "a piercing, violent cry." It would be like saying "he bawled his eyes out," completely undone by what he had done.

What was Jesus's prayer? Not that Peter wouldn't fail, but that his faith wouldn't fail. In many churches it seems there is a gag order in which you have to hide your failures and play a stupid game of pretense with one another. We can never become better, because we are too busy wearing masks. We have created churches filled with people who can't fail, because of the way we interpret failing. In a culture dominated with winning, we forget that God's way of building our faith so often happens through moments of failing. This was a hinge moment in Peter's life, but Peter did what so many of us do when we fail. He quit. He gave up and went back to what he knew before. Look what Peter said in John 21:3: "I'm going fishing." Although he had repented and his heart was changed, Peter felt like his ministry was done. And who wouldn't?

Right now you might also be going through the sifting process. Perhaps you are facing divorce or bankruptcy. Perhaps God is asking you to give up your addiction or you have received a devastating diagnosis. You are tempted to quit, but Jesus is praying that your faith will not fail. The challenge with Peter is the same with us. Peter's heart was open, just not broken. When your heart is authentically broken, your faith will ultimately break through. Don't give up and don't give in.

When God Makes Your Breakfast

In almost twenty years as a pastor, I have witnessed so many people quit before they get to the finish line of what God has started. Here is the thing: guilt always drives us back to what we knew and where we were before Jesus. Such is the case with Peter. Our failures are covered by forgiveness, and yet we can't seem to live beyond guilt. It is almost as if the blood of Jesus isn't enough, but Jesus is never about guilt and always about restoration. Religion says you can't measure up. Grace says you don't have to.

So Peter goes back to the same boat, the same lake, and the same job with the same people. This is a response we recognize. Many of us have been knocked back by failure to the safety of familiar ground. We fall down, then run back to the place where we know we can't fail. But just when you feel like you are done, Jesus shows up. Not to pay you back, but to bring you back. You see the heart of Jesus in this story. He pursued Peter, showing up on the shore where Peter is fishing.

> Early in the morning, Jesus stood on the shore, but the disciples did not
> realize that it was Jesus.
>
> He called out to them, "Friends, haven't you any fish?"
>
> "No," they answered.
>
> He said, "Throw your net on the right side of the boat and you will find
> some." When they did, they were unable to haul the net in because of the
> large number of fish.
>
> Then the disciple whom Jesus loved said to Peter, "It is the Lord!" As
> soon as Simon Peter heard him say, "It is the Lord," he wrapped his outer
> garment around him (for he had taken it off) and jumped into the water. The
> other disciples followed in the boat, towing the net full of fish, for they were
> not far from shore, about a hundred yards. When they landed, they saw a fire
> of burning coals there with fish on it, and some bread. (John 21:4–9, NIV)

Jesus, who has just been denied three times by one of His closest friends, is now making the disciples' breakfast. The scripture says Jesus had a charcoal fire going, which is interesting because this word for "charcoal" appears only two times in the New Testament: here at the shore and when Peter denied Jesus at the fire. Just the smell alone would have reminded Peter of his failure. Jesus doesn't mention it at all, not even a single word. He just offers breakfast, love, and restoration. I love this about Jesus. He could have asked a lot of questions, demanded an explanation, or wanted Peter to explain his actions, but He simply asked him three times, "Do you love me?" Then, after serving breakfast, He essentially said, "Return and do what I made you to do, Peter."

Talk about an incredible, defining moment! Every time I read these words, I get emotional, because I—like you—need this story to be true. We need to return with stronger faith, so we can finish what God has begun.

Words That Change Everything

Will we return to do what God has made us to do? Jesus's first words to Peter just three years earlier were "Follow me" (Matthew 4:19). Now, after Peter's failure, He simply asked him these four words: "Do you love me?" Not guilt, but grace. Not religion, but restoration. Not failure, but freedom. Following is about faith. In faith we will fail, but when we fail we will still hear those words: "Do you love me?"

I have written the following question in my Bible, and it helps me live in God's grace rather than past guilt: "Do I love my past more than my Jesus?" I would ask the same of you today.

I find it so incredible that Jesus knew Peter would fail and yet still loved him, called him, and chose him to be the one He would build His church on. Jesus allowed Satan to sift Peter, so that his faith would be tested, and through repentance he would have a faith that Jesus could build His church on. Jesus knew that Peter's failure would not stop him but would sift away the garbage in his life, making him stronger than before. If we could see ourselves the way God does—as children of a perfect Father—we could see failure as merely a steppingstone to all He has planned.

Don't go back to fishing, but let Jesus restore you and redeem your mistakes. He wants to rebuild your confidence, not tear it down. He will make you breakfast—maybe through the encouragement of a pastor, this book, a wise friend, or a timely e-mail. Don't allow fear to keep you from risking again, but have confidence in a heavenly Father who is perfectly in control.

17

God Is Completely Safe

I love you, LORD; you are my
strength. The LORD is my rock,
my fortress, and my savior; my
God is my rock, in whom I find
protection.

—PSALM 18:1–2

I want to begin this chapter by saying that *God knows*. He not only knows, but He cares deeply. About what? About your every thought, every fear, every hurt, and every hope.

Writing this chapter is emotionally wrenching. I have always been aware of the hurt done to me long ago, but I have only recently begun to realize how I, too, have hurt others. It is so easy to be focused on our own pain and then to overlook the pain we are inflicting on those closest to us. There is an unintentional reflex of an abused person to lash out and keep people at arm's length for fear of being hurt. We even lash out at God and keep Him at a distance. It is often our only way of ensuring no one gets close enough to hurt us again.

Hurt People Hurt People

A massacre occurred in 1999 at Columbine High School in Littleton, Colorado, leaving fifteen dead, including the two students responsible for the attack. It was one of the deadliest school shooting incidents in American history.

The shootings were carried out by Eric Harris, age eighteen, and Dylan Klebold, age seventeen. On April 20, 1999, they entered Columbine High School with semiautomatic rifles, pistols, and several explosives. In less than twenty minutes they killed twelve fellow students and a teacher and wounded twenty-one others. The violence came to an end when Harris and Klebold took their own lives. The following quotes were found in journals of the two teenage killers.[1]

> I hate you people for leaving me out of so many fun things…you people had my phone number and i asked and all but no, don't let the weird looking Eric- kid come along. —Eric Harris

> If you could see all the anger I've stored over the past four years…everyone but my family treated me like the runt of the litter. You made me what i am, you added to the rage. —Dylan Klebold

It is no one's fault that two young men decided to take out their rage on innocent teenagers, but it speaks to the truth of the saying that "hurt people hurt people." We know that somewhere behind their anger was a level of pain that could no longer be managed. The same is often true for an abused child. Over time, unresolved and unforgiven pain will become a physical force that creates walls and divides relationships.

For those who've been hurt, the hope is that you can learn to trust God with the pain you have felt from the abuse you received and allow Him to hold you in His arms so that authentic healing can happen. I want to begin this journey by praying for every person who is reading this with an open heart but is afraid to trust again. I am so sorry for what you have been through, and I believe to the depth of my being that God wants to redeem the horrible pain you experienced. God, the perfect Father, is never about leaving you in abuse, shame, or guilt, but always about redemption, healing, and grace. Let's pray:

Dear Jesus,

I simply ask You to hold Your sons and daughters in Your loving, protective, and perfect arms at this moment. Some have endured beating, bruising, and shoving. For others it has been living in a home of fear and shame. Still for some it is still happening as they read these words. You promise in Psalm 46 that You are our refuge and our strength. You are our ever-present help when we are in trouble. I pray that those promises would be every person's reality right now. The words that follow might hurt before they help, but we thank You in advance for doing in us what we can't possibly do for ourselves. Replace the anger and resentment with hope and healing. Protect us and hide us in Your presence, so that in these moments these words would be both hopeful and helpful. I pray for every person in the name of Jesus.

Amen.

The overarching premise for this entire book is based on one statement from A. W. Tozer: "What comes into your mind when you think about God is the most important thing about you." If you are an abuse victim, what comes into your mind is the image of a God who is ashamed of you, didn't protect you, and allowed the abuse to happen. You see a God who punishes, and who is content for you to feel shame, fear, and rejection. You believe He will never accept you, is out to get you, and does not have good things for you. You're not sure you can trust God not to hurt you, especially a God who is known to be a Father. It's just hard to trust in the good when all you've known is the bad.

The effects of abuse in the life of a child are numerous. Whether it was emotional, verbal, physical, or—even worse—sexual, abuse violates trust and colors every future relationship. Not only does a child lose trust in the abuser, but in anyone and everyone—particularly authority figures. *Can I trust this coach? Can I trust this teacher? This pastor?* In the back of the wounded heart is the ever-present question, *Will I be hurt again?* Those who have been abused often feel alone and live in constant fear until their hearts are healed. Despite the well-intentioned advice of friends and family to "just let it go and get over it," the process may be long and bumpy, often taking many years.

All of this causes a person to have quite a distorted image of God. Perhaps no one struggles more with the concept of God as a perfect Father than an abused child. How can we imagine Him to be a safe refuge and hiding place when our own father was the complete opposite? Bearing anger and an understandable fear of being hurt, these children wonder if God will really protect them.

As I type these words I can vividly remember the fear that my stepdad produced in me. The tension that his presence created was one of complete fear and unpredictability. It was so thick when he entered the room, we could feel it within minutes. He was so mean we were afraid to even talk to him. I always felt like I would be punished if I did anything wrong or said what he considered to be the wrong thing. He would punish for whatever he felt was out of order. It was so difficult to be around him, and yet I still wanted and longed for his acceptance and love.

When I look back to those childhood moments, I can now see that my image of God had become completely distorted. When I was a new Christian, I was thankful for God's grace and that He saved me, but I didn't want God to be a "father." I remember how badly I wished God could just be God and anything but a father, because that meant He, like Dean, would hurt me if I did wrong, or leave me whenever He wanted to. I simply saw God as a bigger version of my earthly father. How could I trust a God who would be like that? I know how wrong I was. I see Him so differently now.

Check out this passage in Romans:

> For all who are led by the Spirit of God are children of God.
> So you have not received a spirit that makes you fearful slaves. Instead, you received God's Spirit when he adopted you as his own children. Now we call him, "Abba, Father." For his Spirit joins with our spirit to affirm that we are God's children. And since we are his children, we are his heirs. (Romans 8:14–17)

We do not have to live in fear, because if we are in Christ, we are adopted into the family of God as His sons and daughters. When we become part of God's family, we are able to live differently, and as our trust in Him grows, so does our ability to forgive and to let go of "what was."

Paul went on to say, "In fact, together with Christ we are heirs of God's glory. But if we are to share his glory, we must also share his suffering" (verse 17). Talk about a difficult and confusing statement. We have to share in the suffering? For some, those words are not comforting, but shocking and discouraging—especially when your suffering is a result of the abuse from someone you expected would protect and take care of you. God does not want anyone to live in abusive situations; that was never part of His plan for us. For those who have felt that the abuse you received is punishment from God, let me be really clear: that is horrible theology. God does not bring abuse into our lives to punish us for being bad—or to punish us for anything. It is never His plan that we should be wounded at the hands of others. However, I understand why anyone who has been abused might wonder why God allows suffering—in our lives and in the world. It's a very fair question!

God Is Not the Bad Guy

First, we must understand that God is not the author of evil and suffering. Humans are the producers of evil. God created us with free will, and every day people use their free will to make bad choices that hurt other people. Not only does God *not* create our suffering, the Bible tells us He is moved by our pain: "You keep track of all my sorrows. You have collected all my tears in your bottle. You have recorded each one in your book" (Psalm 56:8). We learned earlier that God is always present with us and promises never to leave or abandon us. This is true even in abusive situations. Remember Echo, who shared her story of abuse in chapter 8? I want you to hear some of her journey of learning to trust God the Father:

> One thing that really helped me feel like God was more tangible in the healing process was to understand and know that God wasn't just watching from the clouds as the abuse was happening, but was right beside me. He felt every wound that was inflicted upon my body; He felt the violation, He grieved, and He was present. Somehow knowing that He was there with me made a huge difference and has helped me to trust Him. He was with me then, and He will be with me now, even if the unthinkable happens.

Seeing Echo grow in her faith and confidence in God has been a testimony to me personally. She is a devoted follower of Jesus, but understandably, the wounds of her past surface from time to time. God allowed Echo to go through unthinkable pain but was always in control, just as He is in control in our lives. We can be confident that not only is God in perfect and absolute control, there will be a day when He personally will wipe the tears from each of our eyes.

We can also be confident that the day is coming when suffering will cease and God will judge evil: "He will wipe every tear from their eyes, and there will be no more death or sorrow or crying or pain. All these things are gone forever" (Revelation 21:4). God will bring justice for all the wrong done to you and to all who have been hurt. Our part is simply to trust that He is who He says He is and to hold on till He does all that He says He will do. I love Jesus's promise of John 16:33: "I have told you all this so that you may have peace in me. Here on earth you will have many trials and sorrows. But take heart, because I have overcome the world." He is not promising a life free of suffering but reassuring us that He has already won the fight! I pray you will know the peace that comes from putting your life in the hands of the One who knows the future and has guaranteed victory over evil.

A Woman with a Past

The best way to see God undistorted is to see how Jesus interacted with people. In the Gospels, we see who and what mattered, and also what didn't matter as much, to Jesus. Jesus went places the religious leaders would never go, He loved the people others had rejected, and He served instead of demanding to be served. In one of the greatest stories from the New Testament, we see a real story about a real woman who had an incredible encounter with Jesus Christ. She had been abused, disregarded, and disrespected by all of her society and culture. We don't even know her name; she is known simply as "the woman at the well." This encounter is filled with hope for all who have felt abused, misused, and forgotten. In this story, we see a God who is crazy in love with us and is always about truth and grace. Let's walk with Jesus in the gospel of John, chapter 4.

> He had to go through Samaria on the way [to Galilee]. Eventually he came to the Samaritan village of Sychar, near the field that Jacob gave to his son Joseph. Jacob's well was there; and Jesus, tired from the long walk, sat wearily beside the well about noontime. Soon a Samaritan woman came to draw water, and Jesus said to her, "Please give me a drink." He was alone at the time because his disciples had gone into the village to buy some food.
>
> The woman was surprised, for Jews refuse to have anything to do with Samaritans. She said to Jesus, "You are a Jew, and I am a Samaritan woman. Why are you asking me for a drink?"
>
> Jesus replied, "If you only knew the gift God has for you and who you are speaking to, you would ask me, and I would give you living water."
>
> "But sir, you don't have a rope or a bucket," she said, "and this well is very deep. Where would you get this living water? And besides, do you think you're greater than our ancestor Jacob, who gave us this well? How can you offer better water than he and his sons and his animals enjoyed?"
>
> Jesus replied, "Anyone who drinks this water will soon become thirsty

again. But those who drink the water I give will never be thirsty again. It becomes a fresh, bubbling spring within them, giving them eternal life."

"Please, sir," the woman said, "give me this water! Then I'll never be thirsty again, and I won't have to come here to get water."

"Go and get your husband," Jesus told her.

"I don't have a husband," the woman replied.

Jesus said, "You're right! You don't have a husband—for you have had five husbands, and you aren't even married to the man you're living with now. You certainly spoke the truth!" (John 4:4–18)

There are so many little details here that give us a fuller picture of what Jesus was really doing. First of all, although the shortest route from Judea to Galilee was through Samaria, Jewish people would avoid walking there because they despised the Samaritans. Jews considered them an unclean race and would walk miles out of their way to avoid even getting the dust of the Samaritans on their sandals. The Samaritans knew they weren't appreciated or loved. They were outcasts. On top of that, the women of those times were most definitely second-class citizens. At every synagogue service Jewish men prayed, "Blessed art thou, O Lord, who hast not made me a woman." The women sat in a separate section, were not counted in crowds, and were not permitted to touch any man but their husbands. In those times it was the man who divorced the woman, not the other way around. And he didn't need much of a reason. He only had to show there was something "unseemly" about her. Maybe she burned the stew or was having a bad-hair day. All he needed was a buddy to agree and she could be dismissed. The woman at the well had been divorced (rejected) five times. We usually view her as an immoral sinner going from one husband to the next, but I imagine she had a huge distrust of men and an incredibly low self-esteem. She had lost all value in her community; she would be seen as a disgrace and would not even be welcomed by her family. Although her husbands undoubtedly initiated the divorces, she was the one considered to have poor morals. She could not have been employed and would probably have married again or turned to prostitution to avoid starving to death. She was used by men and abused by the women of her town, which is why she went to the well in the middle of the day. Carrying a huge jug of water alone in the noonday heat was still preferable to the hurtful words of the village women who would have come to the well first thing in the morning. The woman at the well was like many of us: wounded, cynical, and fearful. She came to the well that day a mere shadow of who she was created to be.

Jesus Breaks the Rules

Some translations of John 4:4 say, "Jesus had to go to Samaria," but He really had no geographical or physical reason to go there. In other words, this was not a casual encounter at the well, but a divine, deliberate, and calculated decision by the Savior to meet with a particular woman. A Jewish man would never be caught talking in public with a woman who was not his wife, let alone with a Samaritan woman, but Jesus crossed so many lines drawn in the sand by religious leaders. He crossed racial, geographical, and gender lines to intentionally show us who and what matters. He had to go to her that day by divine appointment, to ultimately change a heart and bring the message of hope to a whole city. Although other Jewish men would have ignored the Samaritan woman, pretending she wasn't even there, Jesus struck up a conversation, asking for a drink. This forbidden exchange ended up being the longest recorded conversation between Jesus and any one single person in the entire New Testament—and with a Samaritan woman, no less. He didn't demand, as she was accustomed to, but simply asked for water, and in doing so indicated that He was willing to drink from her cup. Jesus was making a statement about her worth. He didn't have a rope or any way of getting water, so He was in essence saying, "I'll put My lips on the jar that your lips were on." In other words: "I know no one else accepts you, but I do."

Can you see this incredible picture of redemption? Jesus knew her history, her nationality, the history of all of her marriages, her living with a man, her low self-worth. He knew Jewish society considered her unworthy, and yet He still treated her with dignity, as an equal, someone worthy of affection and worthy of God's highest gift: eternal life.

Jesus is not put off by what we have been through. He didn't point a finger at her, nor does He with us. He didn't cast a stone, but accepted her as she was, even though He knew the truth about her. Jesus was addressing her inner pain, not condemning her current situation. The Bible says earlier in John's gospel that Jesus came "full of grace and truth" (1:14, NIV). How much more effective is truth when preceded by grace! Through His acceptance, she could be influenced by His truth. Jesus offers the same unconditional acceptance to us. He makes a divine appointment with each of us and meets us at our own personal well of shame and disgrace.

A Beautiful Exchange

The woman said, "I know the Messiah is coming—the one who is called Christ. When he comes, he will explain everything to us."

Then Jesus told her, "I Am the Messiah!" (John 4:25–26)

Jesus told the woman at the well that He is the God she has been waiting for her whole life. He is the answer to her emptiness. He is the living water that will satisfy her thirst for healing, acceptance, hope, and redemption. He will restore her to love again and be loved in return. In John 10:10, Jesus said, "I have come so that they may have life and have it in abundance" (HCSB). The opposite of an abundant life is one that is lacking. Jesus wants each of us to exchange our emptiness for His life of abundance. The Samaritan woman came that day rejected, abused, and afraid. Jesus accepted, healed, and restored her confidence. She finally got the one thing she had been searching for her whole life: unconditional love. Instead of constant thirst and searching for love in bad relationships, she would now have "a fresh, bubbling spring within [her], giving [her] eternal life" (John 4:14). The water in the well was stagnant, lifeless water, unable to sustain life. The water Jesus offered her was a life-giving, moving, pure water that would provide sustenance for growth and development for all who drink it. This water was the gift of eternal life. God did for her what He wants to do for us. We bring Him our pain, He exchanges it for purpose; we bring our fear, He exchanges it for faith; we bring Him our sin, He exchanges it for eternal life.

From Rejection to Revival

The woman left her water jar beside the well and ran back to the village, telling everyone, "Come and see a man who told me everything I ever did! Could he possibly be the Messiah?" So the people came streaming from the village to see him....

Many Samaritans from the village believed in Jesus because the woman had said, "He told me everything I ever did!" When they came out to see him, they begged him to stay in their village. So he stayed for two days, long enough for many more to hear his message and believe. Then they said to the woman, "Now we believe, not just because of what you told us, but because we have heard him ourselves. Now we know that he is indeed the Savior of the world." (John 4:28–30, 39–42)

Jesus used the woman at the well to launch a spiritual revival in her village. We would be remiss if we missed this point of the story. Jesus picks people everyone else forgets about and uses the abused to change the world. Jesus went beyond the religious dos and don'ts to come to the most broken, hurting person in all of the village to reach a whole city. Jesus saw her. He waited for her. He pursued her. Even though He knew everything about her troubled and broken past, He accepted her and went out of His way to spend time with her. I think it was these actions that changed her. Once a rejected outcast, she was now accepted by Jesus. It was enough for her to leave her jar at the well (in other words, leave who she was) to become who she was meant to be (an evangelist to the very people who abused her and shunned her). I love how Jesus's acceptance gave her immediate confidence to speak to the very people who rejected her. She showed no hesitation in sharing about her encounter with the Messiah. If only we could all so easily grasp what it means to be loved and approved by the only One who truly matters.

Jesus is a safe refuge for us, because He knows everything about us and loves us just the same. I love what it says in Acts 17:28: "For in him we live and move and exist." Jesus has a purpose and plan for your life as well. He is the source of our abundant life. He is not put off by what has happened to you, and He is not planning to punish you. He comes to you today by divine appointment, just as He did for the woman at the well. He knows your journey, and in all of your brokenness and hurt, He is sitting next to you wanting to have a conversation. He doesn't look at your past or see you as a victim; He sees you differently than anyone ever has, could, or will.

The question is, how do you see Him?

It's Your Move

The God who knew the woman at the well the best also loved her the most. It was love that changed her heart and His acceptance that changed an entire city of people who had been rejected and despised. Will you allow God to come to you right now? To help you? He has a massive plan for your life, but it is your move. You have to see Him not as a God that wants to hurt you but as a perfect Father who is safe for you. Jesus wants to meet you in your brokenness; He wants to reclaim you, redeem the pain and the hurt, and then use your story to make history. Jesus comes to us so we will come to Him, but that is not the end of the story. He comes to us so that we might go to the world—a testament to His unconditional acceptance, ever-present love, and all-sufficient grace.

> Those who live in the shelter of the Most High
>   will find rest in the shadow of the Almighty.
> This I declare about the LORD:
> He alone is my refuge, my place of safety;
>   he is my God, and I trust him.
> For he will rescue you from every trap
>   and protect you from deadly disease.
> He will cover you with his feathers.
>   He will shelter you with his wings.
>   His faithful promises are your armor and protection. (Psalm 91:1–4)

18

God Is Always Accepting

To be fully seen by somebody,
then, and be loved anyhow—this
is a human offering that can
border on miraculous.

—Elizabeth Gilbert

My wife and I visited the Winchester Mansion in San Jose, California, as newly-weds. If you're not familiar with the mansion, let me share the story:

Sarah Winchester started building her mansion in 1884, shortly after the death of her husband, William, principal owner of the Winchester Repeating Arms Company, and their only child, the infant Annie. The widowed heiress moved from Connecticut to California and undertook construction at the direction of a psychic, who told her that the Winchester family was under a curse, brought on by the thousands of deaths caused by their invention, the repeating rifle. The spirits of the dead were seeking vengeance, the medium said, and the only relief would come from building them a home. But once started, the project must never stop.

So the Widow Winchester bought a home already under construction, and then built and built and rebuilt. She added dozens of rooms and included features that no human could use, such as stairways leading into ceilings, closet doors that opened to blank walls, and upstairs portals that opened precipitously onto the lawn below. She also built mazelike hallways to confuse the haunts, and if a room's construction went wrong, she simply stopped building it and erected a new one around it. Surely the ghosts would know she was doing it all for them.

With a $20 million fortune that would be worth twenty times as much today, plus a tax-free income of a staggering $1,000 per day, Sarah Winchester eventually wasted a quarter of her wealth trying to appease her haunts and assuage her guilt. But the tortured woman never found relief, and the thirty-eight year project came to its end only after she died in 1922. Now a tourist attraction on San Jose's Winchester Boulevard, the 160-room mansion is a sad monument to the ravages of one of Satan's favorite weapons—guilt.[1]

The Winchester Mansion is an incredible building and an even more fascinating story. I do not know, nor can I pretend to imagine, the guilt and shame she had both lived and died with, but it's clear to see she was tormented till the day she died.

Closely Related, but Worlds Apart

We often tie together the emotions of guilt and shame, but they are in fact quite different. Guilt is not actually an emotion; it is a legal state. You either are or are not guilty of the act. Guilt is tied to what we do, while shame is tied to who we are. Guilt is a by-product of doing something bad; shame is the by-product of believing we are bad. Shame is the devastating result of guilt that is not forgiven and removed.

Children whose fathers blame them feel immense shame, often for things they did not do. They have become scapegoats for their families' wrongs. These children's actions are based on a constant need and pursuit for acceptance and approval. Their shame is not based on truth but on lies created to ease someone else's guilt. The accusations and blame have become such a part of their lives that they now believe the lies to be true, and they see themselves as no-good, unlovable, terrible people who deserve punishment. Shame leaves people with a sense of hopelessness. Their inner world is a dark place where they have no value, no purpose, and often no reason to live. While guilt can be assuaged with reparative actions, shame is a core belief that causes its owner to shrink inside, becoming a mere shadow of his or her former self. Shame cannot be fixed because it is part of the person's character. It is who they are. People with shame believe themselves to be small, lowly, and insignificant, and sometimes they are unable to even make eye contact with others. Shame reaches deep into the soul and steals a person's confidence, happiness, and self-worth. Shame is the bleeding of the soul.

Because of the shame we absorb into our hearts, minds, and actions, we are afraid of not being accepted. We cannot clearly see God as full of His true grace, love, mercy, and compassion. So many people see God as a judge, and although we will stand before Him on Judgment Day, the guilt we deserve has been placed upon His Son, Jesus. The payment has been made for those who place their faith in Jesus Christ. Jesus became the ultimate, once-and-for-all scapegoat to set us free from condemnation, shame, and fear. He restores the weak and is both our healer and our friend. Instead of living in shame, with our heads to the ground and condemnation in our hearts, we can approach God with confidence: "So let us come boldly to the throne of our gracious God. There we will receive his mercy, and we will find grace to help us when we need it most" (Hebrews 4:16).

The Issue of Blood

In the gospel of Mark we see a beautiful picture of Jesus loving and restoring a woman from an incurable disease, fully accepting her in spite of her condition. This woman was considered least among her community, whereas the synagogue ruler was viewed as the leader in his city. Perhaps you can put yourself in this story.

> When Jesus had again crossed over by boat to the other side of the lake, a large crowd gathered around him while he was by the lake. Then one of the synagogue rulers, named Jairus, came there. Seeing Jesus, he fell at his feet and pleaded earnestly with him, "My little daughter is dying. Please come and put your hands on her so that she will be healed and live." So Jesus went with him.
>
> A large crowd followed and pressed around him. And a woman was there who had been subject to bleeding for twelve years. She had suffered a great deal under the care of many doctors and had spent all she had, yet instead of getting better she grew worse. When she heard about Jesus, she came up behind him in the crowd and touched his cloak, because she thought, "If I just touch his clothes, I will be healed." Immediately her bleeding stopped and she felt in her body that she was freed from her suffering. (Mark 5:21–29, NIV)

It's hard for us to imagine these days the full impact of her type of sickness. At this period in history, the issue of blood would have made her unclean and untouchable. She would have been unable to worship in the synagogue at which Jairus was a leader. According to the law of the time, to be touched by this woman would cause the recipient of her touch to be unclean as well. She would also have been unable to have children. At this point she has lived for twelve years with no human touch, no family, no interaction with her community. She would have suffered agonizing loneliness and abandonment, which, in all reality, was probably more painful than her sickness. Can you imagine twelve years of feeling dirty, rejected, lonely, and hopeless? She had visited multiple doctors, who charged a great deal but could not help her, so she continued to get worse. Not only was she physically bleeding, she also was suffering emotionally and spiritually. Her physical problem was very real, but her deepest pain must have come from the shame she carried as a result of her condition. As much as she wanted the bleeding to stop, she must have been equally desperate for acceptance. She was at the end of trying to solve the problem herself, and in her desperation came to Jesus as her last resort and only hope.

Her condition presents a problem. She would not presume to ask Jesus to lay hands on her as Jairus did, for she could not touch anyone else in her unclean state. Certainly her deep-rooted shame and lack of self-worth left her unable to talk to Jesus, yet she believed in His power and knew just a touch could heal her.

She probably pushed through the crowd, head down, face to the ground, unwilling to draw attention, and planning to leave unnoticed, until she got close enough to reach out her hand. She simply touched his cloak and was instantly healed! She could tell immediately that her bleeding had stopped, and there was no more pain in her body. No one else knew what had happened, but Jesus did. Look what He did next:

> At once Jesus realized that power had gone out from him. He turned around
> in the crowd and asked, "Who touched my clothes?" (Mark 5:30, NIV)

Jesus was on His way to the house of Jairus when He was interrupted by the woman with the blood. Two people were desperate for Jesus. One had everything; one had nothing. One had a twelve-year-old daughter who was dying; one had been incurably sick for twelve years. One was a leader in the synagogue; one was rejected by the community. I wonder what Jairus felt in that moment. I imagine he was frustrated or impatient. He needed Jesus to come to his house now, not talk to the woman with the blood! But Jesus always cares about restoring the brokenhearted. He cares about our physical needs, but our spiritual and emotional health are even more important to Him. It makes me pause and wonder how many times I miss what is important in the eyes of God because of what is urgent in my eyes. Jesus always gets it right.

Redefine How You See You

Then the woman, knowing what had happened to her, came and fell at his feet and, trembling with fear, told him the whole truth. He said to her, "Daughter, your faith has healed you. Go in peace and be freed from your suffering." (Mark 5:33–34, NIV)

Jesus calls out to get the attention of the crowd, and then calls the woman "daughter." This is the one and only time Jesus calls someone a daughter. He isn't just physically healing her; she was already healed at this point. He is emotionally healing her from the thing that crippled her the most: her lack of human relationship and the rejection and shame she had lived with for twelve years. Can you imagine that day? For twelve years she has been completely rejected by society. She is literally and legally untouchable. She has no family, no one to love her, her heart is broken, and her soul anguished. She lives a life of shame, not good enough to be with others and unworthy of attention. Then Jesus tenderly calls for her. He pursues her with His love. Jesus didn't need to ask who touched Him. He already knew; He just needed her to know that He knew. He needed everyone to know, so he addressed immediately what they would have considered shocking, unlawful, and unimaginable. Shame grows in silence. Jesus knew this, and perhaps that is why He acknowledged her publicly.

She came to Him trembling with fear, confessing it was she. But it wasn't Jesus she feared; it was the people who had judged and would continue to judge her. Then in front of the leader of the synagogue He called her "daughter" and made her part of His family. Jesus made a statement of both value and belonging. This is the way Jesus is. He reaches out to people who have been forgotten, judged, condemned, and rejected. Imagine, after twelve years of her being an untouchable outcast in society, Jesus welcomed her and restored so much to her life. She would now be accepted in the community and able to live in connection with others. Jesus wanted to make sure she knew who she was created to be, and He wanted those listening to begin to see her in a new way. He wanted to redefine her role in society and restore her to relationship. Instead of being seen as unclean, she was now approachable, lovable, and touchable.

How do you see yourself right now? As rejected, unlovable, shamed? Or do you see yourself the way Jesus sees you? Do you hear Him speaking life into you right now? I imagine this woman could hear people talking around her; they would have been shocked that she dared to touch Jesus. But it wasn't the voices of others that mattered to her, only the voice of God. He is the One who redefines how we see ourselves. See yourself the way God sees you, and listen only to the voice of Jesus, not the mumblings of those around you. God's love for you has never changed. From the foundation of the world, He knew you, He loved you, and—just as with this woman—nothing has or ever can change that. "Even before he made the world, God loved us and chose us in Christ to be holy and without fault in his eyes" (Ephesians 1:4).

Realize That Jesus Is Enough

"Your faith has healed you." It was her faith, not her touch, that drew Jesus's attention. She had faith to believe that simply a touch of His clothes could heal the twelve-year physical calamity that made her unclean and socially rejected. She wasn't expecting a process or a ritual; she knew Jesus was enough to heal her. Too often we complicate the gospel. We add classes, steps, and conditions that just make faith so much harder than it is. We somehow want to add to Jesus, but when we learn that He is enough, we can begin to live in freedom. In fact, just the touch of His garment was enough! This woman whom everyone avoided was desperate enough to see what so many of us miss: that Jesus Christ, the Messiah, is enough. All the world had to offer had failed her; she had tried it all and now was sicker and poorer than before. Jesus was her last and only hope. She just had to get close enough to touch Him. Now, like this unnamed woman, the closer you get to Jesus, the closer you get to realizing your true value and potential. It was her faith in Jesus's ability that healed her.

If you feel crippled physically, spiritually, or emotionally, can you see Jesus as fully capable to heal you in every way? Will you approach His throne not with human logic but with the simple belief that Jesus is enough? So many things that you wonder about will work out in God's time and for God's glory. Are you close enough to touch Him? All you need today is a touch from your Savior.

Perhaps you have lived under condemnation and shame. Somehow God's grace has become a concept rather than an experience. Let today be the day you touch Jesus and let Him touch you. You are valuable, more than you can imagine. You matter. Please begin to shift your thinking to know that you are loved, that you matter, and that you are worth the death of God's only Son. The Bible says, "What is the price of five sparrows—two copper coins? Yet God does not forget a single one of them. And the very hairs on your head are all numbered. So don't be afraid; you are more valuable to God than a whole flock of sparrows" (Luke 12:6–7).

Live Differently

"Go in peace and be freed from your suffering." Here Jesus is telling her to go and live differently. Go now and be freed from your pain and suffering; go and be freed from the shame of being unclean and rejected. Going forward means letting go of the past and moving on from what has been to what can be. Go and live in peace! True healing and freedom from shame will only come as you live differently. That is when suffering ends and peace begins. In this one simple sentence Jesus healed so much more than the issue of blood. He healed her soul. Can you pause and imagine that moment with me? The one who experienced the most rejection and shame had been healed by the God who created the universe. This woman is no longer bound by shame, but free to live again with purpose and stature. You can live differently too. You do not have to continue to be labeled with the guilt and shame. You have a new identity in Christ. No matter what anyone has said, you are part of God's family. He calls you His daughter or His son. You are not a bad person. You are not destined to fail. You have value, purpose, and a destiny. You can look people in the eye now. You can dream about the future. You can live in peace!

Reconcile Your World

We are not exactly sure what happened to this woman. We don't know her name; we don't know if she had a home; we are not sure what her life was like after her healing; but we are sure about this: Jesus publicly did what no one had been able to do for her. He restored her. Jesus allowed His power to heal her physically, and He wanted to make sure that she would not live in guilt and shame any longer. He also wanted everyone in earshot to know the same. He was not going to allow her to hide her healing. He wanted to do more than just stop the flow of blood; He wanted her to testify about what had happened so others would believe. He wanted her life to count! I think Jesus wanted to give her what we humans struggle so much to give. I think He wanted to set an example for the church and for Christians everywhere to follow. We have seen the heart of Jesus to free people from their sickness and restore them to health, not just physically, but spiritually and emotionally. If you are not struggling with shame yourself, you may know someone who is. For healing to take place and for that person to have a life that can be used for God, the shame needs to be exposed in a safe environment. As the church that Jesus started, we need to be that safe place. We need to give others what Christ has given us: the gift of no condemnation.

The Gift We All Want but Rarely Give

John 3:16 is without doubt the most quoted verse in the Bible. I'm sure you know it well: "For God so loved the world that he gave his one and only Son, that whoever believes in him shall not perish but have eternal life" (NIV).

I love this verse, but it is easy to love because it is so hopeful. It's what our faith is built on. God loves, God gives, we believe, we receive. Who wouldn't want to be part of that? The church has done a good job of marketing that verse, and most people get it. I think it's the very next verse that we have failed to embrace fully: "For God did not send his Son into the world to condemn the world, but to save the world through him" (verse 17, NIV). People want to believe the story is true, and they desperately want to be loved, accepted, and pursued by God. They want—finally—to be free from condemnation. But that's where things derail for some. Their image of God is distorted by the guilt and shame they carry, and so they feel judged, unloved, and condemned by the very God who offers freedom from all of it.

John 3:16 is what God does for me that I can't do for others. It is the free gift of eternal life. But John 3:17 is something we are responsible as Christians to both live in ourselves and give to others. Jesus did not come to condemn the world, and neither should we. It is incredible that the only One who has the right to condemn all of humanity does not do so. The word "condemn" used in this verse is a picture of a wrecking ball smashing into a building. It is destructive; it tears down, destroys. That is completely opposite of the abundant life Christ came to give us. Paul reiterates it again in the book of Romans: "Therefore, there is now no condemnation for those who are in Christ Jesus" (Romans 8:1, NIV). This is the promise of God for all who fear being blamed. God gave us the gift of eternal life, and the result of that gift is no more condemnation, no more guilt, no more carrying the past around. So why are you still ashamed? Why do you still see God as a "judge in the sky" just waiting to dole out punishment? Why did Sarah Winchester spend her life trying make up for something that wasn't her fault in the first place? She believed a lie.

Jesus Is the Ultimate Scapegoat

You can set yourself free from guilt by making atonement for your sins (or paying for your crime) but only your heavenly Father can remove your shame. Only He is enough. Only Jesus is the ultimate scapegoat, able to remove our dirt, our blame, and our shame forever. Only He can take the burden on Himself and help you see yourself for who you really are. Only His truth can erase the lie that has stolen your self-worth and made you believe that every bad thing said about you is true. Whether your shame came through the guilt of your own wrongdoing or through the false blame and accusations of your earthly father, Jesus has already made atonement for it. He already paid the price so that you could be restored. It is a burden you do not have to carry. Hold your head up high, and be free from shame today.

The deepest prayer of my heart is that what has been so distorted can become clear. As we complete this journey of discovery about who God is, I hope that what comes into your mind when you think about God is now much clearer and truer than it was prior to reading this book. I pray that each of us, every day and in every way, will grow closer to our perfect heavenly Father. Please continue on with me as we take steps toward wholeness and toward becoming the people God created us to be. I pray these words bring healing to your heart and hope for your future.

Part 3

OUR REFLECTION

Experiencing Healing and Restoration

19

Mirror, Mirror

There are two ways of spreading
light: to be the candle or the
mirror that reflects it.

— Edith Wharton

Have you ever gone into a house of mirrors at a carnival? They distort who you really are. One mirror makes you look short and fat, while another makes you look tall and skinny. For a moment at least you can indulge your desire to appear different than you really are. Or maybe not.

Beyond the Carnival

Mirrors aren't enjoyable for everyone. A friend of mine laughingly said, "The mirror is my enemy." Depending on what you see reflected back, mirrors can either be friends or enemies. They can help us look our best, but don't they also reflect our every flaw? What makes some people happy causes real pain for others.

Sometimes we allow ourselves to look into other "mirrors" as well, such as the opinions of others, media, and culture, or our own expectations and insecurities. These are not helpful mirrors, and they can't be trusted. They are like the carnival mirrors reflecting distorted images. We don't see the truth when we look in the mirror; we only see lies concocted by the Father of Lies (see John 8:44). We desperately want to see God for who He really is, but Satan turns our desperation into distortion. He wants to steal confidence from us and knows wrong words could potentially define us. The mirror of this world is not God's mirror, for sure.

We see ourselves through the eyes of every negative word, insult, rejection, and failure in our past. Who we are today is intrinsically tied to memories and experiences of how things used to be. I once heard a story that illustrates so well the power of our past and the memories that chain us there. What if you knew the chains could be shattered?

Chained to the Past

A man is going through a circus and there is this big elephant. It is bound by a very small chain. And he is with the animal trainer and he said to the trainer, "I have always wanted to ask, how does that chain hold such a large animal?" The trainer said, "It doesn't, but the elephant doesn't know that." He said, "Well I don't understand." The trainer said, "When the elephant is born, we take that same chain and put it on his ankle. It is strong enough then to hold him because he is a baby. As he grows, we continue to use the same chain. Now he is an adult male elephant, which is much stronger than that chain. It is not the chain that binds him; it is the memory of the chain.[1]

Isn't it time to break the chains? I don't know you, but I understand you. I get the pain, I get being stuck, and I get that you are chained to the lies others have told you. Truly I do. The very people who raised us and were supposed to be the safest sometimes became the most damaging. We smile in a crowd of happy people, we laugh at movies, but when the day is over, we are so broken, so sad, and so frustrated with the mirror.

Mirror Memories

The past helped create the image you see when you look in the mirror today—and the journey toward healing starts with another long look. When you look in the mirror, whom do you see? Do you see a child who is loved or one who has been rejected? Do you see a person of great worth or one with no purpose?

I can guarantee it's not the same way God sees you. You are not seeing yourself through God's truth of grace, acceptance, and forgiveness, but you see yourself distorted by lies of guilt, shame, rejection, fear, and insecurity. You look in the mirror, but all you see is your past staring back at you. You see the pain and sting of abandonment and the rejection that made you feel worthless. You see the angry fists that stole your innocence and the controlling behavior that destroyed your confidence. You see the words that pierced your soul and tried to kill your spirit.

The Mirror That Doesn't Lie

Whatever you have been told, wherever your pain has left you, in spite of the scars that you feel and possibly even see, God has given you the only mirror that reflects the truth of who you really are. Not a carnival mirror, but a real, truth-talking mirror that shows you who you are and reveals who you can be.

James, the brother of Jesus, describes the Word of God as a mirror.

> But don't just listen to God's word. You must do what it says. Otherwise, you are only fooling yourselves. For if you listen to the word and don't obey, it is like glancing at your face in a mirror. You see yourself, walk away, and forget what you look like. But if you look carefully into the perfect law that sets you free, and if you do what it says and don't forget what you heard, then God will bless you for doing it. (James 1:22–25)

The Bible is God's incredible and life-giving Word. It is the mirror for your heart. When you read the Word of God, you see your true self reflected back. You see yourself through His eyes. The Word of God cannot lie and does not change; it simply provides a looking glass through which you can see yourself clearly. Knowing God's Word will help you recognize what is a lie and what is truth about you. It gives you a perfect image of who you are to be in Christ: "And you will know the truth, and the truth will set you free" (John 8:32).

As you line up your self-image against the Word of God, it will over time, piece by piece, scar by scar, and pain by pain, strip away the layers of doubt, cynicism, and anger that have built up. Like an old chair that needs to be restored, you have to first strip it down to its original form. Only then can it be made to look brand new.

God wants to give you a new image! Genesis 1:27 says, "So God created human beings in his own image. In the image of God he created them; male and female he created them." You were created in the image of God, and now that you are seeing Him more clearly, you will have a clearer picture of yourself as well. You are His child and a reflection of Him. Ephesians 5:1 says, "Imitate God, therefore, in everything you do, because you are his dear children." It is our responsibility to become Christlike in every way possible, so that He can reveal Himself to the world through us. But we have to heal a bit first and allow Him to mend our broken past.

The next few chapters are about your healing. We'll be talking about what needs to happen and how to get there. What is it for you? Maybe it's time to forgive someone or let go of something. Maybe it is time to climb that mountain staring you in the face.

Whatever the journey looks like for you, there are some truths from the Word of God that will help to get you there. The first one is to know you are a child of God.

20

Getting Off the Orphan Train

I will not leave you as orphans;
I will come to you.

—Jesus (John 14:18, niv)

In 1854 an estimated 30,000 vagrant children were living in New York City. Abandoned kids were everywhere on the streets. "The city's booming immigrant population contributed to overcrowding, poverty, disease, and death. The police did not have a lot of options for homeless children. There were no social welfare programs, no foster homes, no safety net for orphans."[1] In response to the growing problem, two charity organizations developed a program that placed these homeless children into homes throughout the country. The children were transported from town to town by train. This controversial social experiment soon became known as the Orphan Train. "In the seventy-five years from 1854 to 1929, the Orphan Train movement relocated an estimated 150,000 children from the streets of New York to farms and small towns in the Midwest."[2]

A lottery system was implemented to place some of the children into permanent homes, but other kids were taken to the train station and lined up so that prospective parents could inspect them and select the children they wanted. Unfortunately, this was a flawed system because siblings were often split up and there was no screening of the parents to see if they would provide loving homes.

These Orphan Train children just wanted one thing: a family that would accept them and love them. "They wanted to belong."[3]

Although orphanages are virtually obsolete in Western culture, thanks to the foster-care system and advances in welfare, there are still millions of children worldwide separated from both of their parents.[4] I know the devastation of losing a parent as a young child, but I can hardly begin to imagine the horror of losing both parents in the early years of life.

Jesus said, "I will not leave you as orphans; I will come to you" (John 14:18, NIV). Yet there are millions of people all over this planet living as spiritual orphans separated from God the Father. As mentioned in chapter 9, there are also Christians who are living out their lives with an "orphan heart." They have been adopted into the family of God but live as if they haven't. As we move toward wholeness in our relationships with God and one another, and as we continue on the journey to inner healing from the wounds of our past, we have to ask ourselves, *Am I living as an orphan or as a child of God?* How you see yourself makes all the difference in the world. It will determine how you live and respond to those around you and also to your heavenly Father.

Orphan Thinking

The Hebrew word for "orphan" is *yatom*. It is used forty-two times in the Old Testament and literally means "fatherless." Satan loves nothing more than an orphan Christian. His goal has always been to separate Christians from God the Father and children from their birth fathers.

Matt O'Connor, who wrote *Fathers 4 Justice,* begins his book with this awful fact: "In the time it takes you to read this book at least 100 children will have lost contact with their father."[5]

It's so tragic but so true. Satan attacks our relationship with our heavenly Father by destroying the relationship with our earthly fathers. Look what Mark Stibbe, author of *I Am Your Father,* said about Satan's schemes: "The enemy specializes in fatherlessness. Why…? Because he wants to make it as difficult as possible…to call God 'father.' If he can succeed in making the very idea of fatherhood something negative, then he will have gone a long way towards making it next to impossible for a person to have an intimate friendship with the world's greatest Dad."[6]

Many of you can relate to this. The absence of your father's love has left you with wounds that affect the very core of your being. Even if you have made a personal decision to follow Jesus, the very thought of being a child of God is a concept too difficult to grasp.

Listen carefully and prayerfully to what ministry leader Jack Frost has to say concerning the life of a spiritual orphan:

The orphan spirit causes one to live life as if he does not have a safe and secure place in the Father's heart. He feels he has no place of affirmation, protection, comfort, belonging, or affection. Self-oriented, lonely, and inwardly isolated, he has no one from whom to draw godly inheritance. Therefore, he has to strive, achieve, compete, and earn everything he gets in life. It easily leads to a life of anxiety, fears, and frustration.[7]

When you feel as if you do not have a safe and secure place in the heart of Father God, you protect yourself by living outside of His presence. You're a spiritual orphan instead of the beloved child of God you were created to be. You might be wondering by now how to identify yourself as an orphan or a child of God. An orphan sees God as a master, following His rules and obeying His law out of a sense of duty. Orphans will tend to be insecure about their place in the family of God, needing approval and affirmation of their belonging. On the other hand, sons and daughters see God as a loving Father and live according to His law as a response of love. They feel accepted and secure about their place in the family, able to give grace and receive it from others.

We can't change what we don't see. So we need to come face to face with our situation. Are we living like we are God's children or as orphans?

Coming Home

There is a story in the book of Luke that strikes me deeply. It is about a son who, although loved and valued, chose to live away from his home like an orphan. It's the story of the prodigal son. Spiritual orphans are a lot like the prodigal son, choosing to live away from the presence of their Father. Here is Jesus's story of the prodigal:

Jesus continued: "There was a man who had two sons. The younger one said to his father, 'Father, give me my share of the estate.' So he divided his property between them.

"Not long after that, the younger son got together all he had, set off for a distant country and there squandered his wealth in wild living. After he had spent everything, there was a severe famine in that whole country, and he began to be in need. So he went and hired himself out to a citizen of that country, who sent him to his fields to feed pigs. He longed to fill his stomach with the pods that the pigs were eating, but no one gave him anything.

"When he came to his senses, he said, 'How many of my father's hired men have food to spare, and here I am starving to death! I will set out and go back to my father and say to him: Father, I have sinned against heaven and against you. I am no longer worthy to be called your son; make me like one of your hired men.' So he got up and went to his father.

"But while he was still a long way off, his father saw him and was filled with compassion for him; he ran to his son, threw his arms around him and kissed him.

"The son said to him, 'Father, I have sinned against heaven and against you. I am no longer worthy to be called your son.'

"But the father said to his servants, 'Quick! Bring the best robe and put it on him. Put a ring on his finger and sandals on his feet. Bring the fattened calf and kill it. Let's have a feast and celebrate. For this son of mine was dead and is alive again; he was lost and is found.' So they began to celebrate.

"Meanwhile, the older son was in the field. When he came near the house, he heard music and dancing. So he called one of the servants and asked him what was going on. 'Your brother has come,' he replied, 'and your father has killed the fattened calf because he has him back safe and sound.'

"The older brother became angry and refused to go in. So his father went out and pleaded with him. But he answered his father, 'Look! All these years I've been slaving for you and never disobeyed your orders. Yet you never gave me even a young goat so I could celebrate with my friends. But when this son of yours who has squandered your property with prostitutes comes home, you kill the fattened calf for him!'

"'My son,' the father said, 'you are always with me, and everything I have is yours. But we had to celebrate and be glad, because this brother of yours was dead and is alive again; he was lost and is found.'" (Luke 15:11–32, NIV)

I really love this story. It's a story of rebellion and redemption, of sin and salvation; and if we are willing to be honest, isn't this a story of all of us? We have all at times chosen to go our own way, run from God's blessings, and become spiritual orphans.

The Road Back Home

We don't know all the details of the prodigal son story, like why the son left and how long the father waited for him, but there is still so much we can learn about how to return home.

1. Wake up to your destiny.

The Bible says the son "came to his senses" (verse 17). He found his proper perspective in a pigpen and woke up to the cold, awful reality of his life. Nothing he had done while spending his whole inheritance even compared to what he had in his father's home. He had no money, his current employer didn't feed him, and he had hit rock bottom. His desperation caused a spiritual awakening. Why live as a slave when you can live as a child in the family?

Our hurt and the things done to us become the "pigpens" in our lives. If you choose to live in your pain, it will become a barrier between you and the presence of God. But God has a future and a destiny planned for you.

Galatians 4:7 says, "Now you are no longer a slave but God's own child. And since you are his child, God has made you his heir." Nothing the world can offer you even comes close to the blessings your perfect heavenly Father has for you.

2. Repent and return home.

"I will set out and go back to my father" (Luke 15:18, NIV). Are you ready to come home? Maybe you're in the pigpen through your own bad choices, or—more than likely—you have settled there, believing it's all you deserve. Either way, eating with the pigs really stinks. It wasn't the destiny of the son in this story, and it's certainly not what you were created for. The Bible says, "Anyone who belongs to Christ has become a new person. The old life is gone; a new life has begun" (2 Corinthians 5:17). Coming home to the Father may require repentance. Repentance implies many things, but at the root it simply means a change of direction. It is to turn around and walk in the opposite direction. True repentance requires taking in a whole new point of view and looking at things God's way. Maybe for you, repentance will be no longer seeing yourself as worthless but seeing yourself the way God does: valuable and priceless. God wants to change the direction of your life. The pigpen is not for you! To leave the pigpen and come home is to acknowledge your need for a heavenly Father and declare your dependence on Him.

3. Fix what is really broken.

"Father, I have sinned against heaven and against you. I am no longer worthy to be called your son" (Luke 15:21, NIV). It is important to understand that there were no laws in the Old Testament forbidding someone from asking for his inheritance while his father was still alive. The son, although selfish, didn't actually break any rules when he said, "I want my inheritance right now." He didn't break the law of the land or the law of God, but he did break the heart of his father. In the same way, we often want the blessings of God without the attachment to God as our Father.

I wonder how much I have broken the heart of the One who gave everything so I can live abundantly and have eternal life. God does not hold back but is the perfect Father who meets our needs in every way. Yet still we pursue our love of money and other temporary pleasures of our flesh. He lets us go, even though it breaks His heart. Then when we get to the end of ourselves, He is ready to embrace us and restore our full inheritance back to us. That is what grace does! It saves us from what we do deserve and gives us what we don't: another chance to get it right.

If you are feeling conviction in your heart, take a moment now to confess your wrongdoing and ask for His forgiveness. There is nothing in your life too big for God's grace. He is ready and able to remove all your sins from you completely.

4. Accept His embrace.

> But while he was still a long way off, his father saw him and was filled with compassion for him; he ran to his son, threw his arms around him and kissed him....
>
> "Quick! Bring the best robe and put it on him. Put a ring on his finger and sandals on his feet. Bring the fattened calf and kill it. Let's have a feast and celebrate. For this son of mine was dead and is alive again; he was lost and is found." (Luke 15:20, 22–24, NIV)

I hope you are beginning to get a picture of how the heavenly Father loves you. We see a father who has not turned his back on his son but is instead keeping a lookout in the hopes his son might return. When he finally sees his son in the distance, he is filled with compassion and runs to meet him.

You have to think about the setting for this story: The father was a dignified man, a wealthy property owner. He wasn't in the habit of running places, but such was his joy that I imagine he hitched up his robe in a completely undignified manner and ran to his son without concern about what anyone thought. His precious son was home, no longer an orphan! I can only hope to offer my own children the same kind of grace he demonstrated. He did not hold his son's mistakes against him or say *I told you so*. He simply waited and then ran to his son, unrestrained in his joy and unwilling to spare any expense celebrating his return.

The challenge for us is accepting our Father's embrace. While we want to belong, we often find it hard to believe that the past has been erased. While God offers us our sonship back, we are willing to settle for being the hired help. However, as long as we feel we have to earn our acceptance, we cannot rest in our place as a son or daughter. Coming home is the first step, but being restored to the family requires us to put on the ring, wear the best robe, and take our place at the table.

You can make the same choice as the prodigal son. Look around and be honest about your life. Are you living separated from your heavenly Father? Are you settling for scraps when you have a home waiting for you? It's time to come home. Accept the Father's loving embrace. Accept the Father's invitation to live again. Resolve to stay in the presence of your heavenly Father for the rest of your life. It might be the best invitation of your life, but I know it's not the easiest to accept. It's risky to humble yourself and return home, admitting you made a mistake.

A Prodigal Daughter

I will never, in all of my life, forget being invited to get on a plane and go be part of Ruth Graham's ministry to church leaders. I was so honored to become acquainted with Billy Graham's daughter, and in the process I found an incredibly beautiful person who simply wants better for all of us. She knows the embrace of the Father and also gets what it means to live as a prodigal child of God.

Ruth shares the story of her prodigal experience in her book *In Every Pew Sits a Broken Heart*. After a life of broken marriages, and with a broken heart, Ruth decides it is time to return home to her father:

> I wound my way up my parents' steep, mountain driveway in western North Carolina, unsure if I would be welcomed or rejected. I was broken by the choices I had made. Stubborn and willful, I had followed my own path, and

now I would have to face the consequences. I had caused pain for my children and loved ones. I feared I had embarrassed my parents. It seemed I had wrecked my world. The shame was almost unbearable....

I had gone against everyone's advice. My family warned me. They had tried to stop me. But I had not listened. I needed to do what was best for *me,* I had told them. And now my life was a shambles. I was a failure in my own eyes and certainly would be in the eyes of others when they learned what "Billy Graham's daughter" had done. I feared I had humiliated those I held dearest. How would I be able to face them?

Driving up the mountain, my fears multiplied.... My mind was spinning. I tried to remember my mother's insistent tone from our phone conversation a few days earlier. "Come home," she had urged. I was desperate when I called her. I told her of my mistake and was trying to piece together a plan when she interjected with the voice of a loving, protective parent. But how would she and my father respond when they saw me? What would they say to me? Would they say, "You've made your bed; now lie in it"? Would they condemn me? Would they reject me? Despise me? They had every right.

As I rounded the last bend in the driveway, Daddy came into view. He was standing in the paved area where visitors usually park. Rolling the car to a stop, I took a deep breath and prepared to greet my father. I turned off the ignition, opened the car door, and stepped onto the driveway. Then I looked up—Daddy was already at my side. Before I could say a word, he took me into his arms and said, "Welcome home."[8]

Welcome home—the sweet words every orphan longs to hear. It's time for you to get off the orphan train. Your Father is waiting for you, watching out for you, ready to run and meet you halfway. Don't let lies keep you in the pigpen. Don't let fear keep you at the bottom of that winding road. Stop doing what you're doing, turn back to God, and walk up the road to the Father who loves you, who waits for you and who is longing to say, "Welcome home!"

Finding God in the Garbage

Everyone says forgiveness is
a lovely idea until they have
something to forgive.

—C.S. LEWIS

I will never forget the moment I stood at the grave of my biological father on Father's Day, 1998. It was ten years after I became a Christian and a long time after learning that forgiveness was not a suggestion but a command. I knew I had never really dealt with forgiving my father, and after all those years, I still questioned the point.

There I was, standing over the grave of a man I had resented and in reality hated for years, even though I never really knew him. He was the dad I always wanted, dreamed about, and would have given anything to know, but all I had were the stories I made up in my own mind. With only one photo in my possession and one newspaper article in my hand, I was so hurt, so angry, and so frustrated with both him and God. The anger had consumed me as a teenager and became the source of my undoing in many relationships. No one wants to be around an angry person. Even as a Christian, the anger was still controlling and defining me. It affected my marriage, my friendships, my decision making. Yet for years I never put two and two together to truly understand the root of my anger and its impact on my life for so long. How could a dad who died become the source of so much anger? Why would I need to forgive a dad that was dead? How do I even do that?

Anger always takes you somewhere. It took me to places I regret to this day.

Carrying anger and bitterness in your heart is simply like carrying bags of garbage around everywhere you go. It's heavy, stinks like crazy, gets in the way, and has absolutely no value whatsoever. Believe me—I know garbage. When I got out of the air force, I worked as a garbage man for seven months. My job was to hang off the back of a garbage truck up to ten hours a day and pick up around a thousand garbage cans daily. Because I was the new guy, I never drove the truck; I just got the unspeakable joy of dealing with the garbage. (You name it, I have seen it.)

In the summer, the garbage was so hot there would be maggots all through it, and in the winter it was so cold and frozen I could barely get it out of the can. I would go home every night completely exhausted, and all I could do was take a bath, eat, and go to bed. I was on the "extra" list, so they would call when I was needed. I always hoped they wouldn't call or need me.

As I lifted can after can, I would think, *I don't know if I can do this for the next twenty years.* That job became a motivating factor in my decision to finish my bachelor's degree. After receiving my degree, I worked as a tax auditor for the state of Washington, became a business owner, and after coming to Christ, received a master's degree. All of which I directly credit to the discontent of a job I did not want to do.

It's true that good can come out of garbage, yet when we are in the middle of it, there is nothing good about it. The Bible is very clear about how to deal with the garbage and pain in our lives, yet many of us choose to carry around the garbage of past offenses and unforgiven hurts. When we neglect to take out the spiritual trash, we fail to do the very thing that would bring freedom and wholeness to our lives.

Getting Rid of the Garbage

If anger is the garbage, then forgiveness is the freedom from it. Tyler Perry, playwright and actor, said it well: "When you haven't forgiven those who've hurt you, you turn your back against your future."[1] Our salvation began with forgiveness, and your future depends on your ability to forgive others. Forgiveness, while unthinkable at times, is the act of letting go of the offense or the wrong done against you. It is simply releasing the offender from your judgment and realizing that you don't have the right to pay people back. In the Bible there are at least seventy-five different word pictures of forgiveness, and the common Hebrew word for *forgive* means "to lift and carry away." Imagine forgiveness as pounding the courtroom gavel and declaring the defendant "not guilty." It doesn't mean the other person did not offend you or hurt you; it just means you are letting go of the right to stay hurt. Without forgiving there is no future, no freedom, and no healing for you.

I will always remember the words I said at my dad's grave: "You do not owe me, Dad; I forgive you." Forgiveness is turning the key and letting the person, the moment, or the memory you have held in prison go free. It is not a one-time thing but a whole way of life. Standing at the grave of my father that day was simply the beginning of a lifelong process. Once I began to release the bitterness, I realized that I was the one who had been in "prison," not my dad or the moment he abandoned me. I was the one being held captive by my own unforgiveness.

Why Forgive?

People often ask, "Why should I forgive?" But a better question might be, "Why not forgive?" When Jesus took our sin to the cross and forgave all of it with His own life, we lost the right to not forgive others. When I understood what Jesus had done—and what He was asking me to do—the burden of anger became a different burden in my heart. It was now a burden of disobedience to the God who created me and then died for me. The first of seven statements from the cross when Jesus hung there bloodied, beaten, and charged with crimes He didn't commit was, "Father, forgive them, for they do not know what they are doing" (Luke 23:34, NIV). In English it would be better translated as "Father forgive them, forgive them, forgive them!" It wasn't a statement but a cry from God Himself. This is God's heart for us—the true image of a God who desperately wants to reconcile everyone to Himself. True love is not keeping track of wrongs, but doing for others what Jesus has done for you. Why forgive? Because you have been forgiven. Holding on to unforgiveness is like saying, "Thank You, Jesus, for dying for my sins, but Your blood is not big enough for my father's sins and the pain I feel."

What happened to you isn't right. It isn't fair, and there are no answers on this side of heaven that will comfort you. I can only tell you the longer you wait to forgive, the more bitter you will become. The longer you hold someone in prison, the longer you hold yourself there. If you don't eventually deal with your anger, it will deal with you. Whether it is a father, a spouse, or a friend, stop trying to fight it out. Begin to let faith work it out.

None of us deserves forgiveness from God, but it is His nature to forgive us. In all of my garbage, the mess and the stink, He came to rescue me and give me a gift I didn't ask for and didn't deserve. That day at my father's grave has changed every day since. My dad couldn't ask for forgiveness and certainly could do nothing to earn it, but forgiveness is not, and cannot be, dependent on what the other person has to do. It is all about what we have to do. I stood there at the headstone overgrown with grass and asked him, "Why?" Of course he could say and do nothing, so the forgiveness was my choice. I had to take the keys and release him from the debt he owed me as a little boy who needed a daddy. Hard? Yep. Life changing? Undeniably. It was one of the most healing days of my whole life.

Choosing to Forgive

As a pastor, I have seen far too many people who claim to have faith in Jesus never fully let go. We love the fact that God has forgiven us; we just don't want to forgive others who have dared to offend us. But how can you believe Jesus for eternity, trust Him to provide for you, and accept His insane gift of forgiveness—and all the while continue to hold grudges and allow bitterness to take root in your heart? Not very well, in my opinion.

Paul wrote a letter to the church in Ephesus about this very thing. Look at his instructions to them: "Get rid of all bitterness, rage, anger, harsh words" (Ephesians 4:31). From the original language it is better translated "rid yourself completely" of these things. The Greek word used here for "bitterness" is *pikria,* which is a poisonous root that would kill you if eaten. It comes from the root word *pikros,* which means "something pointed and sharp with the ability to pierce and cut deeply." Bitterness will destroy you over time. It is like an arrow shot with the intent to hurt another, and yet it is a poison that ironically hurts you more than anyone else. As Paul said, we need to rid ourselves of it completely.

The truth is, we all have our own forgiveness rules, don't we? "I will forgive if he asks me" or "I will forgive when I can see she is sorry." But that just isn't biblical. I'm so glad Jesus didn't make *His* forgiveness of *us* conditional! I think one of the greatest indicators of our maturity in Christ is what we do with our position of power in the lives of those who hurt us. It is not about allowing that person to hurt us again, but it is about giving up our right to get even. It's taking ourselves out of the judge's seat and allowing God to make things right in His time and in His way. Refusing to forgive is simply our attempt to be God in the situation. Faith requires our acknowledgment that He died for *all* the garbage. His blood is enough for my sins *and* for the sins done to me. The only choice we have is to end the bitterness and end the anger by letting go of the pain and forgiving the past. I will either choose to live a life that reflects God and the values Jesus died for, or I will choose to see God and His commandments as a giant buffet line, from which to take what I like and leave what I don't. That's a surefire way to miss out on the full abundance God has planned for our lives. You have to decide for yourself: will you choose to live as a victim of your circumstances, or as a victor because of what Jesus did for you? C. S. Lewis said, "To be a Christian means to forgive the inexcusable, because God has forgiven the inexcusable in you."[2]

Forgiving someone is not an emotion; rather, it is a choice. For me, it was not an overnight thing. That first day was just the beginning of a process of many choices, many days, many months, and now many years of learning to think and act less like me and more like Jesus. Forgiveness is God's idea, and part of reflecting our perfect heavenly Father is learning to do what He does, even when it doesn't make sense to our humanity. Again, Paul's teaching to the church is our guide. He said in the very next verse, "Instead, be kind to each other, tenderhearted, forgiving one another, just as God through Christ has forgiven you" (Ephesians 4:32). He didn't even give them a process; he just said to forgive one another. Sounds so easy, doesn't it? But in reality it can be really hard.

Let me ask, have you learned to process garbage in a way that honors God? Jesus was very generous with His forgiveness and expects us to be the same. "Then Peter came to Jesus and asked, 'Lord, how many times shall I forgive my brother when he sins against me? Up to seven times?' Jesus answered, 'I tell you, not seven times, but seventy-seven times'" (Matthew 18:21–22, NIV). He isn't saying to forgive exactly seventy-seven times; He is speaking to the process of forgiveness and the multitude of steps it takes to forgive those who have hurt us. Jesus was saying forgive, forgive again, and keep forgiving until the process of forgiveness is completed.

I Forgive

So how do we begin?

I want to give you the "I Forgive" process. As I searched for biblical steps to forgiveness, I learned some things that I hope can help you in your journey too. Also, be willing to get help from others as needed. This journey is not one that can easily be taken alone, and you may benefit from talking to a counselor or therapist.

Now get a piece of paper so you can do the following exercise.

1. Identify who hurt you.

Please do not overspiritualize your betrayals or "kumbaya" yourself into thinking it's okay. Someone hurt you! Who is it? Is it a father or mother? a pastor? a church? a friend? a relative? a neighbor? You've got to identify who it is. Then, and only then, can you begin to walk in the direction of forgiveness. Although at face value identification seems simple, it is often extremely difficult. Some of you who have experienced abuse or abandonment may have come to believe that you deserved it or that it is your fault the bad things happened. That distortion makes it hard for you to lay the responsibility where it belongs. Even picturing your offender may bring back memories you have learned to ignore. As hard as it may be, you have to put a face to the offense. This step is hugely important in the "I Forgive" process. Maybe you have a whole list of offenders, or maybe just one person, but either way, you have to start with the truth. Take a moment to identify who hurt you.

2. Itemize what was taken from you.

You can't let go of something if you don't know what it is. It's not enough to say, "I forgive the debt." You can't truly forgive a debt if you don't know what the full amount is. When my wife, Michelle, and I were first married, we had a burglary. It was the first and only time we have felt the violation of someone walking into our garage and taking our possessions. When the insurance claims person came over and assessed the situation, he gave me a bunch of blank forms on which to list everything that had been taken. I had to recall everything I had in the garage and itemize exactly what was missing in order for the payment to be enough. I believe it is the same with forgiveness. Until you specifically itemize what was stolen from you, you cannot begin the process of healing.

Did someone steal your reputation? Did someone take your innocence from you? Were you in a relationship that you thought was authentic, only to later be betrayed? You have to determine what that person owes. Ask God to shine a light on the dark places of your heart to highlight the hurt you may have hidden there. Name it, write it down, and take as much time as you need to itemize what was taken from you.

3. Incinerate it.

If you don't want to stink like garbage, you have to get it out of your life. Hebrews 12:29 says, "For our God is a devouring fire." The word *devour* means "to destroy or consume something completely." When we incinerate the garbage, it simply means to dispose of it completely—to eradicate it from our lives. The Bible says God removes our sins from us as far as the east is from the west (see Psalm 103:12). Sins are no longer attached to us. The disposal of anger and pain depends on our ability to trust that God is in control. Will you trust that He has a plan for your garbage? Will you be consumed with the past and the hurt you feel, or will you focus on the God who is in the garbage with you? If we allow it, the devouring fire of God will purify us, taking what we have held onto for so long, and burning it completely away. No going back. I encourage you to take what you have identified and itemized and now get rid of it completely. Maybe you need to rip out the page you have been writing on, take it to a fire pit, and burn it up. Forgiveness won't erase the scars you bear or the memories you have, but it removes the sting of them and allows the wound to heal properly. It is with this step that you are giving God your trust and allowing Him to lead you forward.

4. Initiate blessing.

The final step in the process is more about the proof of authentic forgiveness. There will often come an opportunity to either bless or pay back the people who hurt you. What will you do? Jesus said these words: "But I say, love your enemies! Pray for those who persecute you!" (Matthew 5:44). We need to learn to do good to those who have not done good to us. Forgiveness is a gift we can give to others and to ourselves. *But what about revenge? What about getting justice?* It is a natural human response to want people to hurt the way they hurt us, but look at what the Bible says in Romans 12:17–19: "Never pay back evil with more evil. Do things in such a way that everyone can see you are honorable. Do all that you can to live in peace with everyone. Dear friends, never take revenge. Leave that to the righteous anger of God. For the Scriptures say, 'I will take revenge; I will pay them back,' says the LORD."

We have already talked about this, but I want to repeat it: doing right is always more important than being right. We have all heard of family feuds or neighborhood wars that last for years because of the individual's need to be right. The original hurt is long gone, the first offense is long forgotten, but somewhere along the way the need to be right got in the way of normal human relationship. Taking revenge into our own hands removes God's ability to bring good from the garbage.

I shared this process of forgiveness with our church in a message called "God in the Garbage." Our programming team built an environment of garbage in the auditorium. There was trash everywhere—the floor, the stage, the walkways. We moved chairs and made a huge pile of garbage in the middle of the auditorium. As I walked people through these few forgiveness steps, I could see that the issue resonated with many. I asked people to take a piece of the garbage from around them and simply write down the hurt that had been caused, the offender's name, and the unresolved offense. At the end of the message I stepped waist high into that huge garbage pile and lifted out a cross we had hidden beneath the mound. It was a powerful moment as people made their way toward the cross to let go of—and to lay at the foot of the cross—what had held them in bondage for so long. It was a turning point for many. We saw people empty themselves of bitterness and couples stand before a pile of garbage, weeping together and allowing God's work on the cross to devour the things that had held them back. I heard incredible stories of pain so deep that only God could make it right. And He does.

He Gives the Love

If ever there was someone with a pile of garbage to deal with, it is Corrie ten Boom. The Ten Boom family were devoted Christians who opened their home during the Second World War as a hiding place for fugitives hunted by the Nazis. They risked their lives every day, but through their activities they saved the lives of an estimated eight hundred Jews. In 1944 the family was arrested by the Nazis and imprisoned. Corrie and her sister Betsie spent ten months in three different prisons, the last being the infamous Ravensbruck Concentration Camp. Life in the camp was almost unbearable, but the girls shared their love of Jesus, and many women became Christians. Betsie died in Ravensbruck, but Corrie survived and began a worldwide ministry, sharing her powerful message of God's love. In her book *The Hiding Place*, Corrie tells a story of forgiveness that is a challenge to all of us. Surely if she can let go of the atrocities done to her, we can also let go of the offenses we hold on to.

It was at a church service in Munich that I saw him, the former S.S. man who had stood guard at the shower room door in the processing center at Ravensbruck. He was the first of our actual jailers that I had seen since that time. And suddenly it was all there—the roomful of mocking men, the heaps of clothing, Betsie's pain-blanched face.

He came up to me as the church was emptying, beaming and bowing.

"How grateful I am for your message, *Fraulein*," he said. "To think that, as you say, He has washed my sins away!"

His hand was thrust out to shake mine. And I, who had preached so often to the people in Bloemendaal the need to forgive, kept my hand at my side.

Even as the angry, vengeful thoughts boiled through me, I saw the sin of them. Jesus Christ had died for this man; was I going to ask for more? *Lord Jesus,* I prayed, *forgive me and help me to forgive him.*

I tried to smile, I struggled to raise my hand. I could not. I felt nothing, not the slightest spark of warmth or charity. And so again I breathed a silent prayer. *Jesus, I cannot forgive him. Give me Your Forgiveness.*

As I took his hand the most incredible thing happened. From my shoulder along my arm and through my hand a current seemed to pass from me to him, while into my heart sprang a love for this stranger that almost overwhelmed me. And so I discovered that it is not on our forgiveness any more than on our goodness that the world's healing hinges, but on His. When He tells us to love our enemies, He gives, along with the command, the love itself.[3]

God will not ask you to do what He will not also give you the power to do. The love, the strength, the ability you need to forgive comes from Him alone. Sometimes it will seem unreasonable and, yes, unfair. I don't think forgiveness always makes sense, but it does allow you to stop dragging this garbage around everywhere you go. You may be scared that forgiveness makes you vulnerable to being hurt again. However, forgiveness and reconciliation are not the same thing. You can forgive the offender of the past without putting yourself at risk for future hurt. Reconciliation is only possible when authentic repentance is evident, and both parties are walking in a posture of humility. While it is close to the heart of God, it is not always going to be possible. I once heard it illustrated this way:

If someone tracks mud into your beautiful home night after night, forgiving him means the next time he knocks, you go to the door. But if he is still muddy and still willing to track it in, you do not let him in. There has been no repentance, thus there can be no reconciliation. Only repentance (taking off his muddy shoes in respect of your home) can result in an invitation to come in. Forgiveness is simply the willingness to keep going to the door in hopes that repentance may have occurred.

A Personal Confession

If you have tried to forgive those who have hurt you, yet you feel you haven't been able to forgive completely, I respect that. As I type these last words of this very personal chapter, let me be honest enough to say that there are times when I feel I am not quite finished with my own forgiveness journey. I know that what God has allowed me to walk through has made me a better person, a better leader, and in many ways a better husband and father too. We never want the process—we only want the destination—but it is in the process we find God. Seeing God in the garbage helps me as I walk out this journey called *faith*. It enables me to better reflect God to a world filled with hatred and anger.

Thinking back to that day when I went to my father's grave for the first time, I am reminded that, as weird as it sounds, his final place of rest was the place I would begin to find rest in my own soul. The conviction to let go was so overwhelming that I had rehearsed those nine simple words over and over: "You do not owe me, Dad; I forgive you." When I got to his grave and finally said the words for real, they changed my life.

I would still give anything to be visiting a person rather than a grave. How I wish I could go to the home of a dad whom I could look in the eyes, talk to, and forgive. I still long for a dad whose arms might embrace me and whose words might encourage me—a dad who might say, "I love you, John."

How desperately I would give anything to hear those words in the flesh...and yet I have heard those same words from my perfect heavenly Father many times over. I know I am forgiven, I am His son, and I am the heir to all that is His. I have peace now because I have let go of what I could never control or change. In letting go, I was able to embrace my Father in heaven who wants desperately to embrace me as His son. And so it is with you.

Garbage will always be there. Offense will always come. But so too will God be there. He is the God that came to our garbage-filled world to heal the deepest wounds of our lives. It took years for me, but now I can be better instead of bitter. You can too.

The Battle Plan

Only those who see the invisible
can attempt the impossible.

—DICK EASTMAN

W e all have a favorite movie and a favorite scene. Without question, my all-time favorite movie is *Braveheart*. In fact, I'm a bit obsessed with it, to be honest. In the office at my house I have a replica of the sword that William Wallace would have had, made by the same person who made the sword for Mel Gibson. I also have a picture of Scotland, and it is in a killer shadow box. (No pun intended.)

Blue-Painted Faces

If you have seen the movie, you know about William Wallace. The movie is based on the true story of a man who'd had enough of tyranny. As England continued to conquer most of the known world, Scotland was heading for a future of oppression. Who knows what things would be like now had the Scottish given up. My favorite scene in the movie is when a ragtag army of farmers led by William Wallace is ready to engage in the fight that would ultimately take many of their lives. Wallace rides back and forth, stirring up the troops, and with his face painted blue, he yells out, "They can take our lives but they will never take our freedom!" Picture yourself in that intense battle: your heart is beating, and instead of running from the fight, you charge into it. You must surely believe the reward is worth the risk!

I watch that scene in *Braveheart* and get so pumped up picturing a different battle— one where it is the church that is in battle with oppression and tyranny. The church is

God's hope for the world! I imagine us charging into battle, fighting evil. I love it! But I also know we have an actual enemy who wants to bring oppression to our hearts and minds. He wants to distort God and wreck our lives.

Do You Know Your Enemy?

The journey toward wholeness is a battle. A battle for your mind, devotion, and heart. A battle to discourage you from doing anything meaningful and to distort God through your life as the world watches. Satan doesn't want you to be better; he wants you stuck in the past. He wants you to be useless and no good to the world. He knows he can't have you for eternity, but he wants to destroy you in this life. Jesus made it clear what Satan's plan is: "The thief's purpose is to steal and kill and destroy. My purpose is to give them a rich and satisfying life" (John 10:10).

Satan wants to steal, kill, and destroy. But Jesus has a different goal and that is to give you the best, most satisfying life imaginable. If Satan can make you live defeated, he has stolen from the world a valuable tool for the kingdom of God. Sounds like a fight to me! The Bible says, "For our battle is not against flesh and blood, but against the rulers, against the authorities, against the world powers of this darkness, against the spiritual forces of evil in the heavens" (Ephesians 6:12, HCSB).

Despite that verse and countless others about an enemy named Satan, many people still do not believe he exists. I think in a lot of cases they just don't want to believe. The Barna Research Group did extensive surveys in 2001 to determine the beliefs of various categories of Americans about Satan. They discovered that 40 percent of adults say that the devil is not a living being but is a symbol of evil. I can understand that. Most people don't want to believe in the reality of an actual devil, but how can we possibly win a battle if we don't think anyone is fighting against us? It's not surprising so many Christians are then defeated by their problems and unable to gain the victory.

Whether you like it or not, Satan is real, he is evil, and he wants us to live defeated. Peter warns us: "Stay alert! Watch out for your great enemy, the devil. He prowls around like a roaring lion, looking for someone to devour" (1 Peter 5:8).

Your Enemy wants to devour you because he hates you and despises your perfect Father in heaven. It is not a physical fight or a raging argument; it is a spiritual battle fought in heavenly places that manifests itself in the physical realm. I know it sounds a bit like a big version of *The Matrix,* but to think there is not evil in the world means you have been living under a rock. We can see evil all around us: sickness, tragedy, shootings, rape and murder, child abuse. We are in a war! But this is a spiritual war, and children of God fight not with their fists but with one of God's greatest weapons against the Enemy: prayer.

I'm not talking about the holy huddle or the light-a-candle prayer you may be imagining, but the fervent prayer of the Christian who knows he can do nothing in his own strength. Sometimes you will hear Christians say, "I'm really being attacked right now," and it's true there are times that Satan targets us for attack. But what we often forget is that while Satan has a lot of weapons, he has no shield and no armor. There is nothing he can do to defend himself against the prayers of the church. Prayer is not only our best defense; it is the best and most-powerful offense. Our prayers are like arrows, against which Satan has no protection. So if you're going to take him on, you'd better have an arsenal full of prayer! There is a great story in the book of Exodus about the nation of Israel being in a battle and how prayer made the difference. We can learn a lot from their example and particularly that of Moses, Aaron, and Hur.

Every Battle Needs a Warrior

The Israelites, at that point in their journey, were nothing more than a bunch of slaves who had just been set free from Egypt a few months earlier. Their struggle was simply to survive in the desert, day after day. One day the army of Amalek came to fight against them. This was the first real battle for Israel. Moses, the leader of the nation, did an interesting thing; rather than lead his soldiers into combat, he knew whom the battle belonged to and he went up a mountain to pray.

> While the people of Israel were still at Rephidim, the warriors of Amalek attacked them. Moses commanded Joshua, "Choose some men to go out and fight the army of Amalek for us. Tomorrow, I will stand at the top of the hill, holding the staff of God in my hand."
>
> So Joshua did what Moses had commanded and fought the army of Amalek. Meanwhile, Moses, Aaron, and Hur climbed to the top of a nearby hill. As long as Moses held up the staff in his hand, the Israelites had the advantage. But whenever he dropped his hand, the Amalekites gained the advantage. (Exodus 17:8–11)

What Moses knew is what we have to learn: the battle belongs to the Lord. The victory doesn't come through physical battle; prayer wins the battle. As Moses holds up his staff, he is saying, "God, this is Your battle." When we pray, we are saying, "God, this thing with my son, this thing with my daughter, this thing in my marriage—it's Your battle, God. This hurt I can't forget, this memory I can't shake—this is Your battle, God." There is an enemy coming after you. There is a battle heading your way. For my son, it's a drug called heroin. For some, it's crippling debt or a dysfunctional relationship. For others it's greed or pride or pornography. I don't know exactly what it is for you, but I know there's an enemy coming after you who will do anything in his power to keep you disconnected from the one source, God, who will defeat Satan and bring you victory.

To win the battle you need to recognize the Enemy's tactics and implement the Lord's defense through the power of prayer in your life. To do that, you need to understand these three tactics Satan uses in his attacks against us and the three qualities of a prayer warrior that will help us win the battle before us.

1. Overcome the attack of distraction by being desperate for God's presence.

Satan wants to distract us from coming to God with our struggles by making the unimportant things of this world so attractive that you will want them more than the things that are important to God. Matthew 6:19–21 says, "Don't store up treasures here on earth, where moths eat them and rust destroys them, and where thieves break in and steal. Store your treasures in heaven, where moths and rust cannot destroy, and thieves do not break in and steal. Wherever your treasure is, there the desires of your heart will also be."

We live in the most prosperous country in the world, and I would say that in most cases there is relatively no cost to live as a Christian. Compared to the rest of the world, we have access to most every resource and have little true need in our lives. Many times, we have become enamored with getting and having, and so we give all our time and focus to the stuff we think we need. When we are distracted by things of this world, we lose sight of God and our desire to come to Him with our real problems. This can be deadly to our faith. Look at what Jon Bloom said at the *Desiring God* blog: "Love for this present world sets in subtly, like a spiritual leprosy, damaging spiritual nerve endings so that we don't feel the erosion and decay happening until it's too late."[2] Prayer warriors triumph against distraction from the Enemy by focusing on their need for God. Prayer warriors are desperate for God's presence.

Desperation initiates prayer. To be desperate is to have an urgent need and desire. It's not enough to be desperate occasionally; you've got to stay desperate for God the same way you would be desperate to breathe or desperate to live. Moses had to stay desperate for God's presence until the victory was won. He couldn't put his arms down halfway through the fight. When you are desperate, nothing and no one matters more than God. To be desperate is to be at the end of yourself. You climb up a mountain, needing God more than you need anything or anyone else.

You will live desperate or you will live distracted, where your heart depends on what or who has your attention. You can't be desperate for God if you are distracted and busy with what the world has to offer. The battle can't be won when our hearts are not desperate for Him.

2. Overcome the attack of discouragement by being dependent on God's power.

Satan knows that if he can make you look at your problems rather than at God, he will be able to lead you down a road that will leave you discouraged. Focusing on your pain and hurt will take you down a path that will lead to despair and will eventually leave you hopeless. For some, the lack of any hope can lead to destructive thoughts and actions. Remember, Satan is out to kill and destroy you, and he will do anything in his power to do so. I believe we are living in a generation that is seeing more suicides than ever before. According to the Centers for Disease Control, "Each year more than 36,000 Americans take their own lives and about 465,000 people receive medical care for self-inflicted injuries."[3]

When we are discouraged, there is always a lack of courage. We lose sight of hope, and we begin to see God as distant and distorted. When Moses kept the staff raised, it guaranteed the Israelites would gain the upper hand and God would intervene supernaturally for them. God was showing them who the battle belonged to. In contrast, when Moses was tired and inevitably discouraged, he would lower the staff and the Israelites would begin to experience defeat. Discouragement always spirals toward defeat. So how does a prayer warrior fight the Enemy's discouragement? By complete surrender and total reliance on our heavenly Father. He is our source of comfort and strength!

If desperation initiates prayer and gains God's attention, then dependence sustains it. I love this verse in Proverbs: "Trust in the LORD with all your heart and lean not on your own understanding; in all your ways acknowledge him, and he will make your paths straight" (Proverbs 3:5–6, NIV).

Dependence gets God's favor and makes room for His power to move. It says, "I trust You to take it." Being dependent puts the problem in God's hands.

Everything that happens in a battle depends on whose hands the problem is in. All too often I choose to hold on to it myself. I can't tell you how many sleepless nights I had with my son: *Is he safe? Why is this happening? What can I do?* Finally, after a lot of prayer I got to the place where I can authentically say, "He's God's son, and I've got to let him go." I can honestly say it's the hardest thing to do because I want to take control; I want to fight for my son. We see ourselves in physical war, fighting the Enemy hand to hand as Joshua did. But you'll notice the physical battle is hardly even mentioned. Why? Because the real battle is happening up on the mountain. The fight is being won through Moses's lifting up the staff, lifting up hands, lifting up prayers. Our battle requires us to lift up our anxieties and our financial dilemmas, our broken relationships and our broken hearts to God.

Each of us right at this moment is holding in our hands a struggle that leaves us feeling discouraged and defeated. The problem is, we are not the most qualified to deal with it. If you put a basketball in my hands, it's worth twenty bucks. But when you put a basketball in the hands of Michael Jordan, it's worth millions of dollars. If you put a golf club in my hands, it's "Fore!" But if you put a golf club in the hands of Tiger Woods, you have a Master's champion. When I hold a slingshot, it's a toy, but in the hands of a teenager named David it brought down a giant. A staff in my hand is just a piece of wood, but put a staff in the hand of Moses and he can part the Red Sea! Right now, ask, whose hands is your problem in?

When Jesus holds your problem, miracles will happen. Spit and dirt in my hand is just mud (not to mention, gross!), but in the hand of Jesus it healed a blind man. If you take some bread and fish, you can probably make a sandwich. But Jesus made them food for thousands. If you put nails in my hands, I might be able to build you a birdhouse. But if you put nails in the hands of Jesus, He can save the world. Prayer puts the problem in God's hands, and our dependence is on Him alone.

3. Overcome the attack of division by being determined to win together.

Satan's goal has always been to turn Christians against each other—and he's good at it! Now instead of Christians fighting together against the Enemy, it is often Christians fighting against other Christians. Paul wrote this to the church at Corinth: "I appeal to you, brothers, in the name of our Lord Jesus Christ, that all of you agree with one another so that there may be no divisions among you and that you may be perfectly united in mind and thought" (1 Corinthians 1:10, NIV). As a pastor, I have found that one of my greatest joys is being able to support other pastors and know we are together in battle. When we come together to pray for our city or pray for our students—asking God to do what only He can—the blessing and power of God is so evident. If Satan can divide us, it is that much easier for him to hurt us. He will look for opportunities in our weakest places—a difficult relationship, an insecurity, the fear we struggle with—to foster thoughts and actions that alienate others. Do you ever wonder why so many marriages in America will end in divorce? Because Satan hates us to be in unity with others, and marriage is a picture of our relationship with Jesus. If Satan can destroy a marriage, he distorts God's image. God created us to be in relationship with others, and the Enemy wants to destroy God's creation. He does not want God to be glorified as we triumph over brokenness in our homes, communities, and churches. You can expect Satan to use even the smallest of issues to try to create big divisions. We need to come against him with purposeful, deliberate unity.

Moses gave us a picture of what this kind of unity looks like as the battle with the Amalekite army continued: "Moses' arms soon became so tired he could no longer hold them up. So Aaron and Hur found a stone for him to sit on. Then they stood on each side of Moses, holding up his hands. So his hands held steady until sunset. As a result, Joshua overwhelmed the army of Amalek in battle" (Exodus 17:12–13).

Moses finally got to the end of himself. He was praying, depending on God, trusting Him for the victory, and yet he was tired from the battle. Aren't we all? He could not carry the load by himself anymore, so in step Aaron and Hur. Aaron, a priest, was the brother of Moses, so one could expect him to be there as support. But then we have this guy named Hur. He is only mentioned one other time in the Bible and yet plays a huge role in winning this very significant battle. As far as we can tell from the biblical account, Hur wasn't a great leader, but he was a guy willing to step up when needed. He is what I call a "whatever, whenever, however" God-follower. So often we are so focused on Moses holding up the staff and Joshua fighting the battle that we forget about the guy holding up the arms of the guy holding the staff. He was the silent warrior. He was the invisible strength. He was the one who was okay to simply have a supporting role (literally and figuratively) in the story. And he was the one who made the difference. The Bible tells us that Joshua overcame the enemy. I wonder if Hur knew how important his part was in the outcome of the fight.

History does not belong to the powerful, to the wealthy, to the armies, or to the corporations. And it certainty does not belong to the media. The history of our world belongs to the intercessors who are willing to wrestle with God on behalf of someone else. God has chosen to avail Himself and to channel His power through people who pray. That's just the way it is.

Do you think Joshua ever forgot that day? Do you think he ever forgot watching his leader and mentor climb up that hill and raise the staff all day long on his and the nation's behalf? You never forget people who pray for you. You just don't. To this day I have a list of people who prayed for me when I had cancer. Six years later, when I still look at that list, I physically put my hand on it and pray for each person. They were the "Hurs" in my life, and I will never forget.

We all need a Hur. We all need people who will simply hold up our hands when we can't do it anymore, and pray. I hope we can pause to thank those who are like Hur in our lives. The ones who lift our arms, the ones who help us do what God has chosen and called us to do. When you can't lift up your own prayers, somebody will lift up your prayers for you. It may be someone you haven't even met. Some of you are reading this right now because someone prayed for you—maybe an aunt, or a grandma, or a close friend. Someone's praying for you; someone's lifting up your needs; someone's praying on your behalf; someone's interceding for you. It's the number-one kind of prayer you see in the Bible—intercessory prayer—meaning we pray for each other. The Bible says that right now, at this moment, Jesus is praying for you; He's interceding for you. Why? Because the stakes are high, but the battle is yours if you just hold on. We are in this fight together!

When We Work, We Work; When We Pray, God Works

Some of us have been up on the mountain a long time, and our arms are tired. Satan is firing arrows our way, and it's starting to hurt. In moments like these, there is a temptation to start to handle things on our own, to once again rely on our own strength. This in the end only leaves us tired and empty. But God is faithful to us. Just when we feel that we are alone in the battle, we get a word of encouragement from a friend, or a "Hur" steps in to lift our arms. Prayer matters so much. We need one another, and we need God.

Do you know how many people are waging a hidden war right now? Do you know how many people you'll work with tomorrow, next week, or next month who are too tired to fight any longer? Students, do you know how many people you know from school who are right on the verge of committing suicide? You can do something. Be a Hur for others. Go encourage their hearts and serve them in any way you can. Lift their arms up. Pray for them. Do for them what they cannot do for themselves.

I want to share with you an excerpt from a letter I wrote to my son in jail. I will hold his arms up as long as I can, and together we will see the battle won:

Dear David,

I woke up really early today and I'm praying for you in this chapter of your life in jail. I never thought that you would be in jail, and I know you never wanted to be in jail, but guess what? God has allowed you to be in jail now for over seventy days.

You're detoxed physically, but heroin has an emotional and mental addiction as well. I hope you'll take these next words that God put on my heart for you in a way that will help you in the next chapter of your life. David, choose Jesus. Choose to see the battle as God's; choose to see that prayer changes everything; choose to pray and depend on God, David, and choose to let the glory of only God be displayed for everybody to see. God is so desperately in love with you, son; He loves you so much. David, God gives us independence so we can learn to be dependent on Him. He wants His power displayed in my life and your life and the life of every human being who has, who is now, or who will ever walk on this planet.

Heroin is your enemy as the Amalekites were to Israel. It's raising up its ugly fist against our God, and now you are the warrior who will fight. I will be your Moses and other unnamed people will be your Aaron and Hur. I will climb wherever, go wherever, and pray wherever for you to be victorious. Don't give in, buddy, and don't give up. Stay desperately dependent on God because then and only then does God's glory get displayed for the world to see. This is your moment, son. I love, love, love you—but as much as I do, God loves you more. I believe in you—but as much as I do, God does infinitely more. I want the best for you—but as much as I would trade places for you, David, Jesus already has. He became sin for you and for me. David Michael Bishop, I hope these words help you. I hope my words encourage you. I can't wait to see you. Let's do this, let's fight this.

Dad

P.S. When we work, we work; and when we pray, God works.

Will you take your battle and put it in the hands of God? Will you allow the healing to begin in your life, in your relationships, and in your marriage? Will you give the anger that you've had to God? It matters so much whose hands are holding it. Keep it if you want. Walk away from this truth if you want to. Or choose to put your problem in the hands of the One who knows the beginning from the end, the One who created the heaven and the earth, the One who suspended the stars in the sky and named every one of them, the One who numbered the hairs on your head. He knows you best, and He loves you most. Put your stuff in His hands. Pray till the battle is won. Be desperate, be dependent, be determined.

Taking the "T" Out of Can't

Endurance is not just the ability
to bear a hard thing, but to turn it
into glory.

—WILLIAM BARCLAY

Quitting is often the easiest road to take. I can think of many times when quitting seemed the easy way out, but I hate that quitting means you never experience what could have been. You miss out on the reward because you didn't want to keep doing what had to be done. Of all the potential quitting moments in my life, none is more memorable than when I ran and completed (thank you very much) my first and only marathon. My friend Dave and I ran the Portland Marathon in 1998, and although we trained, ran, trained, sweated, and trained some more, nothing you do in training can prepare you for hitting "the wall." I hit mine around mile twenty-one. I will never forget running across the St. Johns Bridge and feeling that my body was shutting down. Quitting felt like the only option. If I hadn't known that most marathoners hit a wall at some point, I probably would have stopped running, like so many of the people around me had. In fact, I remember a couple of people limping off the road with the help of bystanders, and in some cases even being taken away by ambulance.

It is common for runners, and athletes in any endurance sport, to "hit the wall" at some point as they push themselves past their comfort level. Sara Latta shared great examples of this very thing in her article "Hitting 'The Wall'":

"It felt like an elephant had jumped out of a tree onto my shoulders and was making me carry it the rest of the way in."—Dick Beardsley, speaking of

hitting "The Wall" at the second marathon of his career, the 1977 City of
Lakes Marathon

"I wasn't wanting to talk much. And when I'm not talking, you know I'm
hurting." —Don Frichtl, a runner who encountered "The Wall" somewhere
after mile 21 of the 2002 Chicago Marathon

"At around mile 23, I was beginning to feel like the anchor was out."
—George Ringler, speaking of his 1991 Lake County Marathon[1]

Hitting the wall is a very real physical condition. Once carbohydrates and hydra-
tion are diminished, the body wants to stop. Simply stated, it burns out of energy. The
body becomes so tired it can't go forward. Peter Wehrwein, editor of *Harvard Health,*
said this in an article:

Come tomorrow morning, about 27,000 runners will begin the annual
26-mile, 385-yard (42.195 kilometers) mass run from suburban Hopkinton
to Boston. But if past marathons in Boston and elsewhere are any indication,
perhaps up to 40% of these optimistic and determined souls will slam into a
sudden sensation of overwhelming, can't-do-this fatigue several miles (typically about five) before they get a chance to experience the glory of crossing
the finish line.[2]

What is true for the body is true for the soul and is also true spiritually in many
ways. Life is an endurance race, in which we all will at some point "hit the wall" and
want to quit. It's the moment when you have run out of your own ability to carry on,
and quitting becomes the only foreseeable option. At the beginning of a race, we opti-
mistically believe we can finish it, but "the wall" gets in our way. The wall you hit is
simply that moment when *I can* becomes *I can't*. It is that one stupid *t* that prevents us
from completing what we started and finishing the race that truly matters.

It is undeniable that the apostle Paul, who wrote most of the New Testament, probably had more reason to quit than most. He had been beaten, imprisoned, and left for
dead. He was shipwrecked and pursued to be killed. If hitting the wall can be defined
by people who struggle, Paul could be the poster child. Yet Paul never gave up. In his

second letter to his apprentice and friend Timothy, he talked about finishing the race: "I have fought the good fight, I have finished the race, I have kept the faith" (2 Timothy 4:7, NIV).

Paul wasn't the only one who knew about trials. Jesus Himself said in John 16:33, "Here on earth you will have many trials and sorrows. But take heart, because I have overcome the world." It is, of course, completely true for every human that has walked on this planet. Anyone who lives on this earth is going to experience troubles. You are either coming out of a trial, in a trial right now, or heading toward one. Guaranteed. This is when *I can* all too quickly becomes *I can't*.

So, what is the *t* in your life?

Maybe you are reading this book on the bleeding edge of giving up. Life has been too hard for too long, and you have just hit a wall. Perhaps you're a student ready to quit on life because you don't see things changing anytime soon, or maybe you are the father that continues to allow the brokenness of yesterday to break the relationships of today. Maybe it is an addiction. Perhaps you are finally clean and sober, but each day's temptation seems more than you can stand. You simply want to quit. With increasing stress, sadness, or frustration, you hit the wall and end up quitting a race that had brought you so much joy and strength.

You feel like a failure in many ways and your *I can't* is now defining you. It is the address where you learn to live, but it is not the address where God has died for you to live. The truth is, sometimes we can't do it in our own strength. But children of God are not alone. Philippians 4:13 says, "I can do everything through Christ, who gives me strength." Jesus takes the *t* out of can't. He is the walking-on-water, healing, restoring, and accepting God who came to give you abundant life. He came to stomp out the *t*'s in our lives. Pause here and ask yourself, what is causing you to quit right at this moment? Which of the following four *t*'s is discouraging you?

The Four T's That Turn *I Can* into *I Can't*

1. Tiredness

The first *t* that causes us to quit is being tired. I'm not talking about the kind of tiredness you feel when you got only five hours of sleep. This kind of tired can't be fixed by chugging down an energy drink. This kind of spiritual tiredness makes you believe the race isn't worth it and neither are you. It is a deep sense of being weary, exhausted, confused, and ready to quit. You go back to what's easy, because you don't have the energy to go forward. We all have things that make us tired. Our tank gets depleted and life leaves us empty. Because of my brokenness, navigating relationships can be particularly tiring for me. If I am not intentional to do things that refill my tank, I am soon so tired I want to quit.

How about you? Do you feel so tired you can't go on? Chances are, the wounds of your past wear you out and drain you. It all boils down to whom we rely on for our strength. Being tired is not the issue; finding a different source of strength is.

One of my favorite verses is found in Isaiah: "Even youths grow tired and weary, and young men stumble and fall; but those who hope in the LORD will renew their strength. They will soar on wings like eagles; they will run and not grow weary, they will walk and not be faint" (Isaiah 40:30–31, NIV).

The Hebrew word for "renew" used here is *chalaph,* which means "changed, altered, or to show newness." When used in reference to a tree, it describes the production of new buds or leaves. What a beautiful picture of God renewing our strength! He wants to produce new strength for today, not just recycle yesterday's strengths. He not only helps us walk, but enables us to run and soar—like an eagle in the wind.

Did you know that an eagle knows when a storm is approaching long before it breaks? The eagle will fly to some high spot and wait for the winds to come. When the storm hits, the eagle sets its wings so that the wind will pick it up and lift it above the storm. While the storm rages below, the eagle is soaring above it. The eagle does not escape the storm. It simply uses the storm to lift it higher. It rises on the winds that bring the storm.

When the storms of life come upon us—and all of us will experience them—we can rise above them by setting our minds and our belief toward God. The storms do not have to overcome us. We can allow God's power to lift us above them.

God gives us strength to rise above the storms that wear us out. When relationships, temptations, and daily stress make us tired, we can rise up on His strength.

2. Temptation

Perhaps your personal *t* is temptation. We are surrounded daily by temporary pleasures that distract us from God's best for our lives. First John 2:16 says, "For the world offers only a craving for physical pleasure, a craving for everything we see, and pride in our achievements and possessions. These are not from the Father, but are from this world."

Fighting temptation is for some a daily battle that requires constant focus and discipline. When the temptation becomes too much, we find our resolve wavering, our strength diminishing, and doubt taking over. When doubt steps in, discouragement takes over and leads to eventual destruction.

We begin to think we can't succeed. We feel powerless. This is one of the biggest ways that *can't* takes over and controls our lives. There is perhaps nothing more exhausting than the daily fight against relapse to previous addiction. Loran Nordgren, senior lecturer at the Kellogg School of Management, said this about our ability to respond to temptation: "People are not good at anticipating the power of their urges, and those who are the most confident about their self-control are the most likely to give into temptation."[3]

How about you right now, in this moment? Don't dismiss these words. Intentionally ask yourself this question: *Where am I being tempted?* What is the thing, or the person, deceiving your mind and making you believe you cannot go on? The Enemy screams this into your mind and circumstances, but there is always a battle to be fought for your freedom and your testimony. God always, in every situation, allows us to be tempted but also provides a way out. The Bible tells us that God is faithful to help us overcome temptation. Check out Paul's words to the church at Corinth: "No temptation has seized you except what is common to man. And God is faithful; he will not let you be tempted beyond what you can bear. But when you are tempted, he will also provide a way out so that you can stand up under it" (1 Corinthians10:13, NIV).

You might want to write this prayer down and keep it somewhere you can see it daily:

God, help me be all You have created me to be. Help me love and live like You. God, let nothing and no one cause me to give in or give up. Help me have the strength that only comes through You.

Jesus removes the *t* of temptation when we abide in Him. The Bible tells us in John 15 that we are like branches and He is the vine. Our strength comes from staying connected to Him. The Word of God helps us discern right from wrong. It is a light on the path you walk, showing you the right way. The key to overcoming temptation is to have people in your life you trust to keep you accountable. True friends will see what you can't see and help you establish positive boundaries to keep you safe.

3. Talking

We could write a whole book on this one issue, let alone a portion of a chapter. We all in some way have been shaped by what has been said about us—both good and bad. As children we have dreams and make plans, only to be stopped by careless words from a parent or teacher. I bet we can all think of words that have really discouraged us: *You'll never change. You're not good enough. You can't do it.* The Bible tells us that the power of life and death is in the tongue (see Proverbs 18:21). Words truly do have the power to destroy confidence and derail us from moving forward. One word of criticism can in a moment change our hope to disbelief and turn our *I can* into *I can't*. The times I came closest to quitting were the result of words that pierced me like arrows. While writing my first book, *Dangerous Church,* a man I greatly respected said, "You are a preacher, not a writer." To be honest, it hurt. I was so discouraged by that label, it made me question my ability, and for a moment I wanted to quit. But I am learning in my pain to allow the Word of God to be louder in my ear than the voices of others. What is God trying to speak to you right now?

The fact is, truth matters. We talked in a previous chapter about God's Word, which is timeless and unchanging. His Word is always truth, for He cannot lie. When words cut you like a knife, check them against the Word of God. People say we *can't,* but in God's Word it says we *can.* People threaten to hurt you, but God promises shelter and protection. Parents squash your dreams, but His Word says all things are possible! If words don't build you up and make you better, then they are not of God. Do not allow lies from broken people to make you quit. Don't let others tell you that you can't. The Bible lays out the truth: "For I can do everything through Christ, who gives me strength" (Philippians 4:13). Always listen more to the voice of God than the voices of others.

4. Testing

Just when we think we are doing well and have nearly made it to the end, we suddenly hit the dreaded "wall." We get tested. Up until this point we have been running well, staying sober, and controlling our anger, and then a trial comes along to test our endurance. James, the brother of Jesus, gave some instructions for how we should approach the trials of life: "Consider it pure joy, my brothers, whenever you face trials of many kinds, because you know that the testing of your faith develops perseverance. Perseverance must finish its work so that you may be mature and complete, not lacking anything" (James 1:2–4, NIV).

I don't know about you, but I don't always approach trials with joy in my heart. The joy, faith, and perseverance usually come a little bit later in my process—somewhere after the complaining. The fact is, no matter how you react initially, trials do have a purpose, and we can be better because of them. The original word James used for "many kinds" is translated "polka dot" in English. It means "various" or "some big, some small." In other words, we will have various kinds of trials. Some will be small and some bigger than we could ever imagine. Regardless of the size, ultimately all of them are for the purpose of building our faith and developing perseverance within us. A test is not meant to stop us in our tracks but to make us stronger for the next part of the journey. "Blessed are those who endure when they are tested. When they pass the test, they will receive the crown of life that God has promised to those who love him" (James 1:12, God's Word). There is reward for those who do not quit! Stay strong as you walk toward healing. There will be times you want to give up. You will get tired. You will face temptation. You will hear talk that hurts you deeply, and you will be tested to your breaking point, but please don't quit and miss out on the reward at the end of the race. The test God has allowed in your life will one day become the testimony of God's power through your life. Please don't quit.

When Your Test Becomes a Testimony

Sometimes the very thing that tests us the most will one day be our greatest story. God can take even the most broken part of us and turn it into a platform for something great. When I first heard the story of Dick and Rick Hoyt, I was moved to tears. It is hard to comprehend the incredible strength this family has shown in the face of intense challenge and testing.

In 1962, new parents Dick and Judy Hoyt received the devastating diagnosis that their newborn son, Rick, was a spastic quadriplegic with cerebral palsy—a result of oxygen deprivation at birth. Doctors didn't see much hope for Rick to ever lead a "normal" life, so they advised Dick and Judy to institutionalize him. However, Rick's parents took him home, determined to raise him as normally as possible, although he could not walk or talk. A team of engineers built a special interactive computer for Rick in 1972 that allowed him to communicate without actual speech.

At the age of 15, Rick had an unusual request:

Rick told his father that he wanted to participate in a 5-mile benefit run for a lacrosse player who had been paralyzed in an accident. Far from being a long-distance runner, Dick agreed to push Rick in his wheelchair and they finished all 5 miles, coming in next to last. That night, Rick told his father, "Dad, when I'm running, it feels like I'm not handicapped."

This realization was just the beginning of what would become over 1,000 races completed, including marathons, duathlons, and triathlons (6 of them being Ironman competitions)....

In a triathlon, Dick will pull Rick in a boat with a bungee cord attached to a vest around his waist and to the front of the boat for the swimming stage. For the biking stage, Rick will ride a special two-seater bicycle, and then Dick will push Rick in his custom-made running chair (for the running stage).

Rick was once asked, if he could give his father one thing, what would it be? Rick responded, "The thing I'd most like is for my dad to sit in the chair and I would push him for once." [4]

This is such an incredible picture of how Jesus loves you. He knows you are not able to run the race yourself, and so He loans you His arms and His legs for the road. He gives you His strength, His peace, and His courage to endure any trial you face. When you can't go on, He will carry you. He has a purpose and future on the other side of the wall. Don't think you can't make it. Team Hoyt has taken their test and turned it into a testimony. Their team slogan is simply "Yes, you can!"

I love this story so much, and even after hearing it numerous times, it never ceases to elicit emotions that are in some ways painful to share. When I first heard his story, with tears in my eyes, I thought, *I wish I could be a dad like that—a dad who would drop everything in a second to do whatever with my kids.* The second time I saw their story, I was blown away with a different overwhelming thought, *I wish I had a dad like that—a dad who would do anything for me.* Now, as I watch their story—again with tears—I felt God say to me, *"I am a Father like that."* Here I have a God who has done everything for me and who wants to do so much more, and yet I miss it because I'm looking at my problems. What is wrong with us? We have everything and yet miss everything at the same time, it seems. We focus on what we have lost instead of what we have left. We live with an *I can't* view.

Focus on What's Left, Not What's Lost

Who would blame Rick or his parents for being mad at God? It would have been understandable, especially since so many of us blame God for the issues we have been dealt in life. But Rick has graduated both high school and college and has accomplished more than 90 percent of people in the world. Why? Because he lived with an *I can* mentality.

Pain can sometimes hold our attention far longer than it should. Losing my father and being abused left my life a wreck and filled me with rage and anger. I took my anger out on other people, often by fighting. I honestly enjoyed fighting, and whether I won or lost, I loved the feeling of pure rage in the middle of a fight. I knew nothing else except inflicting pain on others for the pain I had inside. I was just a mad person who could not see any good in anything, and I reacted like a stick of dynamite—just a spark would make me explode. I was not safe for myself, my friends, my wife, or anyone around me.

Blinded by my stupid crazy rage, I didn't see God's provision. I missed seeing His love and guidance. I was so mad and angry that I missed the very person God had purposed to be my father: my grandfather, Pop. (I talked about him earlier.) Looking back now, I see that he was an incredible provider, protector, and friend. I guess you could say he was my rock star.

He truly loved me. He believed in me and cared about me, and he was there for me like a father should be, but I missed what was in front of me because I was still consumed by what was behind me. I was so focused on what was lost that I couldn't see what was left. If only I could turn the clock back. If only I could see his face one more time. If only I could tell him thanks.

Pause to see what is in front of you right now. I cannot change the past, nor can you. I cannot know the future, nor can you. All we can change is today. You may have lost your dad, your innocence, your security, or your hope, but you have a mom, a friend, or a sibling who is left. God has given you a church family, or a stepdad, or a grandpa like mine to fill the gap. Hug them, and tell them thanks. Once they take their last breath, you will have no other opportunities to say it.

Finishing Strong

Well done, good and faithful
servant!

—Jesus (Matthew 25:21, niv)

We live crippled by sin, but we should not live disabled by stuff in the past. We are created by God to do great things. Go back, read and reread who your perfect Father is, and learn to think differently. Learn to see differently. Learn to love who you are and who God is through you. This is just a book, but hopefully one that has given you some hope for a different future. Change begins with the choices you make today, not the decisions from your past. Getting past the wall and finishing the race begins with learning to drop one simple letter out of *can't*. Drop the *t* and begin to experience life the way Jesus intended it to be.

Focus your attention on what is left, not what is lost. Stop focusing on your disabled life, and see what is in front of you. You have only one life, one chance to make an impact, one more day to change your world. Will you?

We will never fully comprehend the love of God until the day we step into heaven. That day we will finally be free from pain. There will be no more abandonment, abuse, or rejection. There will be no more tears, no more cancer, no more heart disease, and no more daddy issues. Relationships will be made right and brokenness made whole. I look forward to seeing my Pop that day; I can't wait to embrace him, thank him, and hold him. As Christ-followers we will finally see God clearly for all that He is. Until then, we simply continue to walk, continue to learn, and continue to grow.

The road to healing is, for some, a long one. You may spend years working these issues out with your heavenly Father. It's okay to not be okay for a while. He is in it with you for the long haul. You are worth every bit of His investment. You are His masterpiece, created for a purpose, and you matter so much! If you need to, read the book again. Spend time in the Word of God; listen to His voice. When it gets to be too much, seek out professional help. There are great Christian therapists who can help you get free of the lies from your past.

Remember, journeys take time. There will be roadblocks and setbacks. Satan will attack. You'll want to give up, but there is no relationship worth fighting for more than the one with your Father in heaven.

It has been my goal that you would no longer see God distorted, but that you would have a full revelation of His true nature and find in Him the Father you always wanted. A Father massively in love with you, who is always present, intimately involved, fully pleased, in perfect control, humble, and completely safe, and who does not condemn. You are His beloved child.

I offer up this closing prayer:

Father,

Help us move in our minds and our hearts from what has been, to what is and to what can be. I pray in Jesus's name that You would touch the heart of every person who has been hurt, everyone who has been neglected, abandoned, blamed, and judged, and those who have been around their fathers but never truly known by them. I pray for healing and wholeness in their earthly relationships, and that the distorted image would no longer be the lens by which we see You. God, I know You can do in one second what we cannot do in years, and I ask You to meet every heart's need in the way that only You can.

I also pray for those who have allowed bitterness to enter their hearts and are now being controlled and defined by it. Please help us stop the cycle today. Please help us to authentically forgive, to let go of the past and to walk toward a better—not bitter—future. A future filled with promise and hope for each of our lives and for the lives of the generations to follow us.

For those who are in the middle of unspeakable pain right now as they read these words, help them to know there is hope in the valley and there is peace in the presence of God. May our hearts and minds be filled with the peace of Your presence, Jesus. Thank You that even though we walk through the valley, we don't stay there. Please walk with those who can't seem to walk another day. We trust Your promises are true for our lives today.

Heavenly Father, I pray that as the pages come to an end, the real journey would begin. A journey filled with hope and promise, and a season where we will choose You. I pray we would see You, God, as the perfect Father, that we would allow healing to continue in our journey, and that we would never quit or give up.

Thank You, Jesus, for never giving up on us. It is in Your name that we commit these things.

Amen!

MY PROGRESSION

Letting Go of Daddy Damage

Letting Go of the Fear of Abandonment

Abandonment causes a heart to break into countless pieces. The wounds cut deep and, when not dealt with, turn into an infection that can, and often does, manifest itself in insecurity, fear of rejection, anger, or rage.

Abandonment makes it hard to trust that God will always be there. Deep inside is the belief that He also will leave, and we never fully enter into the kind of relationship we are meant to have with our heavenly Father!

Identify the Distortion

The scars left behind from abandonment are apparent in relationships. There are challenges in areas of trust and security that translate into the way you view God. If it wasn't a father who left you, who was it: a spouse, pastor, trusted friend?

1. In what ways has abandonment played a role in your life? Did your father leave you? If so, was it intentional or circumstantial? How did that moment affect you?

2. Do you ever find yourself becoming excessively angry at other people? What sets you off (lack of recognition, someone not returning your phone call or e-mail, feeling ignored, etc.)?

3. A child who has been abandoned or left can develop traits that negatively affect future relationships. They can become clingy, have difficulty in trusting a loved one to not leave, or overcompensate by lavishing love on others in an effort to cause them to stay. Which of these characteristics, if any, do you see in yourself?

4. Do you have a hard time trusting God because you think He will walk away from you and leave you alone?

Discover What the Bible Says

1. Look up Hebrews 13:5 and write the verse out in the space provided. What does God say about Himself? What will He NEVER do?

2. When a person has been affected by abandonment, the common questions asked are "What did I do wrong?" or "Why did they leave me?" They blame themselves and in turn fear they will do something wrong that will cause God to turn His face from them. Read Romans 8:38–39. What is Paul convinced of that you can be convinced of too?

3. What comfort do you find in the following verses: Isaiah 49:14–16; Psalm 27:7–10; 2 Timothy 4:9–18? How does God's response differ from the responses of the people mentioned in these scriptures?

4. Take a look at Genesis 16:1–13 and 21:8–20. Who was mistreated, rejected, and abandoned? What emotions do you see portrayed? Who was there when no one else was? What name was given to Him?

Take Action Toward Healing

1. Learning to trust people again is difficult, but truly it is more painful to continue to hold people at a distance and isolate yourself than it is to allow them to become a part of your life. According to Colossians 3:12 and Ephesians 4:32, how are we to treat others regardless of their potential to hurt us?

2. Jesus Christ was betrayed by one of His twelve disciples. He knew who would betray Him yet still allowed this man to dine with Him at what became His last meal (see Luke 22:1–6, 20–22). What can we learn from Jesus's example?

3. If God is with you (see Isaiah 43:2, Psalm 23:4) and goes before you (see Deuteronomy 31:8), and won't ever leave you (see Hebrews 13:5), what is there to fear? Even if someone leaves you again, who will still be there? Whom can you trust completely?

4. Scholars believe that Psalm 118 was written after the Israelites returned from Babylonian captivity, a period of time when they felt abandoned by God and alone, living in a foreign land with a foreign culture and foreign leadership. What did the psalmist learn during this heartbreaking time (see verses 5–14)? How can you apply this same lesson to your own life?

5. Joseph was able to forgive his family for abandoning him. He was able to forgive because he saw the bigger purpose behind the pain and trusted God to use his pain for good (see Genesis 50:20; compare Romans 8:28). Who abandoned you? Take a few moments and ask God to help you forgive that person and to give you eyes to see the bigger picture.

6. You can either choose to hang on to the bitterness of the wounds of abandonment, or you can choose to allow God to heal you and make you better. What will God do if you allow Him to (see Psalm 34:18; 147:3)?

Whatever needs you have right now—whether they are physical, emotional, or spiritual—take them to God. Ask Him to provide for you. Believe that He will never leave you or forsake you, and tell Him that you believe this to be true and will stand firm and strong in it. If you feel like God isn't present, tell Him that. Cry out to Him, and *don't stop* crying out to Him. He is fully present and always available to you! Ask Him to help you put your faith in Him, the One who promises to never abandon you.

Letting Go of the Fear of Rejection

The result of having a passive father is a feeling of rejection in the heart and life of a child. The effects are no less detrimental than that of abandonment, abuse, or disapproval, but they are often harder to identify and recognize.

If you had a passive father, the rejection you feel many times exposes itself in loneliness and despair. You find it difficult to see God as an active and involved Father who cares about you, your needs, and your future, but you desperately long for intimacy with Him.

Identify the Distortion

1. When you think back to your childhood, how involved was your father in your development? Was he available or disconnected? If disconnected, describe how his actions portrayed a disinterest and indifference toward you.

2. Do you have a hard time making connection with others? When you walk into a room full of people, are you the social butterfly, mingling and making new friends, or are you a wallflower, remaining safely along the perimeter, longing for conversation but afraid to initiate any?

3. Have you ever felt invisible? Do you feel like God sees you and cares about you? Why or why not?

4. Do you long for intimacy with God and/or with others? Do you feel like you matter? Do you believe the truth in Genesis 2:18, that God does not mean for you to be alone?

Discover What the Bible Says

1. God wants to have an intimate relationship with you as His son or daughter. How does He express this desire (see John 15:12–16)?

2. Jesus Christ experienced rejection. Look at the following scriptures: Matthew 27:27–31; John 1:11; compare Isaiah 53:3. How does knowing that our Savior has experienced what you have comfort you?

3. Spend some time looking at the following individuals who experienced rejection, and then answer the questions below: Elijah in 1 Kings 19:3–15; Moses in Numbers 11:4–17; Joseph in Genesis 37:5–24.

Can you relate to any of these men? If so, in what way?

What thoughts do you imagine were going through their minds?

What did God do to help alleviate the pain of their loneliness and ease their frustration?

How did God use them?

Take Action Toward Healing

1. According to Psalm 139:17–18, how often does God think about you? Does He sound like someone who sits in a recliner watching the evening news while you desperately tug on His shirtsleeve for attention? How intimately does He know you (see Jeremiah 1:5; Psalm 119:73; Psalm 139:13, 15–16)? How does this intimate knowledge differ from what you have known from your earthly father?

2. Write out Jeremiah 29:11 here, then write it on an index card and post it somewhere you will see it every day. Does God care about your future? Does He want to give you the desires of your heart (see Psalm 37:4)? What action do you need to take to see these things come to pass (see Proverbs 3:5–6)? God cares, He loves you, and He wants to see you succeed. Do you believe that?

3. You might feel alone, but are you really? Look around at the people who are in your life. Whom are you thankful for? What relationships make you feel like you matter? God did not create us to be solitary; He created us for relationship. Write

down the names of three of the most important people in your life and what they have done to show you that they see you and care about your life.

4. Think back to a time when you felt like you were in a "pit" or a "cave." Do you remember the loneliness and despair that you felt? What helped you out of it? Those times of isolation can be the most agonizing, yet also the most beneficial because you are not alone there—God is with you and He is working *for* you. What encouragement is there in God's presence (see Isaiah 41:10, Joshua 1:9)?

5. Even if your father didn't come to your defense or if he remained quiet when you needed him the most, God is not silent. When you read the following verses, write down the words or phrases that depict God as a protector and defender: Psalms 28:6–9; 46:1; 144:1–2. Read Jesus's prayer for His disciples and future believers in John 17. Can you see in His prayer the love and concern He has for you?

Today if you are feeling rejected and alone, take some time to just "sit and be" in the presence of your heavenly Father. As difficult as it is, I encourage you to be real and transparent before God. As you sit, allow yourself to be emptied so He can fill you. Ask Him to show you that you are not alone and to give you wisdom in seeking healthy friendships that will support, encourage, and lift you up. If you are in a pit and are feeling hopeless, that's okay—the more you are emptied, the more you will be desperate for God alone.

Letting Go of the Fear of Disapproval

A parent with high expectations for his children usually comes from a similar background of performance-based love. Most of the time these parents are perfectionists themselves, and they demand the same from their children. When a child does not or cannot meet the expectations set by a demanding parent, she is met with disapproval, which leaves her feeling unaccepted, unloved, and unworthy.

If you had a demanding father, you are most likely hesitant when approaching a relationship with your heavenly Father, afraid that your actions or behavior will not be good enough for God. You can't imagine that He knows you the best and loves you the most!

Identify the Distortion

1. Do you tend to be a perfectionist? If so, do you also have high expectations for those around you?

2. Was the love you received from your father conditional? Was it based on what you did or didn't do? Did you receive praise for what you did, or were only your mistakes pointed out to you?

3. In your relationship with God, do you feel like you need to earn His love by doing good things? Do you fear His response if you make a mistake?

4. When you read what God the Father said to Jesus before He started His ministry—before He did His first miracle (see Mark 1:11)—do you feel like God is saying it to you as well?

Discover What the Bible Says

1. Look up the following scriptures and write down the key words and phrases that reflect the way God sees you: Ephesians 2:10; Genesis 1:27; Jeremiah 1:4–5; Zephaniah 3:17.

2. God is never going to be done with you. He does not expect perfection. What does Philippians 1:6 promise? Take a moment to let the words sink in. From this verse alone, do you think God expects perfection?

3. What questions does Paul ask the church in Galatia in Galatians 3:1–14? What point is he trying to make? According to this passage, is God's acceptance of you based on your human effort or on God's grace? How does this change your thinking?

4. Read through the story of Mary and Martha in Luke 10:38–42. What was most important to Jesus: the activity of Martha or the time Mary spent at His feet? Why?

Take Action Toward Healing

1. When you receive nothing more than disapproval from your father, it lends to the mind-set that what you do is never going to be good enough. In contrast, God's love is unconditional. How do the following scriptures describe unconditional love: Lamentations 3:22–25; Titus 3:4–5; Ephesians 2:8–9? Is it something we need to earn?

2. Insecurity is a badge, if you will, of a child who has dealt with the criticism and even condemnation from his or her father. How do these verses affirm God's approval and pleasure with you: Romans 8:1; 1 John 4:13–19? Knowing that God is love (see 1 John 4:8), what more affirmation is there when you read 1 Corinthians 13:4–8.

3. What does Psalm 46:10 say? A person can fill his or her time with busyness and activity, striving for the approval of others because it was not received growing up. But peace comes from inaction. What was Jesus doing when the disciples were panicking in the middle of the storm (see Matthew 8:23–27)? Why do you think He was able to do so? Jesus speaks, "Peace, be still" (Mark 4:39, KJV) to the flurry in your own heart.

196 • My Progression

4. You can exhaust yourself trying to gain approval and accolades from people. Whose approval should we be focused on (see Galatians 1:10)? Whose approval really matters and why (see 1 Thessalonians 2:4; 1 Peter 4:11)?

5. Do you place more value in what you do or in who you are? Is your identity wrapped up in activity or in Christ? Spend some time poring over the following scriptures and rest in who God says you are: Galatians 2:16; 2 Corinthians 5:17; Ephesians 1:4–14; 4:24; John 15:15. Get off the "treadmill of activity," rest at the feet of Jesus and just *be*.

Spend some focused time in prayer to God, your perfect Father. Even if you approach Him with fear and hesitancy, run to Him and put your faith and trust in Him. Believe that He loves you and accepts you and meets you exactly where you are. Ask Him to help you become secure in Him and to not allow the past or any failures on your journey to distract you from God's primary purpose, to complete the work that He has started. It is a journey and a process. Surrender to His perfect will for your life, and know that there is nothing you can do to cause Him to love you more or love you less.

Letting Go of an Attitude of Entitlement

When a father gives too much attention to his son or daughter, they learn to expect the same kind of treatment from other relationships and become upset when they don't receive it. A person who struggles with an attitude of entitlement expects nothing less than good things from God and is never satisfied with what he or she has. Entitlement always leads to expectation. Entitled people look at their lives and see what they are lacking, then think they deserve so much more because of what they've accomplished. Gratitude and humility are replaced by self-centered thoughts and behaviors. If you were raised by a parent who rescued you, you may find yourself disappointed with or mad at God for not answering your prayers the way you want.

Identify the Distortion

Entitlement is an attitude that reveals itself in actions and behaviors reflecting people's belief that everyone owes them something and that they shouldn't have to be held responsible for their mistakes or lack of judgment. If you were enabled, you might not even be aware that you have this viewpoint.

1. What expectations do you have of God? Do you think He should prevent bad things from happening to you and answer all of your prayers the way you want? Why or why not?

2. When something bad happens, do you play the blame game? Do you accuse others or even God for mistakes you have made?

3. Growing up, did you have to face the consequences of your actions, or did your dad bail you out all the time?

4. Do you find it easy to fall into the mind-set that you are owed something? That you deserve to be happy and should be able to do what feels good, regardless of the consequences?

Discover What the Bible Says

1. According to Philippians 2:5–11, what is the attitude of Christ that we should have? What did Jesus do that we can mimic in our own lives?

2. Read James 4:1–6. What opposing words are the themes of these verses? What is the cause of an attitude of entitlement?

3. What do you learn about humility by reading the following verses: Isaiah 66:2; 1 Corinthians 1:28–29; 3:7; 1 Peter 5:5?

4. Look at Deuteronomy 8:2–3. It is easy to wonder why we have to go through hard times, and often we feel like we don't deserve what is happening to us—and that feeling may be right. According to these two verses from the Old Testament, why does God allow these things to happen? In whom does He want you to trust, yourself or Him?

Take Action Toward Healing

1. Entitlement is not something specific only to our generation. Even a couple of Jesus's disciples had this attitude. Take a look at Luke 22:24–27. What was the dispute? How did Jesus respond to them? He had reason to be entitled, yet instead He took the form of a what?

   How can you change your "I deserve" attitude into a "You deserve" attitude, and then stop and serve someone?

2. Read Luke 17:7–10. What is Jesus illustrating? Who had the attitude of entitlement? Who did not, and whom did Jesus exemplify as the way we should all behave and think?

3. Take a look at Romans 3:9–12. Is anyone really better than anyone else? What is the punishment that we all truly deserve (see Romans 6:23)? Take some time to examine your life. What attitudes do you need to change? What behaviors need to be eliminated so you will more appropriately be able to serve rather than be served?

4. One good way to rid yourself of the viewpoint that the world or God owes you something is to be thankful for what you do have. In the space provided, write out the things that you are thankful for.

What has God done for you that you know you could not have ever accomplished without His help?

Read Psalm 118. What is the psalmist thankful for?

Start by examining yourself and asking God to reveal any ways that you have allowed a spirit of entitlement to become your attitude and behavior. Repent, and ask Him for forgiveness. Choose a posture of humility before Him and with others. Spend some time being grateful for what He has given you and the blessings that you enjoy. Ask Him for wisdom and direction in putting others first and valuing them before yourself. Pause to remember that Jesus is enough.

Letting Go of the Fear of Failure

Growing up within the environment of a controlling father often leads to a fear of failure and a tendency toward feeling anxious about performance. The controlling father becomes an authority figure to be feared and the exactor of punishment if he is displeased. This lends itself to a belief that God is also a fearsome dictator who can never be pleased and who will dish out devastating consequences for not being strictly obeyed.

If you were raised in this environment, your actions might become "religious" or even legalistic as you try to adhere to rules and regulations in an effort to earn the approval of your earthly father and your heavenly One, as well. The freedom in Christ that should be enjoyed is a bondage to the victim of a controlling father.

Identify the Distortion

1. Was your father controlling? Were you afraid to express your opinion—especially if it was contradictory to what he said?

2. Do you tend to have anxiety when trying something new or to hesitate when considering taking a risk?

3. Would you describe yourself as being a perfectionist or maybe even struggling with OCD (obsessive-compulsive disorder)? Can you look back to a time in your life when this proclivity began?

4. Do you see God as dictatorial? Do you feel like all He wants and expects from you is strict obedience and adherence to His laws and regulations, and that He is disappointed in you when you don't measure up?

Discover What the Bible Says

1. What do you learn from Peter's restoration in John 21:15–17, coming on the heels of his denial of knowing Jesus three times (see John 18:15–17, 25–27)? Does Jesus hold our actions against us?

2. We are bound to make mistakes, but instead of focusing on the failure, what should we be doing (see Proverbs 24:16; Luke 22:31–32; Micah 7:7–8)?

3. Does God keep a record of what we have done wrong (see Psalm 103:8–12; Isaiah 43:25)?

4. Look at Hebrews 12:1–13. What does God's discipline do for us? What should our attitude be toward His loving correction? How does it benefit us differently from the discipline we may have received from our earthly parents?

Take Action Toward Healing

1. A fear of failure can prevent a person from taking risks or trying new things. Do you see this in yourself? What comfort can we receive from Psalms 91 and 107? Even if we stumble and make mistakes, what does God do when we cry out to Him?

2. When was the last time you would say that you failed at something? Instead of looking at it in a negative light, try seeing the positive in it. What did you learn from it? How can you do better in the future? You survived it and are better for it! Will you challenge yourself to not see failure as failure, but to see it as a valuable tool for your growth and development?

3. Look at Luke 9:1–5. What is Jesus instructing His disciples to do? Does He expect them to have success everywhere they go? How do you know? What does He counsel them to do in the event of what could be perceived as failure of the mission He sent them on? How can you use this same principle in your own life when you don't achieve a goal?

4. Do you feel like giving up right now? Are you hearing the voices of others telling you that you can't do it, that you won't be able to perform? Are you afraid that you aren't going to measure up? What do the following verses in Scripture tell us about giving up: Galatians 6:9; 1 Corinthians 15:58; Hebrews 10:35–39?

5. Failure is not the end of the story, but the beginning of something new. What encouragement do you receive from 2 Corinthians 5:17? Does God want you focusing on what has happened in the past (see Isaiah 43:18–19)? How can you change your viewpoint on failing?

Start by asking God to help you to see Him differently. He is not a dictator, nor does He expect perfection. He simply wants your love and your desire to please Him. Pray for the boldness, courage, and humility to take risks for Him and for the trust and belief that He will not allow you to fail. Pray for an accurate view on what you see as failures and learn to see them as opportunities for learning and growth to ensure future success. Failure is not the end of the story; it is merely the beginning of an amazing work that God wants to do in your life. Just as with Peter, when you run from God, He runs toward you! He is desperately in love with you!

Letting Go of the Fear of Being Hurt

The fear of being hurt by others is common to everyone, but it wraps its tentacles even tighter around a person who has been abused. Abuse lies to the victim by telling her she isn't good enough, or that he isn't worthy of being loved, or that she is nothing more than a doormat meant to be walked on and used. Some even believe they deserved being hurt. Abuse says you are worthless and undeserving of receiving love, grace, and acceptance.

If you have been abused by your father, you probably struggle with accepting and receiving the love of your heavenly Father. Your understanding of God has been shaped by the way your father treated you, so you do not believe that God can love you, you don't believe He will protect you, and you may even blame Him for the abuse. Having not received the love, protection, and care from your earthly father, you do not know how to trust God to provide these things for you.

Identify the Distortion

Abuse can take many different forms. It can manifest itself through physical or sexual harm upon the body or by hurtful words and/or actions. Regardless of the form it takes, abuse is harmful and takes its toll on the individual, affecting the way he or she sees God.

1. How has your father abused you? In what way(s) do you believe that God will or has already done the same to you?

2. Do you believe God wants to punish you? Why or why not?

3. Victims of abuse carry a burden of shame that causes them to withdraw and not feel worthy of love, even going so far as to reject it. They believe incorrectly that they deserved the mistreatment and that they have no value. Do you struggle with receiving God's love and the love of others? If so, why do you feel that you are unworthy?

4. The Bible teaches us that once we receive Jesus Christ as our Lord and Savior, we have been adopted as sons and daughters into God's family (see Galatians 3:26–4:7). Does this fact bring you comfort or fear? If fear, what exactly are you afraid of?

Discover What the Bible Says

1. In Matthew 7:7–12, Jesus is teaching His disciples about prayer.
   a. How is God described in verse 11?

   b. What kinds of gifts does God give His children?

   c. How is this different from what you have experienced from your own father?

    d. How has God answered a prayer of yours recently?

2. If you were in a burning building, what would you do? Where would you go? Whom would you call?

Naturally, you are going to run from danger to safety and contact the professionals that can take care of the fire. The same goes with matters of the heart. When you read the following passages of Scripture, write down what illustrations are used to describe God: Psalms 9:9–10; 46:1; 61:3.

    a. Would you run to someone who didn't make you feel safe?

    b. How does God protect His children? What makes Him safe?

3. Once you have been hurt, it is natural to fear being hurt again. What do the following verses say about the nature of pain: Lamentations 3:22–23; Psalms 30:5; 71:20–21?

    a. Who comforts us and restores us?

    b. What does God do with our pain (see Psalm 56:8; Revelation 21:4)?

4. We all admire the beauty of a diamond and recognize its value, but did you know that diamonds are formed by extreme temperature and pressure in the earth's mantle? After they form, seismic volcanic activity brings them closer to the surface of the earth, where they are mined today. The same can be said of the pain of abuse—the extremity of the harm done to a victim forms something that is so valuable and priceless in God's eyes, and He will use it to benefit others. The apostle Paul suffered a lot of abuse; read what he said in 2 Corinthians 4:7–12.
   a. How did Paul view his troubles?

   b. How can God use your pain to help others? (See also 2 Corinthians 1:3–7.)

Take Action Toward Healing

1. You have already identified how your father has hurt you and how this abuse helped form your viewpoint of God. The next question is, how did his treatment of you formulate the way you see yourself today?

2. Read Psalm 139 and answer the following questions:
   a. How well does God know you?

   b. How close to you is He?

   c. Does He protect you?

   d. How does He see you? (See also Ephesians 2:10.)

3. The Bible teaches us that we are not to memorialize our pain but to remember how God is bringing us through the pain and leading us to restoration and newness. Read Isaiah 43:18–19. The past is behind you, your future is in front of you, and God promises you a great one (see Jeremiah 29:11).

   a. What do you think is holding you back from God's best for your life?

   b. What practical steps can you take to let go of your past and walk toward the future God has for you?

4. First Peter 5:7 tells us we can cast all of our cares and anxieties on Jesus. ALL of them.

   a. What pain do you still carry?

   b. What auto responses do you still have that are affecting your relationships?

   Let Him take your burden (see Matthew 11:28–29). Let it go.

5. Your identity is not in what was done to you; your identity is in the God that formed you. What does God promise YOU in these scriptures?

   a. Jeremiah 29:11

   b. John 10:10

   c. Psalm 37:4

   d. Exodus 15:26

6. You are a victor in Christ, not a victim. Live in victory and not defeat. You don't have to identify yourself with the pain; you can identify yourself with the healer. Read Romans 8:31–39.

   a. According to these scriptures, does the abuse you suffered keep you from God's love and grace?

   b. Who are you according to these verses?

   c. What can separate you from God's love?

   d. Who is for you? How does He show His love for you?

7. Isaiah 61:3 holds such beautiful imagery of how God restores what has been broken in our lives. Write out this verse in the space provided below. What does He promise to give those who have been ravaged by pain and are accustomed to wearing garments of shame caused by abuse?

Ask God to help you heal physically, mentally, and emotionally from the abuse that you suffered. Pray and be willing to forgive the ones who hurt you, and ask for God's eyes to see your abusers the way He sees them. Be willing to take the steps to no longer be a victim, but to be a victor. Allow God to bring you the peace that surpasses all understanding and be the safe fortress that you can always run to for safety and security. Lay your burdens at the foot of the cross, and confess your desire to serve Him and to walk away from your past.

Letting Go of the Fear of Being Blamed

Originally a scapegoat was used to atone for the sins of the nation of Israel, but over time the meaning of *scapegoat* has been distorted—and now children can become the scapegoat to a family's guilt, shame, and insecurity. Blame is wrongfully applied to an innocent child who in turn becomes burdened with a deep sense of failure and an inability to measure up.

If you were raised by an accusing father, shame becomes a motivating force. You may have a deep sense that you have no worth, which can drive you into addictive and compulsive behaviors. You may try to fix what is "wrong" in you, and you can spend your whole life making up for the things you did or did not do to feel loved and accepted.

Identify the Distortion

1. Guilt is connected to our actions; shame is connected to how we feel about ourselves as a result of our actions. In what areas of your life do you feel guilty? In what areas are you feeling shame?

2. In what ways were you used as a scapegoat growing up? What blame was placed upon you? How has that affected the way you see yourself today?

3. Do you believe that Jesus took your guilt and freed you from the penalty of your sin and the "bad things" you have done? Why or why not?

4. What is the motivating factor for your actions today? Could it be that you are trying to make up for things you were blamed for as a child?

Discover What the Bible Says

1. Guilt is a legal condition, not an emotion like shame. What do the following scriptures in Romans say about guilt: 3:9–12, 20–26; 6:22–23; 8:1–4?

2. Read John 8:1–11. Was the woman in this account guilty of sin? What do you learn from Jesus's response when she was brought before Him? Does anyone have the right to judge or condemn you?

3. Whom did Jesus choose to spend time with (see Matthew 9:9–13)? He chooses to spend time with those who aren't perfect and don't have their act together. Does this surprise you? Look at Revelation 3:19–20. Is His invitation only to a select few or to everyone?

4. King David did a lot wrong. He committed adultery (see 2 Samuel 11:1–4) and murder (see 2 Samuel 11:14–24) to name a couple of things. How is he described in Scripture (see Acts 13:22)? Though David was guilty, he was not condemned. When you read Psalm 51, what do you think earned him the title given to him?

Take Action Toward Healing

1. What is the struggle that Paul talks about experiencing in Romans 7:7–25? How do you see this struggle played out in your own life? What is the answer to this dilemma (see Romans 8:1–11)? What has Jesus's death done with our guilt?

2. Romans 6:23 tells us that the wages of sin is death. Three chapters earlier, we learn that ALL have sinned (see 3:23). Though we are guilty, God gives us mercy. How often can we experience this mercy (see Lamentations 3:22–23)? What must we do to receive it (see 1 John 1:9)?

3. Read Matthew 3:13–17. What did God say (see verse 17)? This full approval happened before Jesus started His public ministry, before He did even one miracle. How does this minister to your heart? Do you have to do anything to have God say these same things about you?

4. Take another look at the story of the woman with the issue of blood in Mark 5:21–34. She would have lived in a state of isolation and shame due to her medical condition. What bold move did she make? How desperate was she to have done such a thing? What was Jesus's response? Take some time to write out a prayer, and with the same boldness and desperation, reach out to the One who removes your sin and heals you. Let Him take away not just your guilt but your shame as well.

If you wrestle with shame and guilt, first remember what Jesus has done for you. Go to God and lay these feelings at His feet. It is not His will for you to live with this burden. Be honest about the pain that has been inflicted upon you as a result of being the crux of everything that went wrong. Release the shame and guilt you have lived with. Ask God to show you how He views you as His perfect and spotless lamb and the object of His faithful love, acceptance, and grace. If you struggle with compulsive and addictive behaviors, ask Him for healing and help to overcome. Allow His grace to replace the guilt.

NOTES

Chapter 1: Image Distorted

1. David Popenoe, *Life Without Father: Compelling New Evidence That Fatherhood and Marriage Are Indispensable for the Good of Children and Society* (New York: Free Press, 1996), 163.

2. The Fatherless Generation, http://thefatherlessgeneration.wordpress.com /statistics. Sources for statistics: the US Department of Health; Census; Justice & Behavior, Vol. 14, 403–26; National Principals Association Report; Columbia University; US Department of Census; Texas Department of Corrections.

3. Barron YoungSmith, "Why Do So Many Politicians Have Daddy Issues?" *Slate,* August 22, 2012, www.slate.com/articles/news_and_politics/politics/2012/08 /absent_fathers_political_leaders_like_bill_clinton_ronald_reagan_gerald_ford _and_paul_ryan_often_develop_coping_mechanisms_in_childhood_that_may _make_them_effective_leaders_.html.

4. Gordon Dalbey, "Healing the Wounds," in *The Transformation of a Man's Heart,* ed. Stephen W. Smith (Downers Grove, IL: Intervarsity Press, 2000), 59–60. Source cited as Jeffrey Zaslow, "Julian Lennon on His Dad—and his First Disc in Seven Years," *USA Weekend,* May 28–30, 1999, 22.

5. A. W. Tozer, *The Knowledge of the Holy* (New York: HarperOne, 1978), 1.

6. Juanita R. Ryan, "Seeing God in New Ways: Recovery from Distorted Images of God," The National Association for Christian Recovery, www.nacronline.com /spirituality/recovery-from-distorted-images-of-god-seeing-god-in-new-ways -recovery-from-distorted-images-of-god.

Chapter 3: The Father Who Wasn't There: The Absent Father

1. Richard Rohr, *Radical Grace: Daily Meditations* (Cincinnati: St. Anthony Messenger Press, 1995), 270.

2. The Fatherless Generation, http://thefatherlessgeneration.wordpress.com /statistics.

3. Jack Frost, *Experiencing Father's Embrace* (Shippensburg, PA: Destiny Image Publishers, 2002), 112–13.

4. Donald Miller, *Father Fiction: Chapters for a Fatherless Generation* (New York: Howard Books, 2010), 22–23.

Chapter 4: The Father Who Was There, but Not "There": The Passive Father

1. Lionel Dahmer, *A Father's Story: One Man's Anguish at Confronting the Evil in His Son* (New York: Avon Books, 1995), 32, 33, 35, 214.

2. Substance Abuse and Mental Health Services Administration news release, February 15, 2012, "Report shows 7.5 million children live with a parent with an alcohol use disorder," www.samhsa.gov/newsroom /advisories/1202151415.aspx.

3. National Association for Children of Alcoholics, "Children of Addicted Parents: Important Facts," www.nacoa.net/pdfs/addicted.pdf.

4. Chloe Sekouri, "Roles in the Addicted Family," http://suite101.com/article/roles-in-the-addicted-family-a193018.

5. Bruce J. Ellis, John E. Bates, Kenneth A. Dodge, David M. Fergusson, L. John Horwood, Gregory S. Pettit and Lianne Woodward, "Does Father Absence Place Daughters at Special Risk for Early Sexual Activity and Teen Pregnancy," (Hoboken, NJ: Wiley & Sons, 2003), *Child Development,* 74: 801–821. doi: 10.1111/1467-8624.00569/.

6. Kendra Cherry, "What Is Uninvolved Parenting?" About.com Guide, http://psychology.about.com/od/childcare/f/uninvolved-parenting.htm.

7. Dr. Stephan Poulter, "Is Dad Hurting Your Career?" *Good Morning America,* ABC News, May 30, 2006, www.fatheryourson.com/stephan-poulter-in-the-news-abc-news-good-morning-america-5-20-2006.htm.

8. Kathy Canavan, "Parenting Styles Can Influence Children," *UDaily,* May 3, 2005, www.udel.edu/PR/UDaily/2005/mar/style050305.html.

Chapter 5: The Father Who Expects Perfection: The Demanding Father

1. Jack Frost, *Experiencing Father's Embrace* (Shippensburg, PA: Destiny Image Publishers, 2002), 113.

2. Frost, 116.

Chapter 7: The Father Who Is Always Right: The Controlling Father

1. Dr. Seuss, *Yertle the Turtle and Other Stories* (New York: Random House, 2008), 201.

2. Dan Neuharth, "If You Had Controlling Parents: How to Make Peace with Your Past," WebMD, www.controllingparents.com/webmd_chat.htm.

3. See www.controllingparents.com/Stats.htm.

4. Matthew J. Miller, Psy.D., "Authoritarian Parenting: The Impact on Children," http://cccrd.publishpath.com/Websites/cccrd/images/Authoritarian.pdf.

Chapter 8: The Father Who Hurts Others: The Abusive Father

1. U.S. Department of Health and Human Services, Administration for Children and Families, Administration on Children, Youth and Families, Children's Bureau. (2012). *Child Maltreatment 2011.* Available from www .acf.hhs.gov/programs/cb/research-data-technology/statistics-research /child-maltreatment.

Chapter 9: The Father Who Blames: The Accusing Father

1. "The Scapegoat," Light's House, www.lightshouse.org/the-scapegoat.html #ixzz21aT930Ce.

2. Nicky Cruz sermons, "Testimony" and "Flashback," Living Hope Church, Vancouver, WA, June 17, 2012. See www.livinghopechurch.com/experience-christ/sermons /sermon/2012-06-17/nicky-cruz--testimony- and http://www.livinghopechurch .com/experience-christ/sermons/sermon/nicky-cruz--flashback-.

3. John Bradshaw, *Bradshaw On: The Family* (Deerfield Beach, FL: Health Communications, Inc.), 1990, revised edition, 2–3.

Chapter 11: The Perfect Father

1. Dan B. Allender and Tremper Longman III, *The Cry of the Soul: How Our Emotions Reveal Our Deepest Questions About God* (Colorado Springs: NavPress, 1994), 99.

2. David Nelmes, "God Is Agape Love," Ezilon Infobase, November 10, 2007, www .ezilon.com/articles/articles/7675/1/God-is-Agape-Love.

3. Nicky Cruz sermons, "Testimony" and "Flashback," Living Hope Church, Vancouver, WA, June 17, 2012. See www.livinghopechurch.com/experience-christ

/sermons/sermon/2012-06-17/nicky-cruz--testimony- and http://www.living
hopechurch.com/experience-christ/sermons/sermon/nicky-cruz--flashback-.

Chapter 12: God Is Always with You

1. Randy Rudder, "Achy Breaky Heart," CountryWeekly.com, April 25, 2002, www.countryweekly.com/vault/story-behind-song-achy-breaky-heart.

2. Billy Ray Cyrus Bio, USWeekly.com, www.usmagazine.com/celebrities/billy-ray-cyrus.

3. Sue Anderson, "Dealing with Abandonment Issues," *New Living Magazine,* November 2003, www.newliving.com/issues/nov_2003/articles/abandon .html.

4. Anderson, www.newliving.com/issues/nov_2003/articles/abandon.html.

5. Charles Pierce, "The Sins of the Father," *Sports Illustrated,* March 30, 1992, http://sportsillustrated.cnn.com/vault/article/magazine/MAG1003583/index .htm.

Chapter 13: God Is Up Close and Personal

1. Max Lucado, *Traveling Light: Releasing the Burdens You Were Never Intended to Bear* (Nashville: Thomas Nelson, 2001), 108.

2. Henry Cloud, *Changes That Heal* (Grand Rapids, MI: Zondervan, 2003), 47.

Chapter 14: God Is Fully Pleased

1. "Biography," The Official Whitney Houston Website, www.whitneyhouston.com /us/content/biography.

2. "Kevin Costner on 'The Miracle That Was Whitney'," CBS News, February 18, 2012, www.cbsnews.com/8301-31749_162-57380871-10391698/kevin-costner-on-the-miracle-that-was-whitney.

3. Elyse M. Fitzpatrick, *Because He Loves Me: How Christ Transforms Our Daily Life* (Wheaton, IL: Crossway, 2008), 87.

Chapter 15: God Does Not Owe You

1. Jean M, Twenge, Ph.D, *Generation Me: Why Today's Young Americans Are More Confident, Assertive, Entitled—and More Miserable Than Ever Before* (New York: Free Press, 2006), 68–69.

2. "Full Text of Woods Statement," ESPN Golf, February 19, 2010, http://sports
   .espn.go.com/golf/news/story?id=4928017.
3. Ray Stedman, *Talking with My Father: Jesus Teaches on Prayer* (Grand Rapids, MI:
   Discovery House, 1997), 27–28.

Chapter 16: God Is in Perfect Control

1. Austin Cline, "What Do Americans Think About God?" About.com Guide,
   October 18, 2006, http://atheism.about.com/b/2006/10/18/what-do-americans-
   think-about-god.htm.
2. "Biography," Official Website of John Grisham, www.jgrisham.com/bio/.
3. "Biography," Official Website of Babe Ruth, www.baberuth.com/biography/.
4. "Steven Spielberg Biography," Biography.com, www.biography.com/people
   /steven-spielberg-9490621.
5. Charles C. Manz, *The Power of Failure* (San Francisco: Berrett-Koehler Publishers, 2002), 14.
6. "20 Famous Failures," Present Outlook Website, http://presentoutlook.com
   /famous-failures/.
7. John Maxwell, *Failing Forward: Turning Mistakes into Stepping Stones* (Nashville:
   Thomas Nelson, 2000), 18–19, 114.
8. S. L. Price, "Liu Awes with Tough Mentality but Returns to China Empty-
   handed," SI.com, August 7, 2012, http://sportsillustrated.cnn.com/2012/olympics
   /2012/writers/sl_price/08/07/Liu-Xiang/index.html#ixzz23HMxc0v4.

Chapter 17: God Is Completely Safe

1. "Journal Entries and Quotes: Eric Harris Journal Excerpts," Xanga.com,
   http://klebold-harris.xanga.com/589661390/item.

Chapter 18: God Is Always Accepting

1. Terry Law with Jim Gilbert, *The Power of Praise and Worship* (Shippensburg, PA:
   Destiny Image, 2008), 120.

Chapter 19: Mirror, Mirror

1. Bruce Brodowski, *My Father, My Son: Healing the Orphan's Heart with the Father's
   Love* (Matthews, NC: Carolinas Ecumenical Healing Ministries, 2010), 173–74.

Chapter 20: Getting Off the Orphan Train

1. Frank Rothfuss, "No Longer Orphaned," Saint Luke's Lutheran Church, www
.saintlukeschurch.org/site/index.php?option=com_content&view=article&id
=69&sermon_id=311&Itemid=79.

2. Frank Rothfuss, "No Longer Orphaned."

3. Frank Rothfuss, "No Longer Orphaned."

4. "Orphans in the World," NumberOf.net, www.numberof.net/orphans-in-
the-world.

5. Matt O'Connor, *Father 4 Justice: The Inside Story* (London: Orion, 2007), xvii.

6. Mark Stibbe, *I Am Your Father* (Oxford: Monarch Books, 2010), 105–6.

7. A. J. Jones, *Finding Father* (Maricopa: XP Publishing, 2010), 140.

8. Ruth Graham, *In Every Pew Sits a Broken Heart: Hope for the Hurting* (Grand
Rapids, MI: Zondervan, 2008), 11–12.

Chapter 21: Finding God in the Garbage

1. Tyler Perry, "Aha! Moments," Oprah.com, www.oprah.com/omagazine/Aha-
Moments/3.

2. C. S. Lewis, *The Weight of Glory* (New York: HarperOne, 2001), 182.

3. Corrie ten Boom, *The Hiding Place* (Grand Rapids, MI: Chosen Books, 2006),
247–48.

Chapter 22: The Battle Plan

1. "Religious Beliefs Vary Widely by Denomination," The Barna Group, June 25,
2001, www.barna.org/barna-update/article/5-barna-update/53-religious-beliefs-
vary-widely-by-denomination.

2. Jon Bloom, "God, Make Us Desperate!" *Desiring God* (blog), July 29, 2010,
www.desiringgod.org/blog/posts/god-make-us-desperate.

3. "Preventing Suicide," Centers for Disease Control and Prevention, www.cdc
.gov/features/PreventingSuicide/.

Chapter 23: Taking the "T" Out of Can't

1. Sara Latta, "Hitting 'The Wall,'" *Marathon and Beyond*, September/October
2003, www.marathonandbeyond.com/choices/latta.htm.

2. Peter Wehrwein, "How Boston Marathon Runners Can Avoid Hitting the Wall," *Harvard Health,* April 17, 2011, www.health.harvard.edu/blog/how-boston-marathon-runners-can-avoid-hitting-the-wall-201104172372.

3. "Research Shows Temptation More Powerful Than Individuals Realize," Physorg.com, August 3, 2009, http://phys.org/news168523630.html#jCp.

4. "About Team Hoyt," Teamhoyt.com, www.teamhoyt.com/about/index.html.

Other books by John Bishop

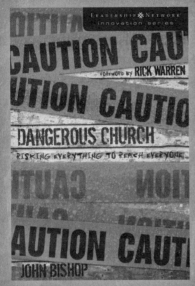

DANGEROUS CHURCH

Many churches gravitate to what is safe and familiar. But reaching out to a lost world was never meant to be easy.

Dangerous churches choose to risk everything - comfort, safety and the security of the familiar - for the sake of the one thing that matters most: reaching out to people who may spend eternity separated from the God who created them.

John Bishop takes us back to the days of the early church in the book of Acts and reminds us that the heartbeat of the church is found not in agendas or human plans but in the mission of God. Through probing questions and amazing stories of God's grace, he challenges church leaders to embrace what matters most to the heart of God, whatever the cost.

DANGEROUS DEVOTIONS 1&2

Each Dangerous Devotion book provides 52 weeks of unique studies that look at a different core aspect of what it means to be fully devoted to Jesus. These devotionals encourage not just information, but life and faith transformation through the study and application of God's word. With practical questions, a "dangerous" prayer and supportive, focused, Bible reading, you will find yourself discovering new things about the Word of God, the life of Jesus and what it means to be fully devoted to following Him and growing in your faith.